MICROPROCESSOR INTERFACING TECHNIQUES

RODNAY ZAKS

AUSTIN LESEA

THIRD EDITION

MICROPROCESSOR INTERFACING TECHNIQUES

RODNAY ZAKS

AUSTIN LESEA

THIRD EDITION

Library of Congress Card Number: 78-55237
ISBN Number: 0-89588-029-6
Printed in the United States of America
Printing 10 9 8 7 6 5 4 3 2 1

ACKNOWLEDGEMENTS

The following persons or companies have supplied valuable information, photographs, programs or schematics of their products or projects: Although not all information supplied could be used, their cooperation is gratefully acknowledged.

Intel, Motorola, Persci (disks), Shugart (disks), Thomson-CSF (CRTC board), David Reinagel (Music Synthesis), Rockwell, Data I/O (programmer), Prolog (programmer), Zilog, Hewlett-Packard (analyzers), Control Data (disks), North Star, Imsai, Altair (S100 bus), Tarbell (cassette interface), Component Sales (keyboards), MOS Technology, Advanced Micro Devices, Fairchild, NEC, Western Digital, Dynabyte (RAM), National Semiconductor, Analog Devices, Lawrence Laboratory, University of California at Berkeley, Power-One (power supply), Fluke, Biomation (analyzer), Trendar (fault analysis)

ALSO AVAILABLE IN:

- *FRENCH*

- *GERMAN*

- *DUTCH*

- *SWEDISH*

- *JAPANESE*

- *ITALIAN*

(more to be published)

TABLE OF CONTENTS

LIST OF ILLUSTRATIONS

PREFACE

Computer interfacing has traditionally been an art, the art to design and implement the required control electronics for connecting a variety of peripherals to the main processor.

With the advent of microprocessors, and of LSI chips, since 1976, microprocessor interfacing is no longer an art. It is a set of techniques, and in some cases just a set of components. This book presents the techniques and components required to assemble a complete system, from a basic central processing unit, to a system equipped with all usual peripherals, from keyboard to floppy-disk.

Chapters two and three are recommended reading for every designer who has not had the experience of designing a basic system. Chapter two presents the construction of a basic CPU, in the case of popular microprocessors such as the Intel 8080, 8085, and the Motorola 6800. Chapter three presents the set of input-output techniques used to communicate with the external world, and a brief survey of the existing chips which facilitate the implementation of these techniques.

Chapter four is an essential chapter: the microprocessor-based CPU will be successively interfaced to every major peripheral: keyboard, LED, teletype, floppy-disk, CRT display, tape-cassette.

The following chapters then focus on specific interfacing problems and techniques, from industrial design (analog-to-digital conversion) (chapter five) to communication with the outside world (busing, including S-100 and other bus standards), in chapter six.

Chapter seven presents a detailed case study, which incorporates the interfacing principles presented in the previous chapters: the design of a . real 32-channel multiplexer.

Finally, chapter eight presents the basic techniques and tools for trouble-shooting microprocessor systems.

This book assumes a basic understanding of microprocessor systems, equivalent to the level of book **C201 - Microprocessors: from chips to systems**.

1

INTRODUCTION

OBJECTIVE

The objective of this book is to present the complete set of techniques required in order to interface a microprocessor to the external world. Because of the availability of new LSI interface chips, which implement most techniques in hardware, it will be shown that interfacing has become simple.

FROM ART TO TECHNIQUE

Microcomputer interfacing has traditionally been the art of designing complex boards of logic managing the data transfers and the synchronization signals necessary for the processor to communicate with external devices. The processor itself has traditionally required one or more boards of logic. Such multi-board implementations are obsolete today in most cases. *Large scale integration* (LSI) has now resulted in the implementation of a complete (or almost complete) CPU in *a single chip*. The new market created by microprocessors has introduced, in turn, the necessity for manufacturers to provide the required support components. Most of the boards required to assemble a complete system have now been shrunk into LSI chips. Since 1976, even device-controller interface chips exist. They do for interface design what the microprocessor has done for CPU design.

A complete interface board, or most of it, is today shrunk into a few LSI chips. The price paid, as in the case of a microprocessor, is that the architecture is frozen inside the LSI chip.

It is now possible to implement a complete microcomputer system, including interfaces, in a small number of LSI chips. *If you are still implementing your interfaces on one or more boards of logic, your design might be obsolete!*

Microprocessor interface chips have not yet reached their maturity. They are still "dumb" chips. In other words, they can execute only a very few commands. It can be predicted that in view of the very low cost of a processing element, most microprocessor interface chips will become fully programmable in the near future. They will become "processor-equipped," and be capable of sophisticated programmed sequencing. They will become "intelligent" interfaces.

Although this next step has not yet been reached, all the techniques presented within this book should retain their validity in the future. There is always a trade-off between software and hardware implementation. The balance will change with the introduction of new components, and with the trade-offs involved in each specific system design.

THE HARDWARE/SOFTWARE TRADE-OFF

Detailed techniques will be presented for solving all the common interfacing problems. As usual in computer design, most of these techniques may be implemented either by *hardware* (by components), or by *software* (by programs), or by a combination of both. It is always up to the system designer to strike a reasonable compromise between the efficiency of hardware, and the lower component count of a software implementation. Examples of both will be provided.

THE STANDARD MICROPROCESSOR SYSTEM

Throughout this book, reference will be made to a "standard microprocessor." The "standard" microprocessor today is the *8-bit microprocessor.* Examples are the Intel 8080, 8085, the Zilog Z-80, the Motorola 8600, the Signetics 2650, etc. In view of the pin number limitation on DIPs (dual-in-line packages), the 8-bit microprocessor has become the norm. The reason is simple:

The number of pins is limited to 40 (or 42) by economic considerations. Industrial testers required to test components having more than 40 pins are either not available, or would be extremely expensive. All standard testers will accept only up to 40 or 42 pins. In addition, naturally, the cost of the package itself increases rapidly over 40 pins.

Because of the limitation of the densities which can be achieved with the MOS LSI process, it is not yet possible to integrate the complete memory, plus I/O facilities, directly on the microprocessor chip. In the standard system, the microprocessor itself (abbreviated MPU), and perhaps the clock, reside on a single chip. The memory (ROM, Read-Only Memory, and RAM, or Random-Access Memory) is external. Because memory and I/O chips are external to the microprocessor, a selection mechanism must be provided for addressing the components: a microprocessor must be equipped with an *address bus*. The standard width of the address bus in 16 bits, permitting the addressing of 64 K locations (where K $= 1,024: 2^{16} = 64K$).

An 8-bit microprocessor will transfer 8-bit data. It must be equipped with an 8-bit *data bus*. This requires 8 additional pins.

At least two pins must be provided for power, and two more for connection to an external crystal or oscillator. Finally, 10 to 12 control lines must be provided for the coordination of data transfers in the system (the control bus). The total number of pins used is 40. No pins are left unused.

Because of this pin-number limitation, a 16-bit microprocessor cannot provide a 16-bit address bus and a 16-bit data bus at the same time. One of the buses must be *multiplexed*. This results in turn in a slower operation, and in the necessity of external components to multiplex and de-multiplex the buses.

It can be expected that the progress of integration will soon introduce a new standard microprocessor, the *16-bit microcomputer-on-a-chip*. A microcomputer-on-a-chip is a microprocessor-plus-clock-plus-memory (ROM + RAM) on a single chip. Since the memory is directly on the chip, there is no longer the necessity of providing an external address bus. 16 pins become available. In such a system, *at least 24 lines become available for data transfers*. They are general-purpose I/O lines. The disadvantage of current microcomputers is that, for the time being, the quantity of memory which may be implemented directly on the microcomputer chip is limited. The current limitation is 2048 words for the ROM, and 512 words for the RAM. Adding external memory involves complex multiplexing and demultiplexing, and is usually not worth it. However, if a system can be implemented in the near future with a significantly larger memory, it can be expected that it will become the next standard design.

For the time being, the 8-bit microprocessor is indeed the standard design used for "powerful" and flexible applications, and will be referred as such. The basic diagram showing the architecture of a standard system appears in Fig. 1-1. The microprocessor itself, labeled

MPU, appears on the left of the illustration. On most standard systems, until 1976, the clock was external to the MPU. It appears here on the far left of the illustration. Since 1976, the clock circuitry has been incorporated in the microprocessor chip itself and all recent products do not require this external clock. However, they always require an external *crystal* or oscillator. It appears here, connected to the clock.

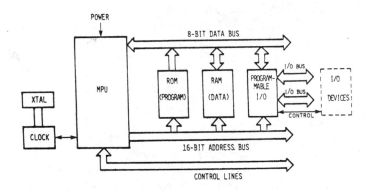

Fig. 1-1: Standard Microprocessor System

The microprocessor creates *three buses:*

The 8-bit bi-directional *data bus* (implemented in tri-state logic to allow the use of a direct-memory-access controller, or DMAC).

A 16-bit mono-directional *address bus,* connected internally, within the microprocessor, to the address pointers, and in particular to the program counter (PC). The address bus is also implemented in tri-state logic in order to allow the use of a DMAC.

Finally, a 10 to 12-line *control bus,* which carries the various synchronization signals to and from the microprocessor. Control lines are not necessarily tri-state.

All the usual system components are directly connected to these three buses. The three basic components appear in the illustration. They are respectively the ROM, the RAM, and the PIO. The *ROM* is the Read-Only Memory. It stores the *programs.* The *RAM* is the Random-Access Memory. It is a read-write MOS memory which stores the *data.* The PIO is a programmable input-output chip which multiplexes the data bus into two or more input-output ports. It will be studied in more detail in chapter three. These ports may be connected directly to input-output devices, or to device controllers, or may require the use of interface circuits.

The interface circuits or *interface chips* required to interface this basic system to actual I/O devices will be connected to these buses, whether it be the microprocessor buses or the input-output buses created by the PIO or by other chips.

Interfacing techniques are precisely those techniques required to connect this basic system to the various input-output devices. The basic interfacing techniques required to connect any microprocessor system to input-output devices are essentially identical. They will be described in detail in chapters three, four, and five. At the level of the microprocessor itself, the logical and electrical interface required is simple. All standard microprocessors have essentially the same data bus and the same address bus. The essential difference is the *control bus*. It is the specific characteristics of the control bus which make input-output interface chips compatible or incompatible from one microprocessor to the next. As an example of basic interfacing characteristics, the basic 8080, 6800, and 6502 SC/MP interfacing characteristics appear in Fig. 1-2.

Interfacing input-output devices requires the understanding of two basic techniques:

1. The assembly of a complete CPU, using a microprocessor chip. This topic will be addressed in chapter 2.
2. The fundamental input-output techniques used to communicate between the microprocessor and the external world. This topic will be addressed in chapter 3.

MICROPROCESSOR CONTROL SIGNALS

It has been shown that a standard MPU creates three buses: the 8-bit bi-directional data bus, the 16-bit mono-directional address bus, and a control bus of varying width, depending on the microprocessor. The data bus is essentially identical for all microprocessors. It is an 8-bit bi-directional bus, normally implemented in tri-state logic. Similarly, the address bus is almost universally a 16 or sometimes, a 15-bit mono-directional bus, used to select a device external to the MPU. The actual use and interconnect of the address bus and the data bus will be pre-

	8080&8228	8085	Z-80	6800	6502
ADDRESS	A0–A15	AD0-AD7 +ALF A8-A15	A0-A15	A0-A15	AB0-AB15
DATA	D0-D7	AD0-AD7 +–ALE	D0-D7	D0-D7	DB0-DB7
CONTROL	HLDA	HLDA	BUSAK	BA&VMA	--------
	HOLD	HOLD	BUSRQ	HALT	RDY
	Ø2	CLK	—	Ø2 stretched	Ø2 stretch
	INT	INTR	INT	IRQ	IRQ
	INTE	—	—	—	—
	WAIT	—	WAIT	—	—
	READY	READY	RESET	—	RDY
	RESET	RESET	M1	RESET	RESET
	SYNC	—	M1&IORQ	—	SYNC
	INTA	INTA	RD&MEMRQ	VMA&FFF8	—
	MEMR	RD&IO/M	WR&MEMRQ	R/W&Ø2	R/W&Ø2
	MEMW	WR&IO/M	RD&IORQ	as above	as above
	I/O RD	RD&IO/M-	WR&IORQ	as above	as above
	I/O WR	WR&IO/M-	—	as above	as above
	BUSEN	—	—	HALT	—
	SSTB	—	—	—	—
OTHER CONTROL SIGNALS	—	RST 5.5	—	—	—
	—	RST6.5	—	—	—
	—	RST 7.5	NMI	NMI	NMI
	—	TRAP	—	—	—
	—	RESET	—	—	—
	—	OUT	—	—	—
	—	SID	—	—	—
	—	SOD	RFSH	—	—
	—	ALE	HALT	—	—
	—	—	—	TSC	—
	—	—	—	DBE	—
	—	—	—	—	SO

Fig. 1-2: Signal Equivalences

sented in the next chapter. The third bus is the only complex one. It carries the microprocessor control signals or "interface signals."

The control bus provides four functions:
1. memory synchronization
2. input-output synchronization
3. MPU scheduling — interrupt and DMA
4. utilities, such as clock and reset.

Memory and input-output synchronization are essentially analogous. A handshake procedure is used. In "read" operation, a "ready" status or signal will indicate the availability of data. Data will then be transferred on the data bus. In the case of some input-output devices, an "acknowledge" is generated, to confirm the receipt of data. For "write" operation, the availability of the external device is verified through a status bit or signal, and the data is then deposited on the data bus. Here also an "acknowledge" might be generated by the device to confirm the receipt of data.

The generation, or non-generation, of an "acknowledge" is typical of the use of the synchronous procedure versus an asynchronous one. In a synchronous procedure, all events take place within a specified period of time. In this case there is no need to acknowledge. In an asynchronous system, an acknowledge must be generated. The choice of a synchronous versus an asynchronous communication philosophy is basic to the design of a control bus. A synchronous design has a potential for a higher speed and a lower number of control lines. However, it imposes speed constraints on the external devices. An asynchronous design will require an additional knowledge, and somewhat more logic, but allows the use of components of varying speeds in the same system.

As examples, the 8080 control signals are illustrated in Fig. 1-3, with the bus timing in Figures 1-4 and 1-5. In contrast, the 6800 bus is shown in Figures 1-6 and 1-7. In chapter two these buses will be explained. Chapter six expands on buses and describes some standard buses in use today.

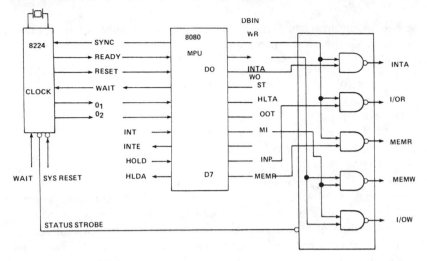

Fig. 1-3: 8080 Control Signals

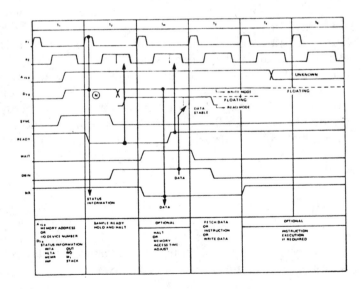

Fig. 1-4: Basic 8080 Instruction Cycle

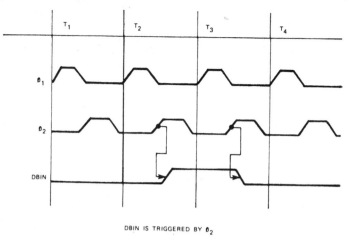

DBIN IS TRIGGERED BY $\emptyset_2$

Fig. 1-5: DBIN Timing

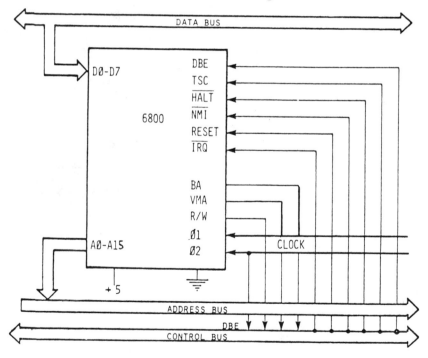

Fig. 1-6: 6800 Bus Signals

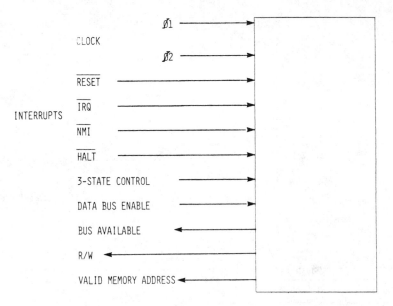

Fig. 1-7: Detail: 6800 Bus Control

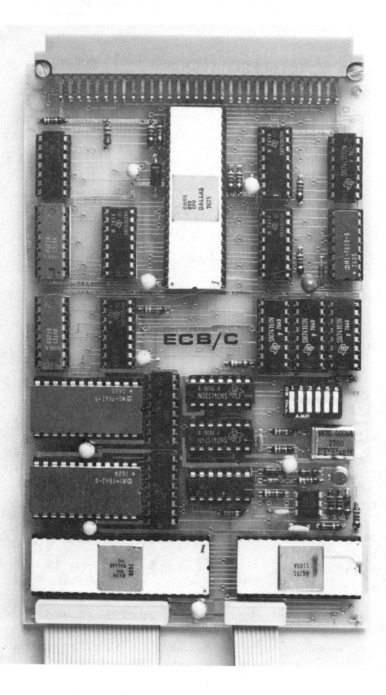

Fig. 2-0: Z-80 CPU Board

2

ASSEMBLING THE CENTRAL PROCESSING UNIT

INTRODUCTION

The heart of any microprocessor system is the *central processing unit or CPU*. A CPU includes the microprocessor and any additional components it may require. Memory devices, buffers, decoders, clock-drivers are all included in the typical central processing unit. Many of these circuits are now being integrated on the same chip as the processor. In fact, since 1976, one-chip microcomputers are a reality. Yet, even with the advent of one-chip microcomputers, there still exist certain limitations on integrated circuit fabrication. There are three basic limits of the present LSI technology: *yield* limits the number of transistors per chip, *packaging* limits the number of pins on the package, and *substrate material* prevents some devices from being integrated.

At first, only single transistors were made on each chip. Later, differential pairs and simple logic gates made their appearance. Present technology allows for up to 30,000 devices to be integrated on a chip. A graph of devices integrated versus time appears in Fig. 2-1. One factor has remained constant throughout this process: process defects limit the maximum size of the individual die. *Yields* are higher for smaller die sizes. (The yield is the number of good devices per batch.) In the design of any LSI chip, the "real-estate" (chip-area) becomes an all-important factor affecting the cost of the final device. Fig. 2-2 illustrates the trade-off between yield and die-size. Yields also increase with manufacturing experience—this is called the "learning-curve"; costs decrease with higher quantities, because of improved yield.

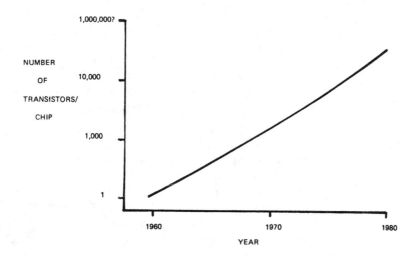

Fig. 2-1: Devices Integrated Versus Time

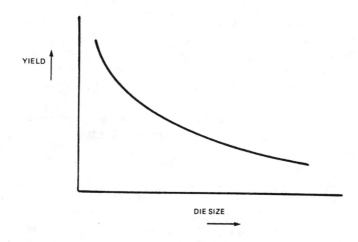

Fig. 2-2: Yield versus Die Size

27

A less obvious factor is the *packaging* of LSI devices. Present testing equipment cannot handle packages with more than 40 pins. Future test systems may overcome this limitation, but, for now, the scarcity of package-pins may require the use of multiplexing techniques. The data bus may also be used to carry *address* or *control* information so that pins may be conserved (e.g. 8080, 8085).

How does the substrate material limit LSI technology? Certain components require a different physical material. The simplest example is the crystal required for timing. A crystal is cut from quartz. The integrated circuit is made from silicon. All systems requiring accurate timing will require a crystal. Because of its bulk, the crystal is external.

In addition to the fact that limitations of LSI technology partition our system into multiple components, additional devices are often needed for system expansion. Large microprocessor systems require a significant amount of "support-logic."

This chapter will present the concepts, techniques, and components required to build a complete CPU: from system architecture to support logic. Four typical systems will be presented, using the 8080, 6800, Z-80, and 8085 microprocessors.

SYSTEM ARCHITECTURE

Fig. 2-3 presents the block-diagram of a typical microprocessor system. All standard microprocessors, such as the 8080 or the 6800, have a similar architecture. Three buses connect the systems' components: data, address, and control bus.

The *data bus* carries information to and from the processor element. It carries the instructions fetched from memory, the data input from input devices, the data stored into memory, and the data output going to the output devices.

To specify where the data are going, or where they are coming from, the *address bus* is used. It selects a location in memory or a register of an input-output device.

The control bus is used to control the sequencing and nature of the operation being performed. The control bus indicates in particular the type of operation to be performed: "read from memory to the processor," "write to memory from the processor," "read from an input device to the processor," or "write to an output device from the processor." Additionally, interrupt, direct memory access, and other control functions are carried by lines of the control bus to implement the scheduling and synchronization of events.

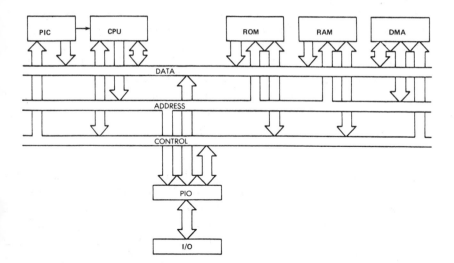

Fig. 2-3: Typical System Architecture

Our standard microprocessor has 8 data lines, 16 address lines, and at least 8 control lines. 8 data bits form a *byte*. The byte is the basic unit of information in our standard system. Half of a byte is sometimes known as a *nibble*. The 16 address lines allow for addressing of 65,536 (2^{16}) different memory locations or bytes. Two methods are used for selecting a memory location, or a device register: linear selection, and fully-decoded selection.

Linear Selection

In the microprocessor world, memory is partitioned into *read-only-memory* (ROM) for programs and fixed data tables, and *random-access-memory* (RAM) for data storage and temporaries, because of the volatility of MOS RAMs.

When more than one type of memory is used, the two types of memory are generally in separate packages. Also, the size of each will be considerably less than the full 65,536 possible locations available to our system. We must place each device in its proper place in our *memory map*. A memory map is the addressing plan for the address bus bits.

Initially, each device, RAM and ROM for our system will have 256 locations. This implies that eight address lines will be needed to select one of the 256 possible locations in each chip. Besides these eight lines, the processor must be able to select one device at a time. RAM and ROM devices have, in addition to their address inputs, at least one "chip-select" (CS). This select line, when activated, allows the operation to be per-formed on the device (Read or Write).

Two basic techniques are used to implement the chip selection. *Linear-selection* connects individual address lines to individual chip-select inputs. For example, if the most-significant address bit (bit 15) is tied to a chip-select, that chip is selected whenever the most-significant-bit is a one. This occurs for half of the total memory locations. Assume that our ROM is selected by this most-significant-bit being "0" and the RAM by this bit being "1." To address the 256 locations available inside each device, we will connect lines A0 to A7 of the address bus.

The essential advantage of linear-selection is simplicity: no special logic is necessary in order to select chips. Each new chip is selected by a dedicated address line. This is, indeed, the approach used in all small microprocessor systems.

For example, a 1K × 8 ROM chip will be used and a 512 × 8 RAM, plus 3 peripheral chips. The 1K ROM requires 10 lines for address selection: A0 - A9, plus one line for the chip-select: A14. The RAM will use A0 - A8 for address selection, and A15 for the chip-select. Lines A10, A11, A12, A13 may be used for additional devices.

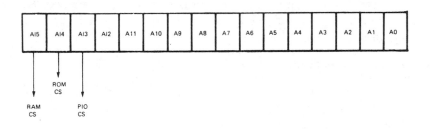

Fig. 2-4: Linear Selection

However, linear selection divides the available memory in half every time a separate address line is used. If the need exists to select more devices than there are available address lines, another method must be used: *fully-decoded addressing.*

Fully-Decoded Addressing

The goal of fully-decoded addressing is to provide a complete 64K addressing capability.

In our example, the 256-location RAM will reside in the last 256 locations of the memory. Expressed in binary, these are addresses 1111111100000000_2 to 1111111111111111_2. Grouping into four-bit groups and converting to hexadecimal this is: FF00 to FFFF. (See appendix for hexadecimal conversion table.) We see that the RAM chip should be enabled when the 8 high-order address bits are equal to "1." "ANDing" these bits together would form our chip select. Fig. 2-5 illustrates the decoding for our example.

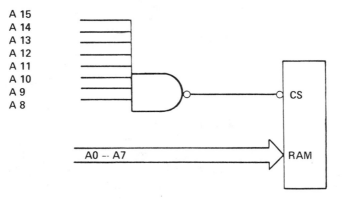

A 15
A 14
A 13
A 12
A 11
A 10
A 9
A 8

A0 -- A7   CS

RAM

Fig. 2-5: Fully Decoded Selection

Instead of using AND gates for every device, there exist general-purpose gating devices known as *decoders*. An example is the 8205 or 74LS138 three-to-eight decoder. The 8205 has three inputs to select one of eight mutually exclusive outputs, in function of three enable inputs. When the three enable inputs are in their proper states, one of the outputs will be active, depending on the three select lines. Examples using the 8205 will be presented in the hardware section to clarify full-decoding schemes.

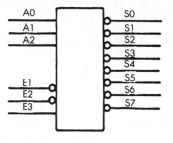

$$S0 = (\overline{A0} \cdot \overline{A1} \cdot \overline{A2}) \cdot (\overline{E1} \cdot \overline{E2} \cdot E3)$$

$$S1 = (A0 \cdot \overline{A1} \cdot \overline{A2}) \cdot (\overline{E1} \cdot \overline{E2} \cdot E3)$$

$$\bullet$$
$$\bullet$$
$$\bullet$$

$$S7 = (A0 \cdot A1 \cdot A2) \cdot (\overline{E1} \cdot \overline{E2} \cdot E3)$$

Fig. 2-6: 8205 Decoder

Complete decoding selects devices without wasting available address space. A contiguous memory may be built where addresses pass from one device to the next without large areas of nonexistent or overlapping memory. The disadvantage of this approach is the cost of decoding. Most systems implement a mix of linear selection and partial decoding.

Storage Chips

The basic devices for storing information now used are the RAM and the ROM. The ROM contains permanent information and *cannot be changed* by the system. The RAM allows for temporary storage and retrieval of information. The program information is usually kept in a non-volatile ROM since it does not change, and the data and intermediate results are stored in RAM.

"RAM" usually refers to a semiconductor device, but is also used for other storage media, such as core memory.

A RAM chip may contain from 256 to 16,384 cells, each cell representing a bit of the information word or byte. Each cell may consist of a flip-flop type structure—in which case it is a *static device,* or it may consist of a capacitor structure—in which case it is a *dynamic device.* The static RAM will retain information as long as power is present, whereas the dynamic device must be refreshed every few milliseconds in order to renew the stored charge in each cell. This means that dynamic memory will undergo a refresh cycle one to five percent of the time. This may be important in some real-time applications, as memory will be "busy" and unavailable for use as long as a refresh cycle is in progress.

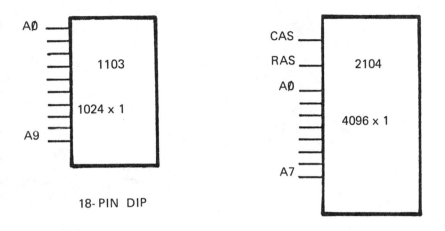

Fig. 2-7: Intel Dynamic RAMs

ROM will refer here to an LSI device, but may also be used to denote other types of read-only memories. Several types of ROMs are available. The masked ROM is "programmed" by the *manufacturer* and will stay programmed for the life of the chip. It cannot be altered. The PROM is programmed by the *user* and may either be of the fusible-link type, where a bit is programmed by blowing a microscopic fuse, or it may be a stored-charge type that will retain the pattern for tens of years. The latter type is also known as an EPROM because it can be erased by ultraviolet light and reused. The EAROM is electrically erasable and could be considered as RAM except that it takes 100 milliseconds or longer (typically) to erase the device. This makes it inconvenient to use as a scratchpad for calculations or data manipulations. The use of EAROMs has been restricted so far to military applications.

Buffering the Buses

Each input of a device presents a load on the output driving it. Most components drive anywhere from one to twenty other components. Every component must be checked for its input and output loading and driving characteristics.

The microprocessor's buses must connect to every memory and peripheral input-output chip in a system. All MOS microprocessors lack the output drive needed for a large system. Because of this, *buffers* or *drivers* are used to boost the driving power of the buses. There are bus *transmitters* for driving the bus, and bus *receivers* for listening to the bus and driving the processor.

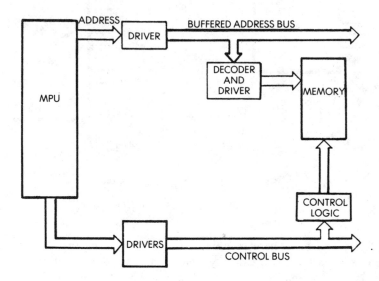

Fig. 2-8: Buffering Address and Control Lines

Fig. 2-8 illustrates the use of transmitters to buffer the address and control buses. The lines on the address and control buses are *unidirectional:* the data flows in one direction.

Fig. 2-9 illustrates the use of bus *transceivers* for the data bus. Data must pass in both directions, so both transmitters and receivers are used. The *bidirectional* data bus will receive data and transmit data, depending on the function being performed.

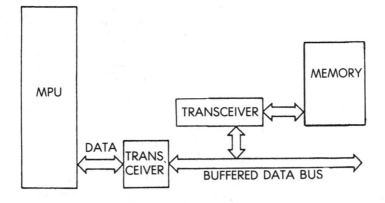

Fig. 2-9: Buffering the Data Bus

The concept of a system architecture will be expanded and completed in Chapter 3 on input and output techniques. To clarify the concepts presented so far, four real systems will now be assembled: an 8080, a 6800, a Z-80 (with dynamic RAM), and an 8085 system.

THE 8080 SYSTEM

Intel's 8080 has been the most widely used "standard"-architecture microprocessor. The 8080 is a popular processor also used in many hobby microcomputers. We will assemble the complete central processing module for a typical 8080 computer system. The connection of the clock, system controller, RAM, and ROM will be presented. The input-output will be covered in detail in Chapter 3.

The Clock

The 8080 requires a twophase non-overlapping clock. This clock must swing between + 11 volts and + 0.3 volts. The clock is therefore not TTL-compatible. Initially, clock-drivers were made from discrete components or special-driving integrated circuits. Intel introduced the 8224 clock chip to reduce parts-count and simplify the clock interface problem. One merely connects the crystal to the 8224, the 8224 to the 8080, and all clock interfacing is complete.

The connection of the 8224 appears in Fig. 2-10 and the structure of the 8224 itself appears in Fig. 2-11.

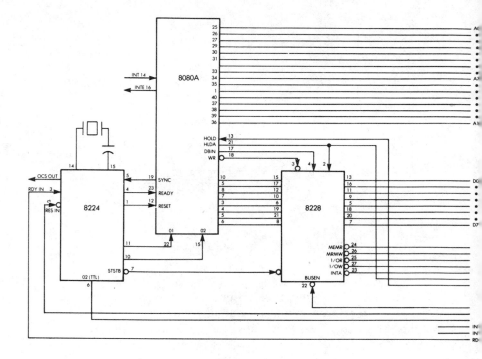

Fig. 2-10: 8080 Completed CPU

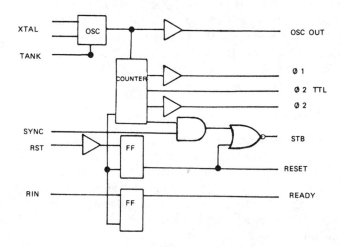

Fig. 2-11: 8224 Schematic

The System Controller

When designing the 8080, the lack of pins became a major limitation. In order to gate out the required control signals, pins have to be multiplexed. Control or address functions would have to share lines with the data bus. In this case, the designers chose to multiplex control information or *status* on the data bus. This status byte may be latched for use at the time of the SYNC signal. The lack of pins is essentially due to the early technology used for the 8080, which required three power levels using four pins.

Early processor designs used latches and random logic to capture these status signals. In fact, this is why the actual S100 bus still retains what is known as the *old 8080 status signals*. The design of what became known as the *system controller* appears in Fig. 2-12. The latch holds the status information, and the gates decode the status along with the other 8080 control lines into control signals for the memory and input-output devices.

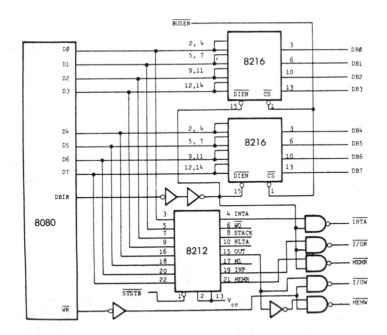

Fig. 2-12: System Controller Using 8212 and 8216's

Intel, realizing early that the system-controller function should be integrated into a single chip, introduced the 8228 chip, shown in Fig. 2-13. This device latches the status and drives the control bus. In addition, it buffers the data bus, i.e. includes a data bus driver.

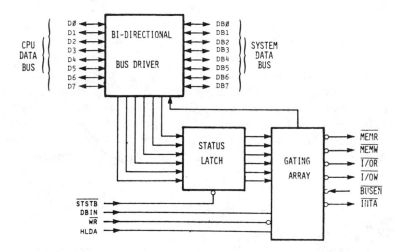

Fig. 2-13: 8228 System Controller

The trio of 8224, 8228, and 8080 now completes the central processor function. The only other component required is the crystal. To complete the CPU we need to add the program memory and the random-access memory (ROM and RAM).

Connecting the ROM

Read-only memories come in two essential varieties: programmable and masked. The programmable ROMs may be programmed once at the time they are to be used (such as fusible link ROMs or PROMs); or they may be programmed, used, and erased (such as ultraviolet erasable ROMs or EPROMs). The mask ROMs are programmed at the time of manufacture and are used only in production systems. The erasable or fusible link ROMs are used for prototyping.

A typical erasable ROM appears connected to our 8080 buses in Fig. 2-14. This device, a 2708 EPROM, contains 1024 bytes of memory. In order to address 1024 bytes, 10 address lines are needed (2^{10} = 1024). In addition, the chip must be selected at its proper place in the memory map. We will choose to put this memory at locations 0000 through 03FF hexadecimal. In order to decode this address space, an

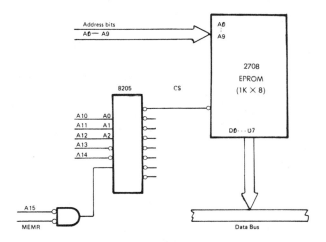

Fig. 2-14: 2708 Selection Using 8205

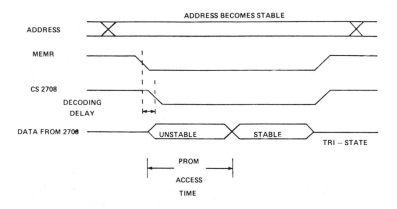

Fig. 2-15: PROM Timing

8205 is used in addition to some other selection logic for controlling the memory-read condition. Note that it can select up to seven additional, contiguously located, 2708's, if required. The data bus connects directly to the data lines of the 8228 system controller. The only control line required is the memory-read line. The timing of a memory-read appears in Fig. 2-15.

The address and memory-read lines activate the 2708. After a period of time called access time, the data byte fetched appears on the data bus. The processor reads this byte and executes the instruction.

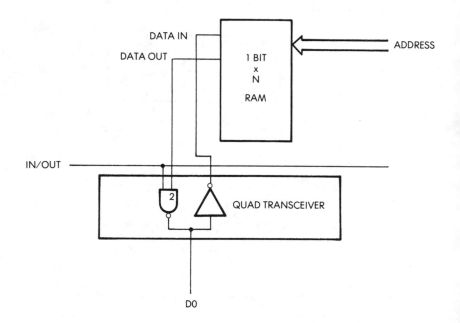

Fig. 2-16: Buffering RAM Data Lines Using a Bus Transceiver

Connecting the RAM

A convenient size for the economical manufacture of ROMs is 1K by 8 bits (1K = 1024). RAMs, however, come in different sizes. The most inexpensive configuration is 1K by 1 bit (least number of pins). We need eight bits for a byte, so that eight devices are needed—one for each bit. Another popular size is 256 by 4 bits. This type of RAM is interfaced here.

40

256 by 4 implies that two devices are needed to complete the byte. The schematic for the 256 by 4 memories, interfaced to the 8080 bus, appears in Fig. 2-17.

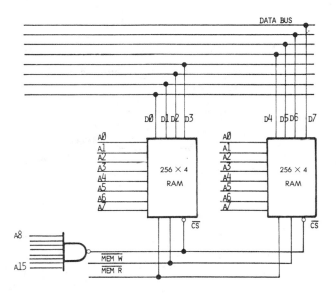

Fig. 2-17: Connecting the 2111 RAM

The address bus lines needed to specify the address are connected to each RAM chip. The eight address lines will select one of the 256 bytes in each RAM chip. The unused eight address lines are decoded by an eight-input NAND gate. As per our earlier discussion, the RAM will be located from FF00 to FFFF hexadecimal. The data bus splits in two, with four bits going to each of the 256 × 4 bit RAMs. Actual data bus connections are shown in Fig. 2-16. Control lines are needed to enable the memories for reading and writing as well as to control the timing of the writing operation. The 2111 RAMs used here have a number of extra enable inputs, as well as read/write lines. The two signals "memory-read" and "memory-write," are used to control the RAMs. "Memory-read" enables the output drivers of the chips to drive the data bus. At all other times, the chip is in a read mode, but will not place information on the bus. "Memory-write" enables the RAM to perform a write cycle and gates data presented on the data bus into the RAMs. Timings of these operations are illustrated in Fig. 2-18.

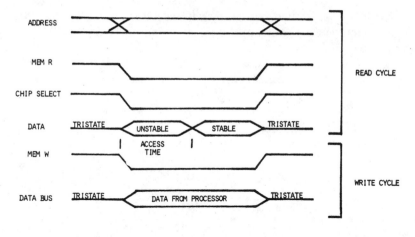

Fig. 2-18: RAM Timing

When the address becomes stable and "memory-read" is brought low, the chip is enabled to drive the data bus. After the byte is accessed, it remains on the bus until fetched by the processor and "memory-read" returns high. The write cycle is similar, except that, this time, "memory-write" is brought low, forcing the data bus contents to be written into the RAMs.

Integrating the processor and memory into an assembled module requires only that we draw them all on the same schematic.

The Complete 8080 System

To make life more interesting, the system module presented here contains only *partial decoding* for the PROMs and *linear selection* for the RAMs. The memory module appears in Fig. 2-19. The PROMs will occupy locations 0000 through 0FFF hexadecimal. The RAM will be at 2000 through 20FF hexadecimal. It will also be addressed for all addresses of the form: XX1XXXXXXXXXXXXX binary—where X is a one or a zero (don't care condition). The PROM is addressed for: XX00000000000000 through XX01111111111111 binary. We cannot add any other memory to this system without further decoding.

The central processor module will be the same as in Fig. 2-10. As an exercise, the central processor assembly of Chapter 8 could be examined at this time and the reader should verify his/her understanding of address-decoding and buffering techniques.

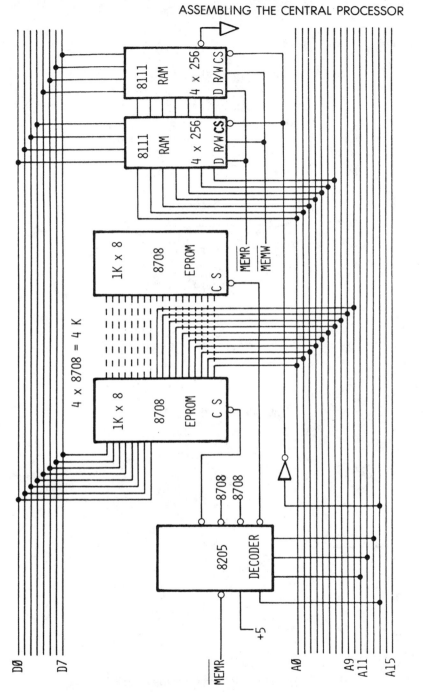

Fig. 2-19: Complete 8080 System Memory

THE 6800 SYSTEM

Developed by Motorola, the 6800 is also a popularly used "standard" type of microprocessor. In comparison to Intel's device, the 6800 implements some design philosophy differences. The most obvious are the lack of pin-multiplexing and the single power-supply requirement. Other differences lie in the instruction set, internal architecture, and control signals. Overall, both devices are essentially similar. Fig. 2-20 shows a schematic of a 6800 system.

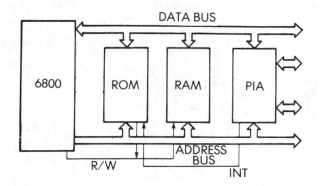

Fig. 2-20: 6800 System Block Diagram

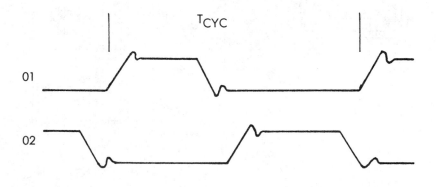

Fig. 2-21: 6800 Non-Overlapping Clock Signals

The Clock

The 6800 requires a non-TTL compatible clock-generator. Since no other useful functions are needed for the twophase clock generation, either simple discrete clock circuits or integrated drivers are used. Motorola produces a hybrid device which contains the crystal and conveniently provides the necessary clock phases. Fig. 2-21 details the 6800 clock requirements.

6800 Buses

The 6800 architecture uses memory-mapped input-output (see Chapter 3) and requires only a single power-level, versus three for the 8080. As a result, no multiplexing is required to gate the control signals. However, the buses need to be buffered in any large system, making the parts count essentially equal to 8080 and 6800 systems. (The 8228 system controller includes a data bus driver).

The data bus is a bidirectional 8-bit bus. It requires buffering for most applications. The suggested Motorola components appear in Fig. 2-22.

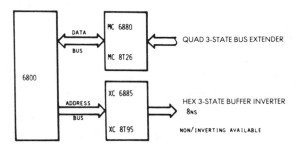

Fig. 2-22: Buffering 6800 Buses - Suggested Devices

The address and control buses are unidirectional with 16 address lines and ten control lines respectively. Fig. 2-23 illustrates the 6800 bus signals. For memory interfacing, the R/W, $\overline{\phi}2$, and VMA signals are required. They are the read/write control, phase two of the clock and valid-memory-address control line.

TSC	High forces address bus and R/W into high impedance mode
DBE	Low forces data bus into high-Z mode
R/W	MPU is in read mode when low
VMA	Is valid memory address. A high enables RAM, PIA, ACIA
IRQ	Is interrupt request line. PC is loaded from FFF8, FFF9
RESET	Starts the 6800 from power-down. PC is loaded from FFFE, FFFF. 8 cycles are required before
NMI	Is non-maskable interrupt. PC is loaded from FFFC, FFFD.
HALT	Allows program execution by external source and stepping
BA	(HALT or WAIT) indicates that address bus is available

Fig. 2-23: 6800 Control Signals

The ROM

Motorola manufactures a line of 6800 compatible products which facilitate the interface requirements in small or medium-size systems. Their 1K by 8-bit mask ROM includes *four chip-select lines* for selecting the ROM as shown in Fig. 2-24.

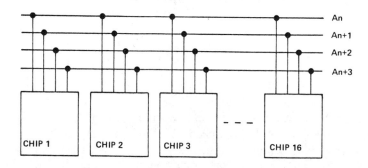

Fig. 2-24: 4 Chip Selects Allow Connection of up to 16 Devices

In the example of Fig. 2-25, the chip selects are connected to three of the high-order address bits, and to the VMA signal ANDed with the $\phi 2$ signal. In this way, the ROM is selected for any valid memory address cycle from 1C00 to FFFF hexadecimal. Of course, the ROM is only 1024 bytes, so the large area it takes up is due to the "don't cares" or the undecoded address bits: A15, A14, and A13.

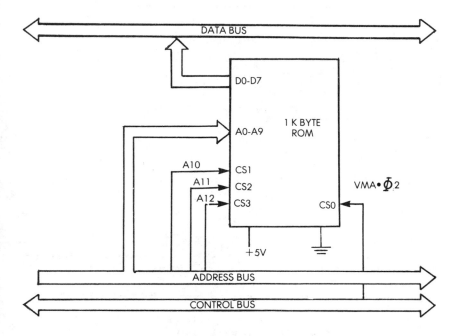

Fig. 2-25: 6800 ROM Connection

The RAM

Motorola is one of the few manufacturers that make a 128 by 8-bit RAM. This is a convenient size for small systems. The interface to the 6810 RAM is aided by the large number of decoded chip selects that are provided on the chip.

The interface of the RAM appears in Fig. 2-26. Note that only seven address lines are needed to select one of the 128 RAM bytes. The other 9 address lines must be used in some combination to select the chip. In this example, RAM is selected when A11 through A7 are all low. This would be address 0000 through 00FF hexadecimal. Since the highest four address bits are not fully decoded, the memory is also enabled for addresses 1000 through 10FF. Similarly, it is enabled for 2000 through 20FF, and so on, ending with F000 through F0FF.

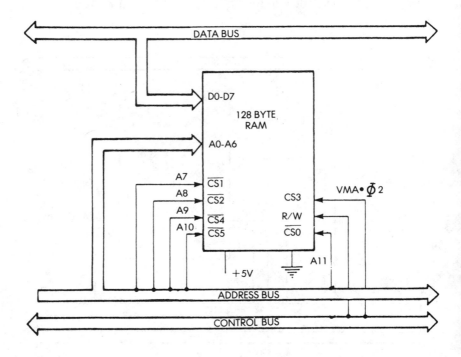

Fig. 2-26: 6800 RAM Connection - The 6810

In order to use our RAM with our ROM, we must select those places where the two do not overlap. One example is ROM from FC00 through FFFF and RAM from 0000 through 00FF.

The VMA and $\phi 2$ signals select the device for the memory cycle, and "read/write" controls the function—fetching or storing.

The Complete 6800 System

In Fig. 2-27, the complete 6800 system is presented. Note that an input-output device is included here. This will be explained in Chapter 3.

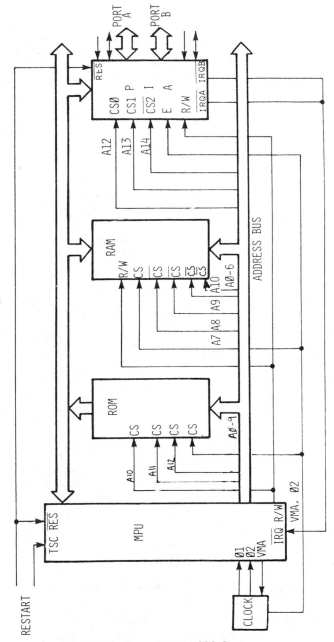

Fig. 2-27: Completed 6800 System

THE Z-80

Up to this point, the processors used were developed at about the same time. Zilog, created by the designers of the Intel 8080, was determined to improve the power of the original device. The Z-80 is software-compatible with the 8080. (In addition, it has some additional instructions and registers which improve its processing capability.) In particular, the Z-80 provides the necessary signals for interfacing with the larger *dynamic memory* devices. A small Z-80 system appears in Fig. 2-28.

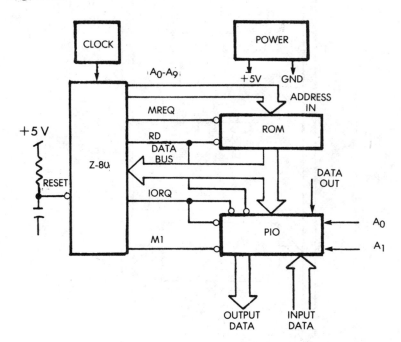

Fig. 2-28: Z-80 System

Dynamic RAM Interface

In our previous examples, the memory devices used were *static* RAMs data and are retained as long as power is applied. *Dynamic* RAMs need to be *refreshed* periodically. A dynamic RAM stores information in a FET capacitor. Such a device can only retain its charge for a few milliseconds. The cell must be accessed every few milliseconds, in order to renew, or "refresh" the cell. The Z-80 provides the refresh address using a design trick.

After an instruction is fetched, the address bus no longer needs to remain stable. Instead of wasting this time, the Z-80 outputs a *fresh address* on the lower 7 address bits. This address increments once each instruction cycle, and with the additional internal refresh register, dynamic memories may be interfaced easily to the Z-80.

Otherwise, the processor would have to wait while a separate circuit, called the *refresh controller,* stepped through the dynamic memory rows refreshing the cells. The dynamic memory interface appears in Fig. 2-29.

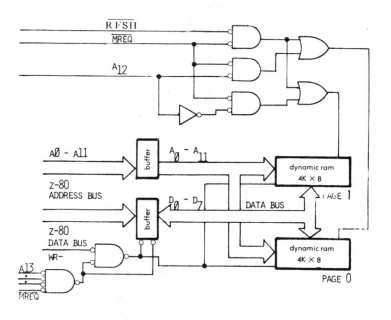

Fig. 2-29: Z-80 Dynamic Memory Interfacing

In Fig. 2-30, the timing of the Z-80 refresh cycle is presented. Note how, whenever an instruction is fetched, we get a "free" refresh cycle. Using the RFSH and MREQ signals, we can do a column refresh, thereby maintaining our data.

In any other system one would have to provide an address multiplexer, column counter, and refresh control logic on each memory board. Fig. 2-31 illustrates such a system.

51

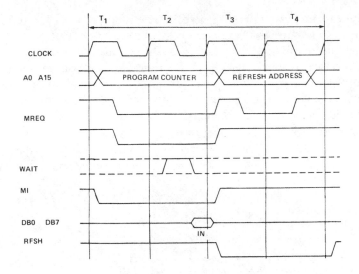

Fig. 2-30: Z-80 Refresh Timing

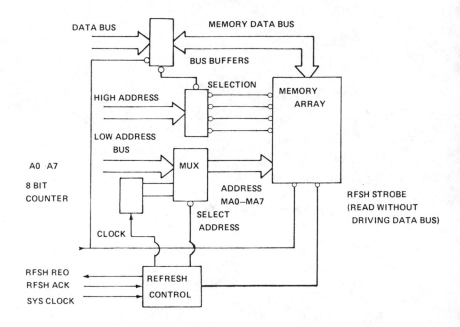

Fig. 2-31: General Refresh Controller

The *Refresh Control Section* will vary with each different microprocessor bus timing specifications. Besides the timing, one must choose the method of refresh.

The control section may wait 2 milliseconds and then refresh all the columns, or it may refresh after every few instructions one column at a time. The latter method is preferred, because it upsets system timing the least. For a complete discussion, see "Dynamic RAM Interface," p. 240.

An efficient scheme is *transparent refresh.* This is what the Z-80 does automatically. If one knows the intricate timing of the bus exactly, sometimes the designer can find a time in which the memory is not being used. Then, during that time the hardware can "hide" a refresh cycle.

Mostek, which second-sources the Z-80, produces a single-board CPU, with 16K bytes of RAM, 20K bytes of ROM and various input-output ports. The RAM bank consists of eight 16K by 1-bit dynamic memories, and the ROM bank of five 4K by 8-bit ROMs. This one board uses few chips to implement a powerful processor. Compared to the 8080, the chip-count reduction is due to the elimination of the 8224 clock, 8228 system controller, and refresh logic.

THE 8085

Intel naturally also had to improve the 8080 design. Then, the 8085 reduces the parts count of an 8080 system while increasing the speed. Essentially, it integrates the 8080, the 8224, and the 8228 into a single chip.

This time, to provide expanded control functions, 16 address lines and 8 data lines, the decision was made to multiplex the low eight address bits. At the beginning of every instruction cycle, the low eight address lines appear on the data bus. To be used, they need to be latched. The multiplex control line ALE ("address-latch enable") is used to latch and hold the lower address bits.

Fig. 2-32 shows the 8085 system. Right away it should be apparent that *no latch is used for the low address bits!* Intel has created a new line of special RAM, ROM, PROM, and input-output chips which *contain the low-address latch.* Thus, the 8085 bus has 8 data, 8 address, and 11 control lines.

The special peripheral chips contain combinations of RAM, PROM, and input-output. In this way, complete systems with as few as three LSI chips may be built. An 8277 PROM I/O chip is presented

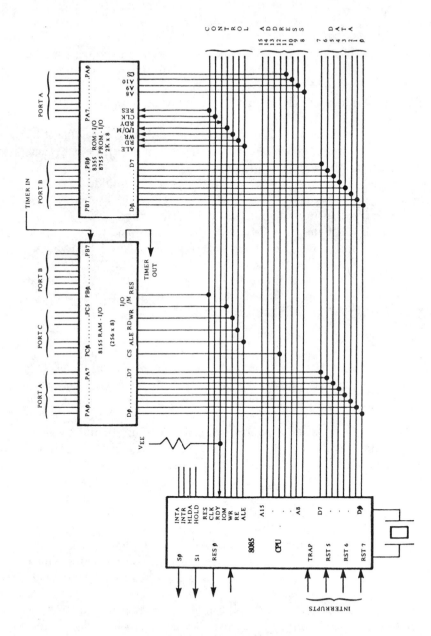

Fig. 2-32: 8085 System

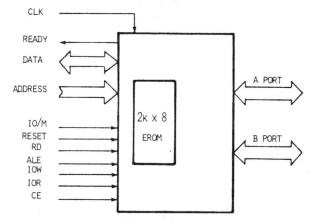

Fig. 2-33: 8277 PROM + I/O

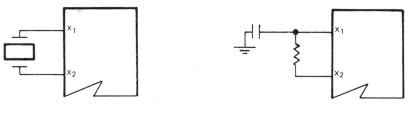

WITH A CRYSTAL   WITH AN R-C NETWORK

Fig. 2-34: Clocking the 8085

in Fig. 2-33.

The clock circuitry has also been built into the 8085. The connection of a crystal to two pins finishes the interface for the basic CPU.

SUMMARY

The standard microprocessor architecture, with its three buses, controls the assembly of our complete microcomputer. The memory devices, RAM and ROM, are easily connected to the standard microprocessor buses. Small systems use partial or linear decoding to select the memory. Larger systems use full-address decoding. The 8080, 6800, Z-80, and 8085 systems were presented to illustrate the simplicity of CPU assembly. Future processors will contain almost everything—except for the crystal, making CPU assembly obsolete. The only task remaining will be signal buffering and input-output interfacing. The basic input-output techniques will now be presented, before the interfacing of actual peripherals.

55

3

BASIC INPUT-OUTPUT

INTRODUCTION

Now that the processing section of our microcomputer is complete, the next step is to communicate with the peripherals. Information about the outside world must be gathered and processed. Once processed, the information must be displayed and sent to control the various devices. the chapter will present the input-output techniques and illustrate them with design examples. This will be done in two steps.

Basic input and output interfacing will first be described: serial input-output, and parallel input-output. The concepts will be presented, then the chips which implement the algorithms.

The scheduling techniques required for sequencing the input-output devices will then be presented: polling, interrupts, and direct memory access.

A terminology problem will first be clarified. Larger computers have traditionally been equipped with memory-type instructions, and with I/O-type instructions. *This distinction is obsolete for microprocessors.*

MEMORY VS I/O MAPPING OF INPUT-OUTPUT DEVICES

The traditional implementation of computers distinguishes memory and I/O instructions:

Memory-Mapped I/O

Memory-mapped I/O refers to the use of memory-type instructions

56

to access I/O devices. Memory-mapped input-output allows the processor to use the same instructions for memory transfers as it does for input-output transfers. An I/O port is treated as a memory locations. The advantage is that the same powerful instructions used for reading and writing memory can be used to input and output data. In a traditional computer, there are usually many more memory instructions than I/O instructions. For example, in memory-mapped I/O, arithmetic may be performed directly on an input or output latch, without having to transfer the contents in and out of temporary registers.

What are the disadvantages? First, each I/O port used in this way makes one fewer location available for memory. Thus, if all 65,536 memory locations are needed as memory, memory-mapped I/O should not be used. Clearly, this is virtually never the case in a microprocessor system. Second, instructions that operate on the memory normally require three bytes to address the location of the port (there can be 65,536 locations, which require 16 bits of address), whereas special I/O instructions may need only eight bits to specify a port. Third, memory-mapped I/O instructions may take longer to execute than special I/O instructions because of the need for extra address bytes. This problem is usually solved by allowing "short addressing," i.e., the use of 2-byte memory instructions.

I/O Mapped Input-Output

In I/O-mapped input-output, the processor sends control signals indicating that the present cycle is for input or output only—not for memory. Two special lines are supplied for I/O read and I/O write. Fewer address lines may be used to select input-output ports, since systems need fewer input-output ports than memory locations.

There are three advantages to I/O-mapped input-output. One, since separate I/O instructions are used, they can be easily distinguished from a memory-reference instruction while programming, which is a convenience. Two, because of shorter addressing, less hardware is necessary for decoding. Three, the instructions are shorter. The disadvantages are two: One loses the processing power of memory-mapped I/O, and, most important, two control pins must be "wasted" for I/O read and I/O write. For this reason, this technique is almost never used with microprocessors (except the 8080).

Fig. 3-1 shows a memory-mapped input-output system, where the control signal, which determines whether the address is for memory or

I/O, depends on the state of A15. If A15 is high, then all addresses on bits A14 through A0 specify an I/O device. If A15 is low, A14 through A0 specify a memory location.

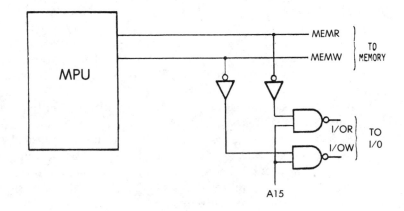

Fig. 3-1: Memory-Mapped Input-Output

Fig. 3-2 shows an I/O-mapped input-output system with separate control lines for memory and I/O-control functions. The address bus will select a device and a register or location within the device. This is illustrated in Fig. 3-4. The control bus will specify the operation to be performed. This is the standard design in almost every microprocessor system.

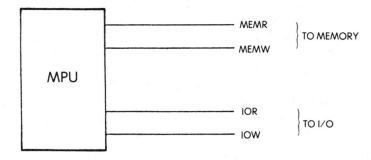

Fig. 3-2: Input-Output Mapping

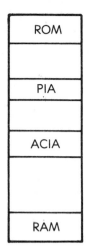

Fig. 3-3: A Memory Map

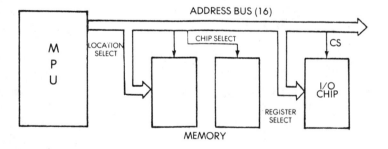

Fig. 3-4: Selection of an I/O Port

PARALLEL INPUT-OUTPUT

A minimum parallel interface requires *latches* and *bus drivers*. Let us look at a basic LSI input-output port. In Fig. 3-5, a port is equipped with an input buffer, which latches input signals from a device and holds them stable, until the microprocessor requires that information, and with an output buffer to latch microprocessor data, to hold

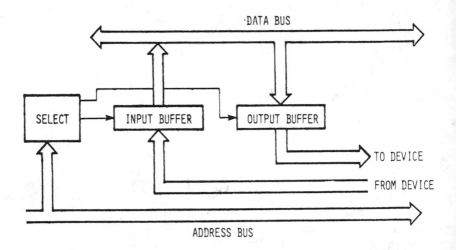

Fig. 3-5: Basic I/O Port

them as long as the external device requires. In addition, there must be a *selection* mechanism and *read/write control* for the registers or ports. Figs. 3-6 and 3-7 illustrate conceptually what a simple I/O port requires..

This device has the following: an input latch that can hold external information until the system reads it; an output latch to hold data from the system stable until output; and bus buffers to receive and drive the data bus. Additionally, there should be an internal status register indicating if there are data to be read, or whether the data have been output. Although such ports can be constructed from discrete devices, a new component, the PIO, has made them essentially obsolete.

Programmable Parallel Input-Output Device

The programmable parallel LSI input-output device (PIO) will perform the following functions: address decoding, data input-output buffering and multiplexing, status for "handshaking," and other control functions, to be described.

The address decoder will select one of the internal registers to be read or written. These registers may be the input latch, output latch, direction register, or status register. Usually, three address bits, as well as the chip select, will be required for 6 to 8 internal registers. In addition, *the PIO is "programmable."*

The new concept is the use of a "data-direction register": it is possible, on a bit-by-bit basis, to define a port as having the first three bits configured as inputs and the last five as outputs, or as having any other combination.

The direction of every line of the PIO ports is programmable. Each bit of the "data-direction register" specifies whether the corresponding bit of the PIO port will be an input or an output. Typically, a "0" in the data-direction register specifies an input, while a "1" specifies an output. A PIO is programmable in other ways. Each PIO has one or more command registers which specify other options, such as the configuration of the ports and the operation of the control logic.

Finally, each PIO multiplexes its connection to the microprocessor data bus into 2 or more 8-bit-ports. The maximum is 3, including control lines for the I/O device, because of the 40-pin limitation on the package. A typical PIO appears in Fig. 3-8. In this case, the device has two ports each equipped with its own direction register. In addition, a status register is used to indicate the status of each port.

Example 1: the Motorola 6820 PIA

The internal diagram of the 6820 appears in Fig. 3-9. It has six registers, two sets of three registers per port. One set is for port A and the other is for port B.

Let us examine the control register. Its format is shown in Fig. 3-10. Bit 7 indicates a transition of the CA1 input. It is used as an interrupt flag. The same is true of bit 6, except that it monitors the CA2 pin of CA2 used as an input. Bits 5, 4, and 3 establish the eight different modes of the device and the function of the CA2 pin. Bit 2 indicates whether the direction register or data register is to be selected, as they have the same address. Bits 1 and 0 are the interrupt enable/disable control bits.

A clarification is needed here: Motorola's PIA has 6 registers and only two register select (RS) pins, because of the 40-pin limitation. The DR and the DDR in each port share the same address! They are differentiated by the value of bit 2 of the control register, a programming nuisance.

Fig. 3-11 indicates how the registers are selected by use of the RS1 and RS0 pins and the state of the internal bit 2 of the control register.

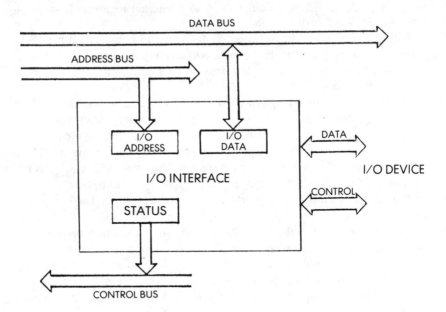

Fig. 3-6: Simple I/O Port

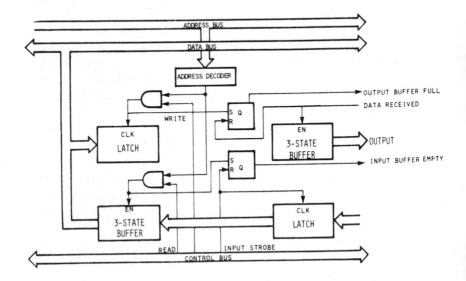

Fig. 3-7: Simple Bidirectional I/O Port (Strobed)

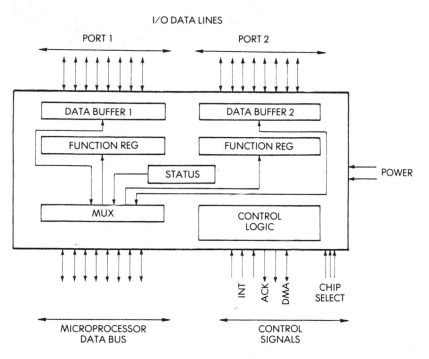

Fig. 3-8: Typical PIO

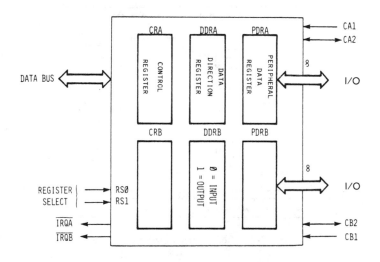

Fig. 3-9: 6820 PIA

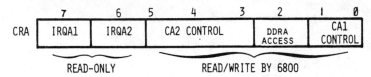

	7	6	5	4	3	2	1	0
CRA	IRQA1	IRQA2	CA2 CONTROL			DDRA ACCESS	CA1 CONTROL	

READ-ONLY   READ/WRITE BY 6800

Fig. 3-10: 6820 Control Register Format

SELECTING PIA REGISTERS USES 2 LINES (RSØ, RS1), PLUS BIT 2 OF CR:

RS1 = Ø   SELECTS PORT A REGISTER
RS1 = 1   SELECTS PORT B REGISTER
RSØ = 1   SELECTS CONTROL REGISTER (A OR B)
RSØ = Ø   SELECTS DATA DIRECTION OR BUFFER REGISTER

RS1	RSØ	CRA(2)	CRB(2)	REGISTER	
0	0	0	-	DATA DIRECTION REGISTER	
0	0	1	-	BUFFER REGISTER	A
0	1	-	-	CONTROL REGISTER	
1	0	-	0	DATA DIRECTION REGISTER	
1	0	-	1	BUFFER REGISTER	B
1	1	-	-	CONTROL REGISTER	

Fig. 3-11: 6820 Register Selection

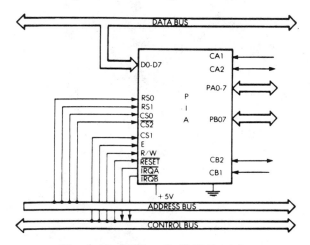

Fig. 3-12: 6820 and 6800 Interface

Fig. 3-12 shows the connection to the 6800 buses, and Fig. 3-13 illustrates a typical application with the bits shown for the control and data-direction registers.

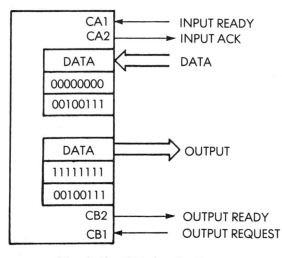

Fig. 3-13: 6820 Application

As a last note on the 6820, it is a good idea to buffer the data bus to this chip as it cannot drive a heavily loaded data bus. Fig. 3-14 gives a suggested buffering arrangement for the data lines.

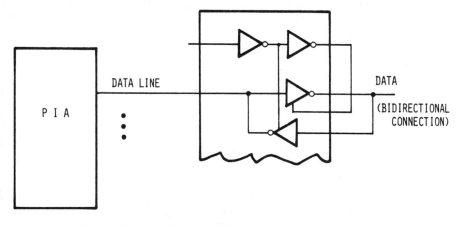

Fig. 3-14: Data Bus Buffering

Example 2: Intel 8255 PPI

The 8255 contains four ports, two with eight bits each, and two with four bits each. Each port can be programmed via the mode-control register to be either all inputs, all outputs, or a special function. The 8255 appears in Fig. 3-15.

Table 3-16 indicates how the ports are addressed. There are several modes of operation, where each half of port C is used for interrupt flag inputs or handshaking signals. The Intel device is not programmable by bit, but offers 4 more lines for control. Overall, the functions performed are essentially analogous. In fact, a PIA can be used on an 8080 system, and conversely. Each major microprocessor manufacturer has its own version of a programmable parallel interface. Their function is essentially similar.

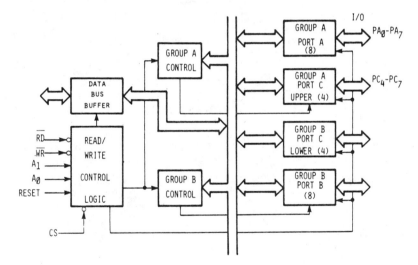

Fig. 3-15: 8255 Addressing

SERIAL INPUT-OUTPUT

Several devices require serial communication: teletype (TTY), tape, and disk.

Instead of latching eight bits of parallel data, we could pass each bit in the byte to a single line one at a time. Known as bit-serial interfacing, there are serial standards that cover this kind of transmission. Such standards are discussed in Chapter 6. The format of the serial input-output to a teletype is shown in Fig. 3-17.

CS	A1	A0	RD	WR	OPERATION	
0	0	0	0	1	PORT A TO DATA BUS	MPU
0	0	1	0	1	PORT B TO DATA BUS	READ
0	1	0	0	1	PORT C TO DATA BUS	(A,B,C)
0	0	0	1	0	DATA BUS TO PORT A	MPU
0	0	1	1	0	DATA BUS TO PORT B	
0	1	0	1	0	DATA BUS TO PORT C	WRITE
0	1	1	1	0	DATA BUS TO CONTROL	
0	1	1	0	1	ILLEGAL	
1	-	-	-	-	DATA BUS TO 3-STATE	(DISABLE)

Fig. 3-16: 8255 Addressing

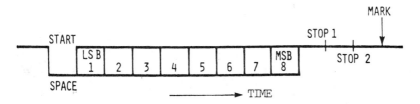

Fig. 3-17: Serial Character Format

Since microcomputers are parallel systems, we need to convert an eight-bit byte of data to serial form before output, and from serial form to input. There are two ways to perform this conversion: by software, or with a *UART* (universal asynchronous receiver-transmitter).

Software Serial I/O

In software, a program can simply accomplish the serialization-deserialization. On input, the program will wait until it senses a start bit, then sample at the proper times to read the data bits. On output, the program will send the series of ones and zeroes to a single line, with a programmed delay between each bit.

An example of a teletype output program appears in the flowchart of Fig. 3-18 and the 8080 program listing in Fig. 3-19.

It will be described in Chapter 4. The principles of a serialization routine are to assemble an 8 (or more)-bit word in the accumulator and to shift it out, one bit at a time, at the proper frequency. The simplest way is to output the contents of the accumulator to an output port which is connected only to line 0.The accumulator is then shifted right, by one bit position, a delay is implemented, and the next bit is output. After 8 (or more) outputs, the initial parallel data have been serialized.

Conversely, assembling serial data into parallel form by program is just as simple. Bit 0 is read into the accumulator. The accumulator is shifted left. After a specified delay, bit 0 is read again. After eight shifts, a byte has been assembled.

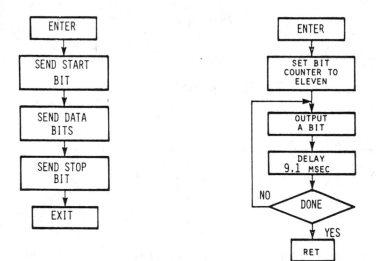

Fig. 3-18: Flowchart for Serial Conversion

The advantage of a programmed implementation is simplicity and the elimination of external hardware. However, it is slow and might impair the microprocessor's performance. Also, no reliable delays can be implemented in a system using interrupts. A hardware implementation is required.

UART and USART

One of the earliest standard LSI devices was the UART. A UART is a serial-to-parallel and parallel-to-serial converter. The UART has two functions: to take parallel data and convert it to a serial bit stream with start, parity, and stop characters, and to take a serial bit stream and convert it to parallel data.

The functional block diagram of the UART appears in Fig. 3-20. Each UART has 3 sections: a transmitter, a receiver, and a control section. Almost all the manufacturers have a pin-compatible or "improved" version of the standard UART.

```
;
;  THIS SUBROUTINE ENTERED WITH CHARACTER TO BE OUTPUT IN THE C REGISTER
;
TYOUT:   MVI    B,11    ;  SET COUNTER FOR 11 BITS
         MOV    A,C     ;  CHARACTER TO ACCUMULATOR
         ORA    A       ;  CLEAR CARRY-FOR START BIT
         RAL            ;  MOVE CARRY TO A(0)
MORE:    OUT    2       ;  SEND TO TTY
         CALL   DELAY   ;  KILL TIME
         RAR            ;  POSITION NEXT BIT
         STC            ;  SET CARRY-FOR STOP BITS
         DCR    B       ;  DECREMENT BIT COUNTER
         JNZ    MORE    ;  DONE?
         RET            ;  YES
;
;  9 MSEC DELAY (ASSUME NO WAIT STATES)
;
DELAY:   MVI    D,6
DLO:     MVI    E,200
DL1:     DCR    E       ;  0.15 MSEC
         JNZ    DL1     ;  INNER LOOP
         DCR    D
         JNZ    DLO
```

Fig. 3-19: 8080 Serial Conversion Program

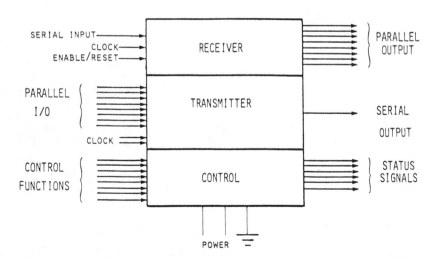

Fig. 3-20: UART Block Diagram

The UART requires both an input port and an output port to interface to a microcomputer system, so subsequent UARTs were designed to be directly bus-compatible with microprocessor buses. Two of these are: the Motorola MC6850 ACIA (asynchronous communications interface adaptor), and the Intel 8251 USART (universal synchronous and asynchronous receiver-transmitter).

Example 1: The Motorola 6850 ACIA

The internal block diagram of the ACIA appears in Fig. 3-21. Besides the input and output serial/parallel registers, the control circuitry implements the control functions of the EIA RS232C standard. (See Chapter 6 for details on RS232C.)

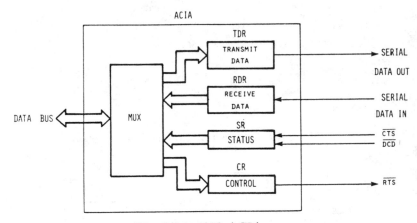

Fig. 3-21: 6850 ACIA

Fig. 3-22 breaks down the inputs and outputs into their functions: the serial data, the modem control, the clocks, and the buses. The serial data in and out are TTL-compatible signals and must be buffered to provide the level necessary for driving serial devices. (See Chapter 4 for a full explanation of how to connect a teletype to an ACIA.) The modem control controls the interface required in an RS232C modem link.

The clocks control the bit rate of the serial data and may be different for transmit and receive sections. The bus signals are the signals used in a 6800 system. The truth table showing the addressing of the internal registers appears on Table 3-23.

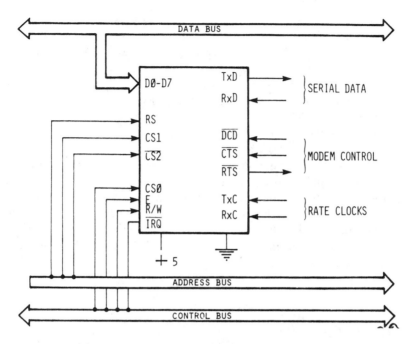

Fig. 3-22: 6850 ACIA Functions

RS	R/W	REGISTER
0	0	CONTROL
0	1	STATUS
1	1	RECEIVE DATA
1	1	TRANSMIT DATA

Fig. 3-23: 6850 Internal Register Addressing

Example 2: The Intel 8251 USART

The block diagram and control signals for the 8251 USART are shown in Fig. 3-24. This device differs from the ACIA: it also provides *synchronous* data transmission and reception, in addition to asynchronous transmission. (Motorola supplies a separate USRT, the "SSDA" for synchronous communication.)

The 8251-to-8080 system interface appears in Fig. 3-25. Some of the internal circuitry of the 8251 is dynamic, hence the need for the ϕ2 clock signal. The rest of the signals are straightforward.

The USART has five internal registers: receive data, transmit data, mode, status, and control. Upon reset, the first byte sent to the 8251 as control will set the *mode*. The next byte sent as control will be latched in as *control*. The *mode* determines whether the 8251 is to be used in synchronous, or asynchronous, mode. The *control* indicates the word length and other transmit parameters. Table 3-26 is a truth table of the 8251 bus control signals.

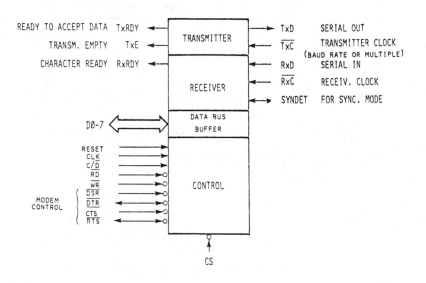

Fig. 3-24: 8251 USART

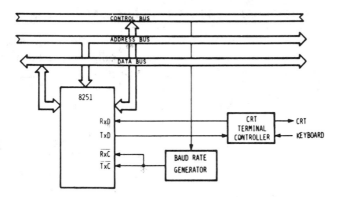

Fig. 3-25: 8251 to 8080 Interface

Serial Interface Summary

The two methods presented, hardware and software, illustrate the traditional trade-off decisions to be made even in the simplest interface design. Most small systems use a software serial interface, whereas larger systems tend to use the UARTs. Still more sophisticated circuits are being introduced to perform new types of synchronous serial communications. These LSI components implement the other serial standards described in Chapter 6.

C/D RD WR CS	OPERATION
0 0 1 0	8251 TO DATA BUS (READ)
0 1 0 0	DATA BUS TO 8251 (WRITE)
1 0 1 0	STATUS TO DATA BUS
1 1 0 0	DATA BUS TO CONTROL
- - - 1	DATA BUS TO 3-STATE

Fig. 3-26: 8251 Addressing Truth Table

73

THE THREE INPUT-OUTPUT CONTROL METHODS

We have now introduced the components and techniques required for basic I/O interfacing: we can create parallel and serial ports.

The next problem is to manage data transfers, i.e., to implement a *scheduling-strategy*. Three basic methods are used, and will briefly be described. Additional chips will be introduced to facilitate each of these strategies.

These three methods are illustrated in Fig. 3-27. They are called polling, interrupt-controlled, and DMA. (Combinations may also be used.)

Programmed I/O or Polling

In programmed input-output, all transfers to and from devices are performed by the program. The processor sends and requests data; all input and output operations are under the control of the program being executed. The transfers must be coordinated by a "handshaking" process. The basic method for determining if an I/O operation is needed or possible is through the use of *flags*. A flag is a bit which, when set, indicates that a condition has occurred that needs attention. For example, a flag indicates "device-ready" = buffer full for an input device, or buffer empty for an output device.

The flag is continually checked: it is *"polling."* The characteristic of this approach is to use a minimal amount of hardware at the expense of software overhead.

A flowchart for a *polling loop* appears in Fig. 3-28.

The program continually loops through a series of tests to determine if input or or output can/should be performed. When a device needing service is found, the proper service routine is activated and polling resumes after its completion.

Two basic methods of sensing device-ready flags are employed: the use of a simple input-status port, and the use of a priority-encoder input-status port.

The simplest technique is to drive the data bus with the device-ready flags of eight devices when executing a read-status input-port instruction. Fig. 3-29 illustrates such a system. The input-status port may be any convenient decoded address. Usually, the first or last I/O port address is used for this port. When the port is read in, the program will check each bit, determine priority, and branch to the proper service routine.

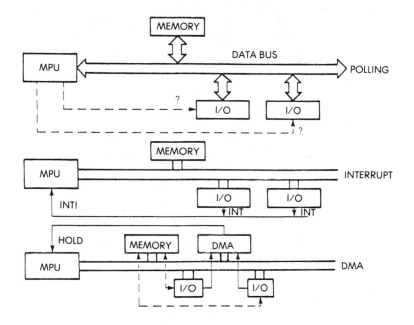

Fig. 3-27: Three Methods of I/O Control

The second method is to perform the priority encoding with a look-up ROM or a priority-encoder chip. This way, the status port holds the actual address of the highest priority device requesting service. Figs. 3-30 and 3-31 show the byte format and the hardware required.

By changing the upper five bits to any other code, other port addresses may be generated. This will save looking up or generating the port address from the device-ready status-port, *since that port holds the address of the ready device.*

Polling is the most common and simplest method of I/O control. It requires no special hardware and all input-output transfers are controlled by the program. Transfers are said to be synchronous with program execution.

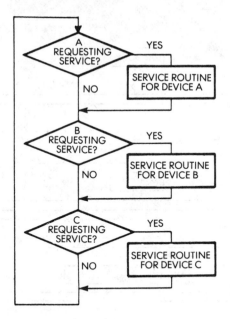

Fig. 3-28: Polling Loop Flowchart

Interrupts

The polling technique has two limitations:

1. It is wasteful of the processor's time, as it needlessly checks the status of all peripherals all the time.

2. It is intrinsically slow, since it checks the status of all I/O devices before coming back to any specific one. This may be objectionable in a real-time system, where a peripheral expects service within a specified time. In particular, when fast peripherals are connected to a system, polling may simply not be fast enough to satisfy the minimum service requirements. Fast devices such as the floppy disk or a CRT require a near-instantaneous response time in order to transfer data without loss.

Polling is a synchronous mechanism, by which devices are serviced in sequence. Interrupts are an asynchronous mechanism. The principle of interrupts is illustrated in Fig. 3-32. Each I/O device, or its controller, is connected to an interrupt line. This line will gate an interrupt request to the microprocessor. Whenever one of the I/O devices needs service, it will generate an interrupt pulse or level on this line to request the microprocessor's attention.

A microprocessor will check for interrupts at the end of every instruction. If an interrupt is present, it will service the interrupt. If no interrupt is present, it will fetch the next instruction. This is illustrated in Fig. 3-33.

During the execution of some critical processes, it must be guaranteed that the program in execution will not be disturbed by external interrupts. One such example is the execution of a power-fail routine. Power failure can easily be detected. If the system is equipped with a battery back-up for the memory, the processor may preserve the contents of its registers in memory and shut down the entire system in an orderly fashion. Several milliseconds of processing time are normally left, by the time the power failure is detected. A power-failure routine is then activated which should execute regardless of other less important requests which might occur. Other requests should be "masked-out." (Power failure is considered a "non-maskable interrupt.")

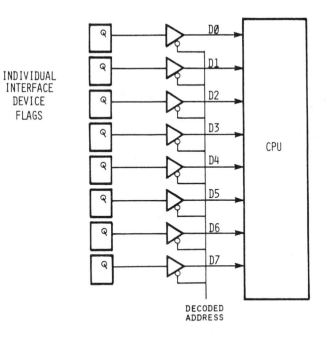

Fig. 3-29: Device-Ready Flag Status Port

This is the purpose of the mask bit (or mask register when several interrupt levels are available) in the microprocessor. Whenever the mask bit is on, interrupts will be ignored (see the chart in Fig. 3-33). The "mask" facility is also often called the "enable." An interrupt will be enabled whenever it is not masked.

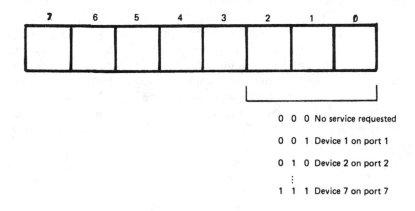

0 0 0 No service requested

0 0 1 Device 1 on port 1

0 1 0 Device 2 on port 2

1 1 1 Device 7 on port 7

Fig. 3-30: Byte Format

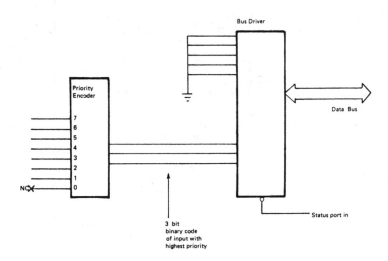

Fig. 3-31: Polling Priority Encoder Hardware

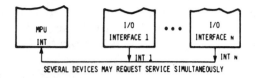

SEVERAL DEVICES MAY REQUEST SERVICE SIMULTANEOUSLY

Fig. 3-32: Interrupt Sequence

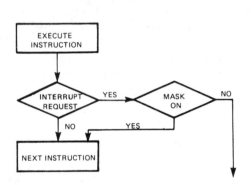

Fig. 3-33: Interrupt Logic

Once the interrupt request has been received, and accepted, by the microprocessor, the device must be serviced. In order to service the device, the microprocessor will execute a specialized service routine. Two problems occur.

First, the status of the program in execution on the microprocessor at the time of the interrupt must be preserved. This implies saving away the contents of all the registers of the microprocessor. These registers will be preserved in the *stack*. At the very minimum, the program counter (PC) must be pushed in the stack, in order to install a new branching address in the PC, for execution of the interrupt handler. Preserving the rest of the registers can be done in hardware, by the microprocessor, or else may be the responsibility of the interrupt-handling routine. Once the PC (plus possibly the other registers) has been preserved in the stack, the microprocessor will branch to the interrupt handler's address. This is where the second problem arises.

A number of input-output devices are connected to the same interrupt line. Where should the microprocessor branch in order to service this device? The problem is to identify the I/O device which triggered the interrupt. This identification of the device may be done in hardware, in software, or by a combination of both methods. Branching to the I/O device address is called *vectoring the interrupt*. The simpler system, from a hardware standpoint, will not provide vectored interrupts. A *software* routine will determine the identify of the device which requested service. *Polling* will be used. The technique is illustrated in Fig. 3-36. The interrupt identification routine will poll every device connected to the system. It will check their status register, usually testing bit 7. The presence of a 1 in a given bit position will

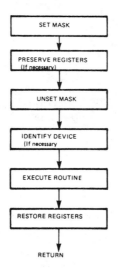

Fig. 3-34: Interrupt Control

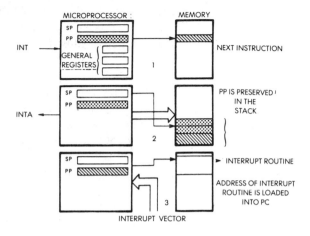

Fig. 3-35: The Three Steps

signal that the device did request the interrupt. Having identified the device which has triggered the interrupt, it will then branch to the appropriate interrupt-handling-routine address. The order in which the polling is conducted will determine which device is serviced first. This implements a *software-priority* scheme, in the case where multiple devices might have triggered an interrupt at the same time.

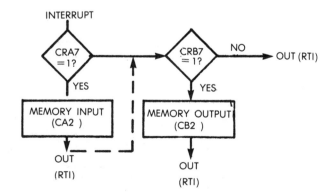

Fig. 3-36: Polling the Interrupts

A second method, software-driven, but with the help of some additional hardware, is significantly faster. It uses a *daisy-chain* to identify the device which triggered the interrupt. This is illustrated in Fig. 3-37. After preserving the registers, the microprocessor generates an interrupt-acknowledge. This acknowledge is gated to device 1. If device 1 did generate the interrupt, it will place its identification number on the data bus, where it will be read by the microprocessor. If it did not generate the interrupt, it will propagate the acknowledge signal to device 2. Device 2 will follow the same procedure, and so on. Because of the physical arrangement of devices, this interconnect mechanism is called a daisy-chain. This mechanism can be implemented by most PIOs.

The fastest method is the *vectored interrupt*. It becomes the responsibility of the I/O device controller to supply both an interrupt and the *identity* of the device causing the interrupt, or better yet the branching address for the interrupt-handling routine. If the controller just supplies the identity of the device, it is a simple software task to look up a table containing a branching address for each device. This is simpler, from a hardware standpoint, but does not achieve the highest possible performance. The highest possible performance is achieved when the microprocessor receives an interrupt and the direct 16-bit branching address. It can then directly branch to the required location in the memory, and start servicing the device. The new PICs (Priority-Interrupt Controller chips) have made this a practical reality now.

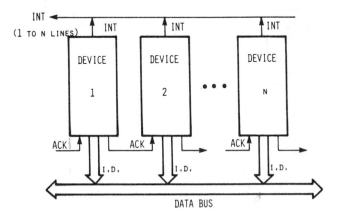

Fig. 3-37: Daisy Chain Technique

Priorities

One more problem arises: several interrupts may be triggered simultaneously. The microprocessor must then decide in which order they should be serviced. A priority is attached to each device. The microprocessor will service each device in the order of its priority. In the computer world, priority level 0 is, by convention, the highest one, priority 1 is next, and so on. Typically, level 0 will be for a power failure (PFR or Power-Failure-Restart), level 1 will be for a CRT. Level 2 may be left vacant for the possible addition of a second CRT. Level 3 could be a disk. Level 5 will be a printer. Level 6 will be a teletype. Level 7 will be external switches. Level 4 is unused in this example. Priorities may be enforced in hardware or in software. The software enforcement of priorities has been described above. The routine looking at the devices will simply look at the device with the highest priority first. Enforcing priorities in hardware is also possible. It is indeed accomplished in the recent PICs. In addition, these priority-interrupt controllers provide a full 8-bit mask which allows the programmer to mask selectively any interrupt level. The basic structure of the PIC logic appears in Fig. 3-38. It does not show the address vectoring but simply the generation of the level vector. Such a device typically accepts 8 interrupt levels. They appear on the right of the illustration and will set a bit in the interrupt register. The mask register is used by the programmer to mask-out interrupt levels selectively. Typically, unused interrupt levels will be masked. However, it is also possible to mask levels at specific times in the program. A simple AND gate will allow the propagation of unmasked interrupts. The level of the interrupt of highest priority will be converted to a three-bit code by an 8 to 3 encoder. One more facility is provided: the level of the interrupt is compared to the contents of the three-bit priority register. The priority register is set by the user. It will prevent any interruption by an interrupt of level higher than n, where n is the priority. It is a global masking process for any interrupt of level higher than n. A comparator in the PIC determines that the level of the interrupt is acceptable, and will then generate a final interrupt request. The microprocessor will have available the three-bit interrupt vector. A more sophisticated PIC will do more. Recent PICs will directly supply a 16-bit branching address. This is simply accomplished by including a RAM of 8 × 16-bit registers within the PIC. The three-bit level vector is then used to select the contents of one of these eight registers. The contents of these 16 8-bit registers are then pulsed on the microprocessor data bus or sometimes on its address bus. This causes an automatic branch to the specified address. Naturally, these registers are loaded by the programmer. A recent PIC design is shown in Fig. 3-39.

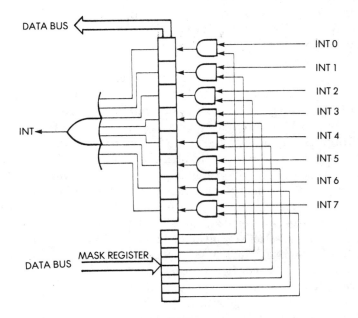

Fig. 3-38: PIC Logic

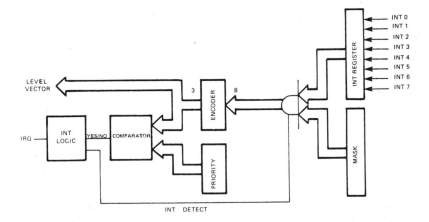

Fig. 3-39: Interrupt Controller with Priority

Fig. 3-40 illustrates the sequencing of events during an interrupt. Going from left to right on the illustration, program A is in execution until an interrupt request is generated at time T_{RQ}. This interrupt will be taken into account at the end of the instruction, at Time T_B. The control unit of the microprocessor will then implement the branch to the necessary address. Once this branch is accomplished, the interrupt handler (the third line of Fig. 3-40) starts execution. The interrupt handler may have to spend some overhead time in preserving the registers, which might not have been preserved automatically by the control unit of the microprocessor. The service routine for the device then executes. At the end of execution, registers must be restored (time T_F to T_R). A return instruction is then executed, and the control unit restores the previous contents of the program counter (fetched from the stack), so that execution of the previous program A may resume. Program A resumes at time T_P.

The time T_{RQ} to T_S is the interrupt-response time, i.e. the total time that has elapsed between the interrupt request and the effective time at which the service routine has started doing its useful work. Some manufacturers consider that the response time is only T_{RQ} to T_H. The total length of time lost to the program is T_B to T_P. The total overhead involved in the interrupt is really T_B to T_S + T_F to T_R. These numbers vary significantly from one microprocessor to another.

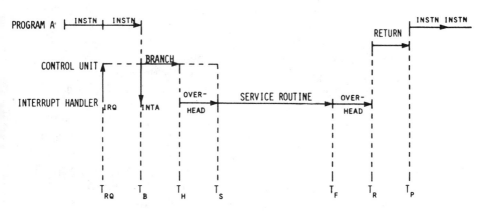

Fig. 3-40: Interrupt Sequence

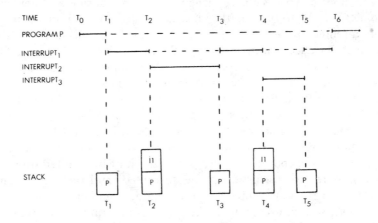

Fig. 3-41: Stack during Interrupts

Multiple Interrupts and the Stack

Fig. 3-41 illustrates the role of the stack during multiple interrupts. At time T0, program P is in execution. At time T1, interrupt I1 is accepted. The registers used by program P are then pushed in the stack (see the bottom of the illustration, on the left). Interrupt I1 executes until time T2. At time T2, interrupt I2 occurs, and it is assumed here that I2 is of higher priority. Interrupt I1 is suspended just like program P before. The registers used for interrupt I1 are pushed in the stack. This is illustrated in Fig. 3-41 at the bottom of the illustration, by time T2. Interrupt I2 then executes; this is the third line of Fig. 3-41. Interrupt I2 executes to completion, at time T3. At that time, the contents of the stack will be popped back in the microprocessor and only P is left in the stack (see Fig. 3-41)—the stack contains only P at time T3. Interrupt I1 resumes execution, and, at time T4, it is interrupted again by another interrupt, I3, of higher priority. Again two levels are in the stack at time T4: I1 and P (see Fig. 3-41). Interrupt I3 executes to completion, at time T5. At that time I1 is popped from the stack (see Fig. 3-41) and resumes execution. This time it runs to completion until time T6, at which time program P is popped from the stack and resumes execution. It should be noted that the number of levels contained in the stack is equal to the number of suspended programs, i.e. to the number of dashed horizontal lines at any time. This

86

example illustrates the use of the stack during multiple interrupts. Clearly, if a large number of interrupts may occur simultaneously, the programmer should allocate a large enough stack to contain the successive levels.

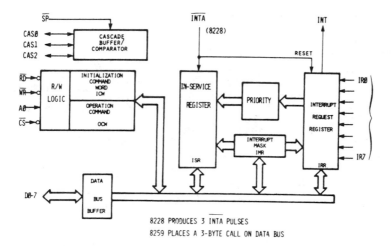

Fig. 3-42: 8259 Interrupt Controller

Direct Memory Access

Interrupts guarantee the fastest possible response to an input-output device. However, service to the device is accomplished by software. This may still not be fast enough for processes involving fast memory transfers such as disks and CRT displays. Again, the solution is to replace software by hardware. The software routine performing the transfer between the memory and the device is replaced by a specialized hardware processor, the DMAC, or Direct Memory Access Controller. A DMAC is a specialized processor designed to perform high speed data transfers between memory and the device. In order to perform these transfers, the DMAC will require the use of both the data bus and the address bus. DMAC philosophies differ in the way they obtain access to these buses. For example, a DMAC may suspend a processor, or it may stop it, or it may steal memory cycles from the

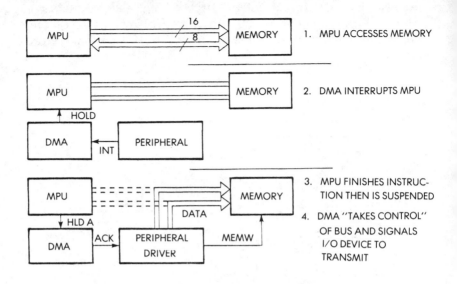

Fig. 3-43: DMA Controller Operation

processor, or it may stretch clock pulses. Some sophisticated DMAs, such as dynamic-memory-refresh DMAs, can also use some portions of the instruction cycle, when they "know" that the processor will not require the use of the data bus and the address bus. A complete discussion of DMA philosophies is beyond the scope of this book. The simplest approach, and the one usually implemented for most microprocessors, is to suspend the operation of the processor. This is the reason for the tri-state buses used for the data and the address bus. The organization of a DMA system is illustrated in Fig. 3-43. Each device will send its interrupt to the DMAC, rather than to the microprocessor. When the DMAC receives an interrupt from a device, it generates a special signal for the microprocessor, the HOLD signal. The HOLD signal will suspend the microprocessor and place it in a dormant state. The microprocessor completes its instruction, then releases the data bus and the address bus in the high-impedance state. It is said to "float" its buses. It then goes to sleep and responds with the "HOLD-acknowledge" signal. Upon receipt of the HOLD-acknowledge, the DMA knows that the buses are released. It will then automatically place an address on the address bus, which specifies the memory address at which the data transfer is to take place. A DMAC connected to 8 I/O devices will contain 8 16-bit address registers for this purpose. Naturally, the contents of these registers have been specified by the programmer for each device. The DMAC specifies the address at which the transfer is to take place, then generates a "read" or a "write" signal and lets the I/O device generate the data, or receive the data, on the data bus. In addition, a DMAC contains an automatic sequencing mechanism for block transfers. This is particularly valuable for transmitting blocks of data (in the case of a disk) or sequences of data (in the case of lines in a CRT). The DMAC is equipped with a counter register for each device. Typically, an 8-bit counter is used which allows automatic transfers of 1 to 256 words. After each word transfer, the counter is decremented. The data transfer stops whenever the counter goes down to 0, or whenever the DMA request from the device disappears.

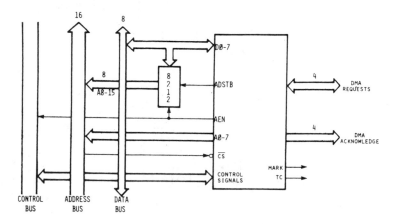

Fig. 3-44: Intel DMAC

The advantage of a DMA is to guarantee the highest possible transfer speed for the device. Its disadvantage, naturally, is to slow down the operation of the processor. The DMA is a very complex device whose complexity is analogous to that of a microprocessor. It is also expensive, since DMAs do not sell in the same quantities as microprocessors. In many instances, it may be cheaper to dedicate a microprocessor plus memory to doing dedicated block transfers, than

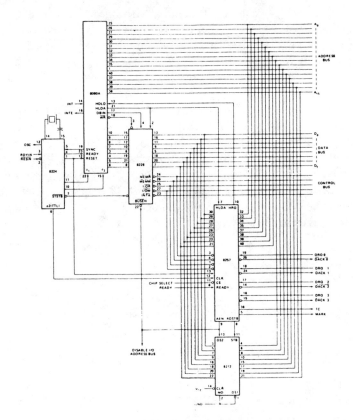

Fig. 3-45: DMA CPU Board

to use a DMA chip. As an example, the structure of an Intel DMAC appears in Fig. 3-44, and the structure of a Motorola 6800 DMAC appears in Fig. 3-46. The DMA controller shown in Fig. 3-46 is a cycle-stealing DMA controller. The address bus and the R/W float up to 500 ms. However the maximum duration of the suspension may not exceed 5 microseconds, as the dynamic registers of the 6800 would lose their content after this time. The new Motorola 6844 DMAC may operate in three modes: halt-burst, halt-steal (1-byte transfer), and TSC steal. In "halt-burst," a transfer request on T × RQ halts the 6800, and a byte-count of 0 restarts it. This is a block transfer. In halt-steal, only one byte is transferred. It has four DMA channels with

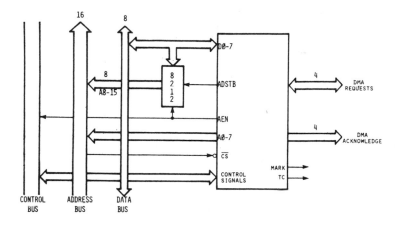

Fig. 3-46: Motorola DMAC Connections

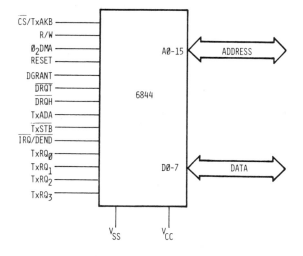

Fig. 3-47: The DMAC Chip

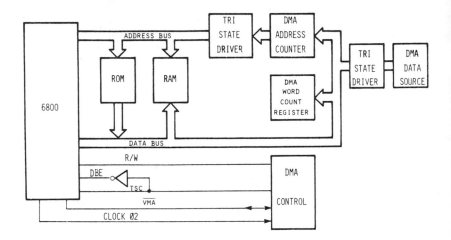

Fig. 3-48: Conceptual Operation

16-bit address and 16-bit counter. The maximum transfer rate is 1 megabyte per second. This is illustrated in Figs. 3-49 and 3-50. The Intel 8257 provides four channels and operates by simply suspending the 8080 (for any length of time). It requires an external 8212 latch for bits 8-15 of the address bus. It is illustrated in Fig. 3-45 and 3-50. Finally, the interconnect of the Am 9517 of AMD to an 8080 system is shown in Fig. 3-51.

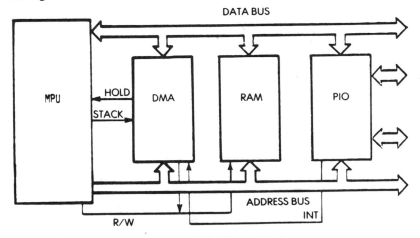

Fig. 3-49: DMA Block Diagram

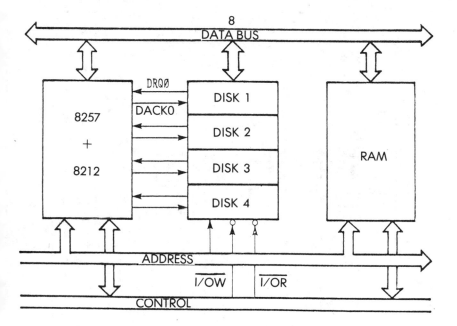

Fig. 3-50: 4 Channels of 8257

SUMMARY

The basic input-output techniques and components have been presented in this chapter. In an actual system, the designer will select the combination of hardware and software algorithms required to meet his performance criteria and cost constraints. More chips will be introduced in the future which offer still greater efficiency for high-speed input-output management.

Before leaving the CPU interface and I/O problems, there are always some simple circuits required to tie a system together. Presented in Figures 3-52 through 3-57 are some useful circuits. These include one shots, a reset circuit, and code conversion. They are described below.

The next, and most important, problem to be solved, is to interface the peripherals. This will be done in Chapter 4.

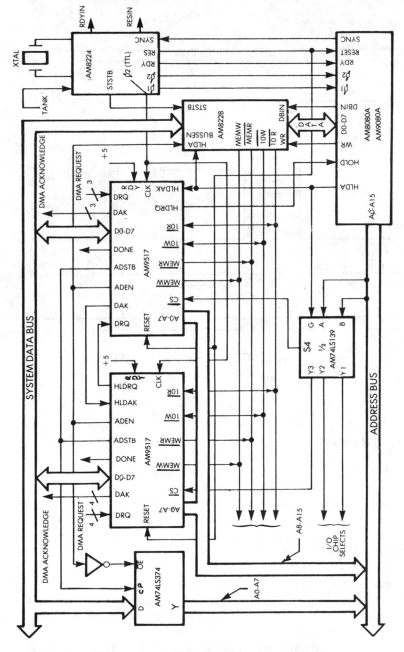

Fig. 3-51: AM9517 Application Example

MISCELLANEOUS USEFUL CIRCUITS

Besides the microprocessor elements, the microprocessor chip, RAM, ROM and I/O, miscellaneous random logic elements can be required for the complete assembly of a system. These are gates, inverters, one-shots, multiplexers, counters, and Schmidt triggers.

The AND, OR, NAND, NOR and inverter devices will not be covered here. It is assumed that the reader is already familiar with these types of logic devices. (See reference C201 for a discussion of logic gates.)

The first element to be discussed is the *one-shot*, or asynchronous monostable device. The one-shot is in reality an analog circuit. When a pulse is applied at the input, the one-shot will generate a pulse of varying width at the output. The width of the output pulse will not depend on the width of the input pulse. The width will be determined by two timing elements, usually a resistor and capacitor. One-shots are useful when a pulse must be stretched. Two examples are: reset pulses and interrupt pulses. The fact that it is an analog element implies that

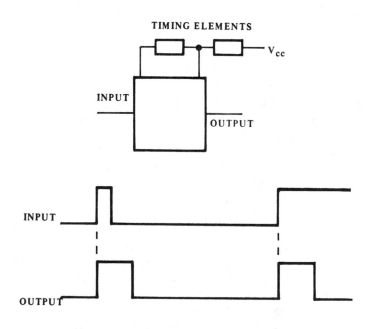

Fig. 3-52: One-Shot Stretches Pulses

its reliability is usually less than that of the other elements in the circuit. It is by its very nature more sensitive to power supply noise and decoupling problems. It is considered good design practice to try to avoid using one-shots as much as possible. A typical one-shot is illustrated in Fig. 3-52.

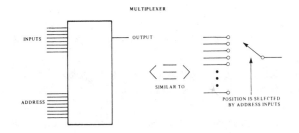

Fig. 3-53: Multiplexer Operation

Multiplexers and *demultiplexers* act as digital switches. A multiplexer accepts a number of inputs and multiplexes them onto one single line. A demultiplexer separates these signals from the one line onto many lines. In this way, multiplexers and demultiplexers are very similar to rotary switches, which can be digitally controlled via address inputs. Multiplexers are necessary for the multiplexed dynamic RAM chip memory designs and scanned input interfaces. Demultiplexers are often used as decoders, besides their regular function of unraveling the tangle made by the multiplexer. Multiplexer operation is described in Fig. 3-53.

The *Schmitt trigger* is an interfacing element to take noisy TTL signals and convert them into glitch-free TTL signals. It accomplishes this function by the use of input *hysteresis*. The input signal must pass through two threshold values before the output can change. A clean transition is generated from a slow varying or noisy input signal by this dual threshold action. Shown in Fig. 3-54 is a typical application for a Schmitt trigger using the 7413. Used with a one-shot for the clean reset generation, the Schmitt trigger will fire the one-shot upon power-up. The one-shot will then generate a reset pulse that will last the minimum required number of clock pulses according to the particular microprocessor data sheet of the manufacturer.

In many cases, on reset, a different starting address is desired. By using a multiplexer, as in Fig. 3-55, new address lines are generated as needed. In this application, the multiplexed address is switched to the new address line whenever a reset occurs. In order to get back to the old address lines, the flip-flop is reset to 0. This will choose the old address lines when the reset program has finished executing.

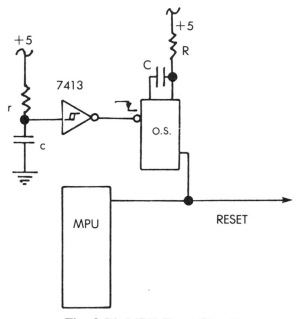

Fig. 3-54: MPU Reset Circuit

Along with these devices, which are the needle and thread of a system, there are other applications for ROMs besides storing programs. In Fig. 3-56, the use of a standard ROM is illustrated as a code converter. Inserting this ROM in the parallel data path between the input device and the microcomputer, or between the microcomputer and the output device, will convert your ASCII code to EBCDIC code. Other conversion schemes are also possible. Another use is as a software watchdog. A ROM pattern is generated from a pattern derived by using a logic analyzer. That static pattern is then compared with the same information which generated it. If there is ever a change, this would indicate a possible software failure. In Fig. 3-57, the elements

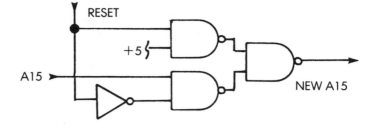

Fig. 3-55: Address Vector on Reset to a Different Reset Vector

of this watchdog circuit are shown. Once a software failure has been detected, the hardware can interrupt the microprocessor. This interruption will tell it that a software failure has occurred. Self-check programs may be run at this point to try to determine the cause of the problem.

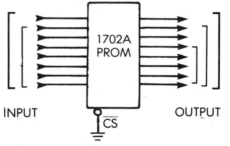

Fig. 3-56: Code Conversion Using PROM

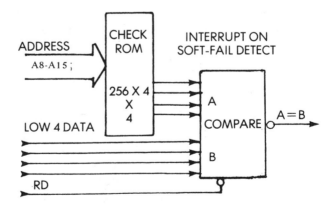

Fig. 3-57: Software Failure Detect ROM with Table Derived from a Logic Analyzer

Fig. 3-58: Texas Intruments 2716 EPROM

4

PERIPHERAL INTERFACING

INTRODUCTION

Now that the CPU, memory and input-output are connected and working, how do we connect to the teletype in the corner? What about the paper-tape punch, keyboard and telephone line? These are all *peripherals* that allow the user, or another computer, to communicate with the system. In this chapter, a number of common peripherals will be interfaced:

— Keyboard (including ASCII keyboard)
— LED Display
— Teletype (TTY)
— Paper-tape Reader (PTR)
— Stepping Motor
— Magnetic Stripe Credit Card Reader
— Tarbell Interface
— Cassette Recorder
— CRT Display
— Floppy Disk
— Music Synthesizer
— Dynamic RAM Interface

KEYBOARDS

A keyboard consists *of pressure- or touch-activated switches arranged in a matrix fashion.* To detect which key has been pressed usually requires a combination of hardware and/or software means.

Two basic types of keyboards are available: *encoded* and *non-encoded*. Encoded keyboards include the hardware necessary to detect which key was pressed and to hold that data until a new key stroke. Non-encoded keyboards have no hardware and must be analyzed by a software routine or by special hardware.

Bounce

One of the most common problems with a single switch is *bounce*. Keybounce refers to the fact that when the contacts of a mechanical switch close, they bounce for a short time before staying together. This is also true when the switch opens. Fig. 4-0 is a time-versus-resistance plot of a typical switch contact.

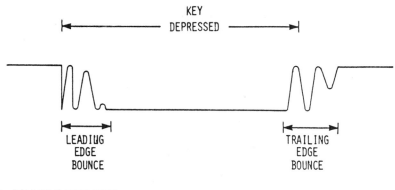

- BOUNCE IS 10-20 MSEC
- HARDWARE SOLUTION: R-C FILTER
- SOFTWARE SOLUTION: VERIFY KEY STATUS FOR 20 MS

Fig. 4-0: Key Bounce

The solution is to wait for the status of a key to remain stable for perhaps 20 milliseconds. This may be done by *hardware-filtering* or by a *software-delay* routine. The hardware circuit appears in Fig. 4-1 and requires the same circuitry for each key. This circuit is useful for the few front-panel switches in a system. In the case of a larger number of keys, software is often used.

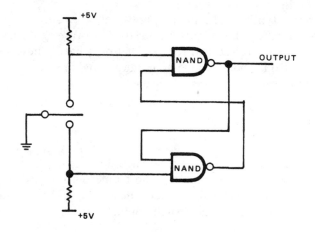

Fig. 4-1: Debounce Circuit

0	1	2	3
4	5	6	7
8	9	A	B
C	D	E	F

Fig. 4-2: A Hex Keyboard

Non-Encoded Keyboard

Usually, the keyboard is arranged in a row-and-column fashion, with an n by m key organization. We can scan one set of lines with a "walking one" pattern and sense the other lines for a coincidence. (See Fig. 4-3.) This key-identification technique is known as "row-scanning." Once a coincidence is found, it is checked for 20 milliseconds or so, to see if it is stable, and then the corresponding data are generated.

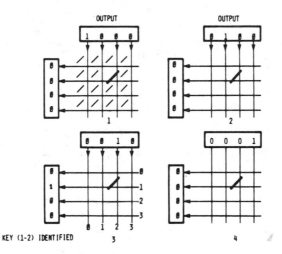

Fig. 4-3: Walking Ones Keyboard Decode

Larger keyboards require more select or sense lines. Fig. 4-4 shows how a four-to-sixteen-line decoder allows for a 64-key matrix with four bits of output and four bits of input from the microprocessor I/O ports. Fig. 4-5 shows a simple twelve-key matrix using four output bits and three input bits on an F8 microprocessor system.

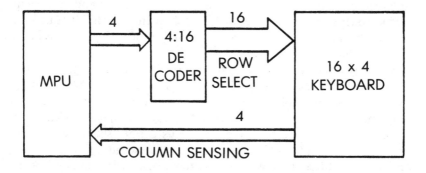

Fig. 4-4: 4-to-16-Line Decoder with Keyboard

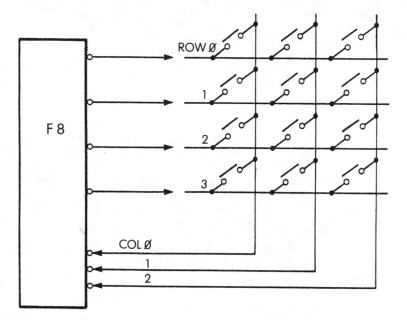

Fig. 4-5: Twelve-Key F-8 Matrix

Rollover

Rollover is the problem caused when more than one key is held down at the same time. It is essential to detect this fact and to prevent wrong codes from being generated. The three main techniques used to resolve this problem are the *two-key rollover,* the *n-key rollover,* and the *n-key lock-out.*

Two-key rollover provides protection for the case in which two keys are pressed at the same time. Two techniques are used. The simplest two-key rollover simply ignores the reading from the keyboard until only one key closure is detected. The last key to remain pressed is the correct one. This philosophy is normally used when software routines are used to provide keyboard scanning and decoding. The second philosophy is often used by hardware devices. The second key closure is prevented from generating a strobe until the first one is released. This is accomplished by an internal delay mechanism which is latched as long as the first key is pressed. Clearly, for better protection, rollover should be provided for more than two keys.

N-key rollover will either ignore all keys pressed until only one remains down, or else store the information in an internal buffer. A significant cost of n-key rollover protection is that most systems need a diode in series with every key in order to eliminate the problem created when three adjacent keys at a right angle are pressed ("ghost key"). This increases the cost very significantly and is seldom used on low-cost systems.

N-key lock-out takes into account only one key pressed. Any additional keys which might have been pressed and released do not generate any codes. By convention, it may be the first key pressed which will generate the code, or else the last key pushed. The system is simplest to implement and most often used. However, it may be objectionable to the user, as it slows down the typing: each key must be fully released before the next one is pressed down.

Line-Reversal Technique

The basic technique used in identifying the key which has been pressed on a keyboard is row-scanning, as described above. However, because of the availability of the universal parallel interface chip, the PIO, another method can now be used. This is the line-reversal technique. This method will use a complete port on a PIO, but will be more efficient software-wise (faster). This method is illustrated below. In the example, a 16-key keyboard is used. One port of the PIO is dedicated to the keyboard interface. The identification of the key is performed in essentially four instructions only. In practice, some more instructions may be needed, because of the specific structure of the PIO used.

Step One: Output

Initially, the 8 lines of the PIO are configured as 4 lines in and 4 lines out. This will be accomplished by loading the proper data pattern in the direction register, which controls the direction of the lines. In the example, the direction register is loaded with the value "00001111". This results in configuring the data lines D0 through D3 as inputs, and the data lines D4 through D7 as outputs. D0 through D3 are row outputs of the keyboard. D4 through D7 are the column inputs to the keyboard. It is assumed that the intial value of the data register is all zeroes. In other words, four zeroes are output on lines D4 through D7, the row inputs to the keyboard. Whenever a key is pressed on the keyboard, the normal output on the column, which is a "one," is grounded by the key closure. As a result, a "zero" appears on line D1 (the third column from the left of the keyboard). The other three column outputs, i.e. lines D0, D2, D3, have not been grounded by any key closure and supply a "one" output. Detecting the key closure itself can be accomplished in two ways. A NAND gate, appearing under the keyboard in the illustration, may be used to generate an interrupt to the microprocessor. As an alternative, as usual, a polling program may read the contents of the data register and detect the fact that a zero is present on any one of lines D0 through D3. The problem to be solved here is to identify which key was pressed. The information available so far in the data register, i.e. '10110000'' is not sufficient. The column is identified, but not the row. This problem was solved in the row-scanning technique by supplying a "one" on each row in turn. Here a more "elegant" method will be used, which will supply the same information in fewer steps.

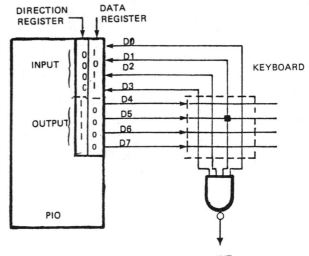

Fig. 4-6: Line Reversal: Step 1   INT

Step Two: Line Reversal

At this point, the direction of the eight lines is simply reversed. Inputs become outputs, and outputs become inputs. This is illustrated on the right of the drawing. To perform this line reversal, a single instruction is necessary: "complement the contents of the direction register." Naturally, this assumes that such an instruction is available. On some microprocessors, two, or even three instructions might be required to perform this on an external location.

The contents of the direction register are now "11110000". As a result, the contents of the bits D0 through D3, which were previously inputs, are now outputs. The value "1011" is therefore output on the columns of the keyboard. As a result, lines D4 through D7 are conditioned by the rows of the keyboard. In this example, the resulting value for D4 through D7 is "1011". Wherever a key is pressed, a "zero" is generated on input. Finally, it is sufficient to read the contents of the data register to know which key was pressed. The contents of the data register in our example is "10111011". It indicates that the key at the intersection of the third column and the third row was pressed. It is then a simple matter of using a branch table, or any other conversion technique, to obtain the code corresponding to the key. In addition, if more than one "zero" is present either in the first "nibble" (group of four bits) or in the second one, it detects a *multiple-key closure,* i.e. a *rollover* problem. This is usually handled by the jump table. Such a code, having illegal zeroes, will result in a branch to a table entry which is invalid. This can be detected, or else this may cause the whole process to be restarted again, therefore ignoring the input until only a single key is pressed.

The advantage of this technique is to require a very simple software program, and to eliminate the circuitry needed to scan rows. The disadvantage is to dedicate one port of a PIO to keyboard management. However, in view of the very low cost of PIOs, this can indeed be a very inexpensive alternative.

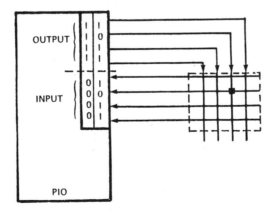

Fig. 4-7: Line Reversal: Step 2

Encoded Keyboard

Not everyone enjoys writing the software required for keyboard encoding. Various types of LSI interface circuits are used to encode keyboard. Usually, the circuit will scan the matrix, discover a coincidence, provide for some amount of debounce and rollover, and latch the data for use in the system. Some units also provide an internal ROM look-up table to generate the proper code for the key pressed, such as ASCII or EBCDIC.

With this one chip and the microcomputer system, a complete *entry and display* interface is acomplished. Note in Fig. 4-13 that the 8279 forms the complete entry and display section interface for a point of sale terminal using the 8048 single-chip microcomputer system.

Keyboard Encoders

The basic role of the keyboard encoder is to identify the key which has been pressed and to supply the 8-bit key code corresponding to it. In addition, a good keyboard chip should also solve the problems we have described above. It should *debounce* and provide *rollover*-protection. Three essential types of encoders are available: *static* encoders, *scanning* encoders, and the *converting* encoder.

A *static encoder* simply generates the code corresponding to the key. In order to simplify the key-protection problem, the linear keyboard can be considered. A linear keyboard is, for example, a 64-key keyboard which provides a wire for every key pressed. Detection here is easy. The pulse appears on the wire corresponding to the key pressed. This pulse is then simply transformed into the suitable 8-bit code. However, this means 64 separate incoming lines to produce one of 64 8-bit codes. In order to reduce the cost of the wiring and the necessity for encoders, most keyboards are arranged in matrix fashion, for example 8 by 8. In an 8-by-8 keyboard, only 16 wires are used. The price paid is that the process necessary to identify the key becomes more complex. This then requires a *scanning encoder*, or the use of a *scanning routine*. Expensive ASCII keyboards (full keyboards) can afford the luxury of a linear arrangement in view of the cost of every key. No scanner is then necessary to identify the key. However, most keyboards have the matrix arrangement.

Scanning Chip

A *scanning chip* solves the problem of key identification when using a matrix-keyboard array. Each row of keys is scanned in turn by using a counter. As long as no key is pressed, the scanning goes around in a circular manner. As soon as the key is pressed, a key closure strobe is generated, and scanning stops. The counter can be read; it identifies the row and column on which the key has· been pressed. Such a straightforward scanning mechanism may not provide the desired two-key rollover protection. Scanning in this system stops with the first key down which is encountered. When two keys are pressed in close sequence, one which is identified might well be the second one which was pressed. A better scanning mechanism will scan the entire keyboard for key closure and will generate a valid code only if only one key is pressed. Whenever more than one key is pressed, it will simply keep scanning until only one is held down. This has the added advantage of providing intrinsic *automatic debouncing* for the key.

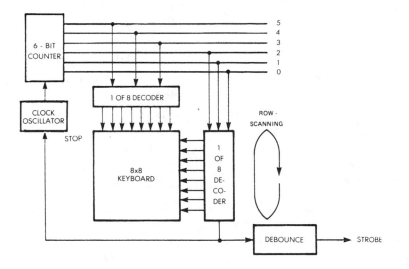

Fig. 4-8: Scanning The Keyboard

The above discussion was, in fact, simplified. In order to provide the reading of the key down, it is necessary to supply the voltage on the columns. If all columns were activated at the same time, it would be impossible to determine which column was pressed. In reality, a one is supplied on a column, then on the next one, then on the next one. Whenever a key closure is detected, the column is known, and the rows are scanned for another closure.

The operation of the scanner is usually the following: a single 6-bit counter is used. The top three bits of the counter are decoded by a 1 to 8 decoder and are used to activate each one of the 8 column in sequence. The lower three bits of the counter, which change faster than the other ones, are also decoded by a 1 to 8 decoder which is used to scan the rows. This guarantees that every time a one is generated on one of the columns, the 8 rows are scanned in turn. Then the next column is activated. Whenever a key-closure occurs, the detection will occur when the row is selected, and this will stop the six-bit counter. The contents of the counter can then be read. They identify the column and the row which correspond to the key closure.

Good keyboard encoders are equipped with a read-only memory which automatically supplies the output code corresponding to the key pressed. They should also have separate shift and control inputs. In particular, this eliminates false output codes whenever wrong keys are pressed.

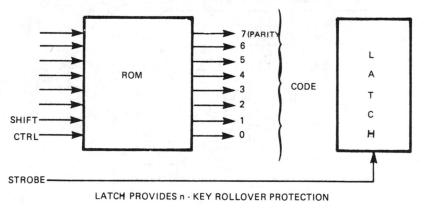

ADDING MEMORY TO SCANNED KEYBOARD CREATES FINAL CODE

LATCH PROVIDES n - KEY ROLLOVER PROTECTION

Fig. 4-9: ROM and Latch

As an example, the NECuPD 364D-02 2 keyboard encoder appears in illustration 4-10.

It provides n-key lock-out, n-key rollover and debounce, frequency control oscillator, and 3 mode selections: shift, control, and shift plus control. It is equipped internally with a 3600 bit ROM. It provides a 10-bit output for 90 keys in 4 modes. The 90 keys of the keyboard must be organized as a 9-by-10 matrix. It is equipped internally with a 10-stage ring counter for the columns, and a 9-stage ring counter for

110

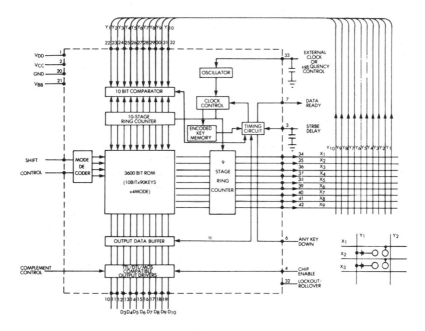

Fig. 4-10: NEC Keyboard Encoder

the rows. In addition, its memory output is equipped with an output data buffer. This guarantees that there will be no random code outputs, while scanning occurs with no keys pressed. Other similar encoders are available from a variety of manufacturers, such as General Instruments. The on-chip ROM can be mask-programmed to provide any desirable coding scheme—such as ASCII or EBCDIC.

This device may be used in a microprocessor system as an input port *during the bus*. The data-ready line can be used to flag the processor when a keystroke is ready to be read.

Fig. 4-11: ASCII Keyboard

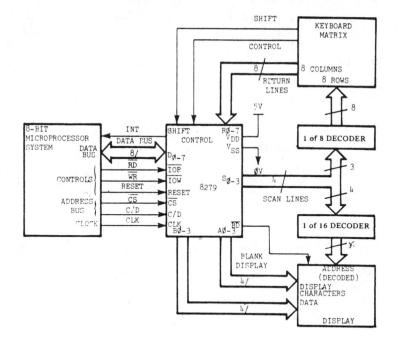

Fig. 4-12: 8279 Keyboard Display Controller

Pictured in Fig. 4-12, this LSI circuit provides for an 8 × 8 keyboard matrix with shift and control keys. In this way, up to 256 codes can be generated. For example, pressing control *and* shift and the letter "p" would be one of the codes.

In addition to encoding the keyboard, the device will also scan a display and light the display to display data stored in an RAM bank in the 8279. Similar devices are available from Rockwell and GI.

ASCII Keyboard

Keyboards may be purchased with the standard teletype or typewriter layouts that generate the seven-bit ASCII code. These keyboards contain the keys, plus the LSI keyboard-controller chip. The output is usually seven parallel bits with a strobe pulse. To interface this to a standard serial input, a UART and clock may be added. The complete design appears in Fig. 4-15.

The UART takes the seven bits of data and transmits them in a serial 10-or-11 bit format when the stroke pulse occurs. The keyboard

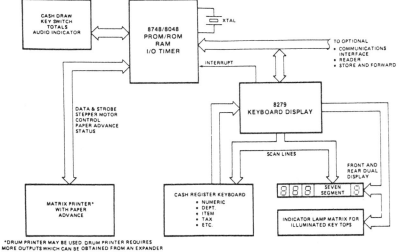

*DRUM PRINTER MAY BE USED. DRUM PRINTER REQUIRES
MORE OUTPUTS WHICH CAN BE OBTAINED FROM AN EXPANDER
DEVICE.

Fig. 4-13: 8048 Point-of-Sale Terminal with 8279

BIT NUMBERS								0	0	0	0	1	1	1	1
								0	0	1	1	0	0	1	1
								0	1	0	1	0	1	0	1
b_7	b_6	b_5	b_4	b_3	b_2	b_1	HEX 1 / HEX Ø	0	1	2	3	4	5	6	7
			0	0	0	0	0	NUL	DLE	SP	0	@	P	`	p
			0	0	0	1	1	SOH	DC1	!	1	A	Q	a	q
			0	0	1	0	2	STX	DC2	"	2	B	R	b	r
			0	0	1	1	3	ETX	DC3	#	3	C	S	c	s
			0	1	0	0	4	EOT	DC4	$	4	D	T	d	t
			0	1	0	1	5	ENQ	NAK	%	5	E	U	e	u
			0	1	1	0	6	ACK	SYN	&	6	F	V	f	v
			0	1	1	1	7	BEL	ETB	'	7	G	W	g	w
			1	0	0	0	8	BS	CAN	(	8	H	X	h	x
			1	0	0	1	9	HT	EM	)	9	I	Y	i	y
			1	0	1	0	10	LF	SUB	*	:	J	Z	j	z
			1	0	1	1	11	VT	ESC	+	;	K	[	k	{
			1	1	0	0	12	FF	FS	,	<	L	\	l	¦
			1	1	0	1	13	CR	GS	_	=	M	]	m	}
			1	1	1	0	14	SO	RS	.	>	N	^	n	~
			1	1	1	1	15	SI	US	/	?	O	□	o	DEL

Fig. 4-14: ASCII Table

is locked out while transmitting. The serial clock runs at 16 times the bit rate. For 110 baud, the oscillator is tuned to 1760 hertz. For 300 baud, it is tuned to 4800 hertz.

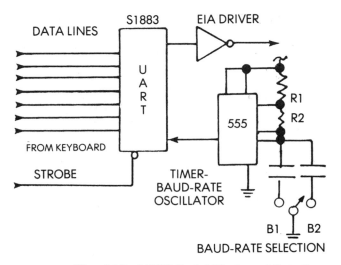

Fig. 4-15: ASCII Serial Keyboard Interface

LED DISPLAYS

Light-emitting-diodes (LEDs) are commonly used to indicate status or other information to the user. LED displays may take a number of forms. Three of these are: single LED, seven-segment LED, and dot-matrix LED displays.

The *single LED* is a diode with a voltage drop of 1.2 to 2.4 volts, depending on the type. It is a device that emits a narrow wavelength band of visible or infrared light. The most-used LEDs are red LEDs. Others used, although more expensive and sometimes not as efficient, are green, orange, yellow, and infrared LEDs.

Fig. 4-16 shows an LED interface to an output port bit.

The current, I, that passes through the LED will determine its intensity. The formula given can be simplified to: $I = 3.5/R$ for a five-volt supply. Typical currents are from two to twenty milliamps. When the input is less than 0.6 volts, the transistor is off and no current flows. When the input is greater than 0.6 volts, the transistor turns on and allows current to flow, lighting the LED.

114

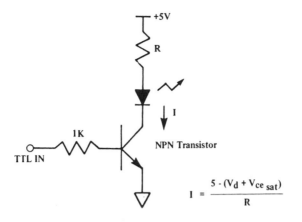

Fig. 4-16: Single LED Interface

Seven-Segment LED

A seven-segment LED display consists of a group of seven elementary LEDs arranged as in Fig. 4-17.

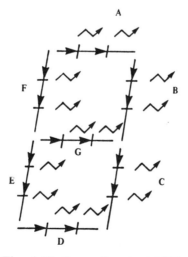

Fig. 4-17: Seven-Segment LED

With these segments, we can display the numerals 0 through 9 and some letters of the alphabet. In this way, we have a *readout* of the seven drive signals.

115

A common interface device is a *BCD-to-seven-segment decoder/driver*. It will convert 4-bit BCD directly into the proper

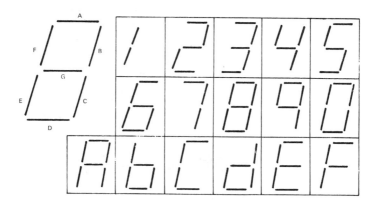

Fig. 4-18: Seven-Segment Characters

numerals and also drive the LEDs directly with internal driver transistors. An example is the 7447 pictured in Fig. 4-19. An output port may drive the 7447 with four bits of BCD data to light the proper segments. The truth table appears in Fig. 4-20.

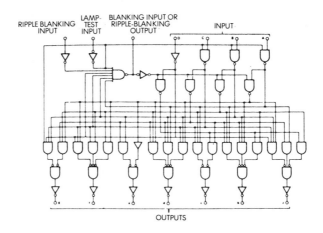

Fig. 4-19: 7447 Seven-Segment Decoder-Driver

TRUTH TABLE

DECIMAL OR FUNCTION	INPUTS							OUTPUTS							NOTE
	LT	RBI	D	C	B	A	BI/RBO	a	b	c	d	e	f	g	
0	1	1	0	0	0	0	1	0	0	0	0	0	0	1	1
1	1	x	0	0	0	1	1	1	0	0	1	1	1	1	1
2	1	x	0	0	1	0	1	0	0	1	0	0	1	0	
3	1	x	0	0	1	1	1	0	0	0	0	1	1	0	
4	1	x	0	1	0	0	1	1	0	0	1	1	0	0	
5	1	x	0	1	0	1	1	0	1	0	0	1	0	0	
6	1	x	0	1	1	0	1	1	1	0	0	0	0	0	
7	1	x	0	1	1	1	1	0	0	0	1	1	1	1	
8	1	x	1	0	0	0	1	0	0	0	0	0	0	0	
9	1	x	1	0	0	1	1	0	0	0	1	1	0	0	
10	1	x	1	0	1	0	1	1	1	1	0	0	1	0	
11	1	x	1	0	1	1	1	1	1	0	0	1	1	0	
12	1	x	1	1	0	0	1	1	0	1	1	1	0	0	
13	1	x	1	1	0	1	1	0	1	1	0	1	0	0	
14	1	x	1	1	1	0	1	1	1	1	0	0	0	0	
15	1	x	1	1	1	1	1	1	1	1	1	1	1	1	
BI	x	x	x	x	x	x	0	1	1	1	1	1	1	1	2
RBI	1	0	0	0	0	0	0	1	1	1	1	1	1	1	3
LT	0	x	x	x	x	x	1	0	0	0	0	0	0	0	4

Fig. 4-20: 7447 Truth Table

In order to save the cost of having one decoder for each LED digit display, the displays may be multiplexed. Each digit is on for a short time before a new digit is selected and turned on. In this way, one decoder can serve a number of displays. There are many ways to multiplex. Two are presented here:

Fig. 4-21 shows the first scheme, which scans both digit and data. Note how *external drivers* are used. This is because, when multiplexing, each display must be N times as bright as when it operates alone, since it is on 1/N times as long. Thus, currents needed are N times as large. Most integrated circuits cannot provide this current, so external discrete transistors must be used.

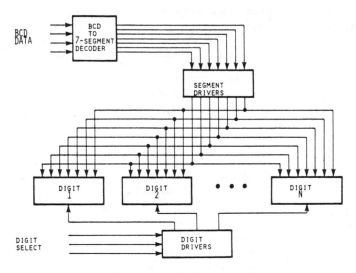

Fig. 4-21: Multiplexing LEDs

The second scheme, in Fig. 4-22, uses a *counter* to advance the digit count. The count is input to the processor and is used to address the proper data for the digit. The data are placed on an output port which drives the 7447 decoder. Note again that current-buffering is needed to increase the brightness.

118

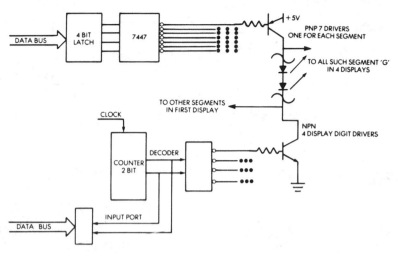

Fig. 4-22: Drivers for Scanning

Matrix LED

The LED matrix consists of five rows of seven columns of LEDs. These 35 LEDs can display upper and lower case letters and numbers. A typical arrangement appears in Fig. 4-23.

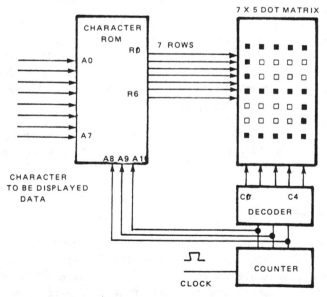

Fig. 4-23: 7 × 5 Dot Matrix LED

119

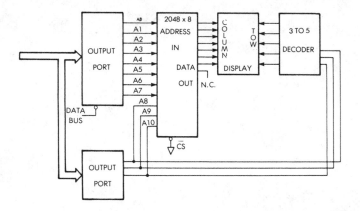

Fig. 4-24: Counter-Multiplexed-Matrix LED

The first output port selects the column data and the second output port selects the row, through the decoder. With this technique, the program will step through the five rows, displaying whatever character has been programmed into the 2048-by-8 read-only memory.

Another technique is to have external hardware step through the rows and display the proper data. Such a method is illustrated in Fig. 4-24.

The counter will start at 0 and count to 4. The character ROM is being addressed to the character "S". Column 0 addresses the row data to be displayed. They are from R6 to R0: 1001111_2. The clock advances the counter to column 1. The row data are now 1001001_2. This continues through row Column 4 and then repeats. All the letters of the alphabet may be generated this way. A typical character ROM is shown in Fig. 4-25.

Note that this part is for imporved-resolution 7 x 9 displays. Also, this character ROM may be used with ASCII, Baudot or EBCDIC code, depending on the table ordered.

Summary of Displays

There are many other displays. However, LED-type displays are reliable, easy to interface, and illustrate the techniques used in most all other display interfacing techniques. CRT interfacing will be covered also in this chapter, and the dot matrix methods will be presented in that section.

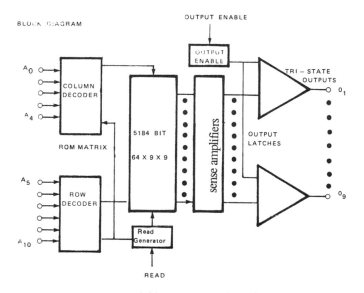

Fig. 4-25: Dot Matrix ROM

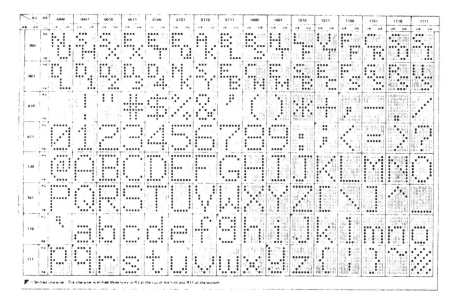

Fig. 4-26: Dot Matrix Characters

TELETYPE

A teletype is a serial mechanical input-output device which usually operates at 110, 150 or 300 baud depending on the model and manufacturer. Three methods of interfacing will be presented here: one for a UART, using a model 33 Teletype [R], one for a Motorola ACIA, using a model 33 Teletype [R] with opto-isolation, and one RS232EIA interface. A model 33 Teletype operates at 10 characters per second. Each character is encoded by eleven bits/ one start bit, 8 data bits, and 2 stop bits. The resulting transfer rate is, therefore, 110 baud. The only significant interfacing problem is to assemble the 8-bit parallel data-byte from these 11 bits. Transmission is asynchronous. The universal interface for a TTY is the UART, which was described in the previous section. It performs automatically all the required functions, and may operate in both directions.

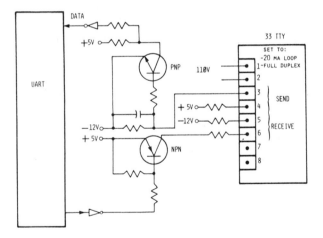

Fig. 4-27: UART TTY Interface

In Fig. 4-27, the UART is used for serial to parallel and parallel to serial conversion of the data. Fig. 4-28 illustrates the serial format, and Fig. 4-29 illustrates the timing sequence. The schematic of the interface shows how the TTL signals are converted into 20 milliamp current loop signals required by the TTY.

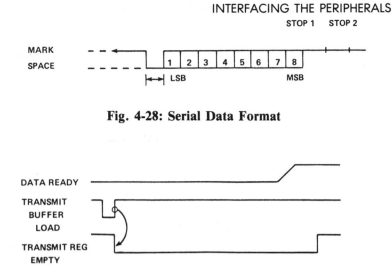

Fig. 4-28: Serial Data Format

Fig. 4-29: UART Timing

In fig. 4-30, *opto-isolators* are used to isolate the teletype electrically from the microcomputer system. *This requires that the + and − 12 volts levels also be isolated from the microcomputer.* The ACIA performs the conversion and interfaces directly with the 6800 bus.

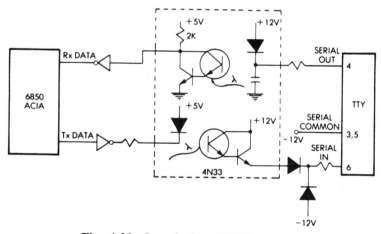

Fig. 4-30: Opto-isolated TTY Interface

Some teletypes are equipped with EIA-RS232C in serial configuration. In RS232C teletypes, + and − 12 volt pulses rather than the presence or absence of 20 milliamp currents are used. Fig. 4-31 illustrates a common set of devices for EIA to TTL to EIA level conversion. These are the MC1489 and MC1488 integrated circuits. There are four translators in each package so a number of lines may be interfaced.

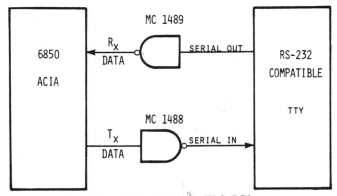

Fig. 4-31: MC1489 EIA IC's

```
NEXT 1    LDA A STACON       LOAD STATUS
          ASR A              SHIFT RDRF BIT TO C-BIT POSITION
          BCS FRAM           CHECK RDRF BIT
          ASR A
          ASR A              SHIFT DCD BIT TO C-BIT POSITION
          BCC NEXT 1         CHECK DCD BIT
          BR ERROR 2         CARRIER LOSS - BRANCH TO ERROR ROUTINE
FRAM      ASR A
          ASR A              SHIFT FE BIT TO C-BIT POSITION
          BCC OVRN           CHECK FE BIT
          BR ERROR 3         FRAMING ERROR - BRANCH TO ERROR ROUTINE
OVRN      ASR A              SHIFT OVRN BIT TO C-BIT POSITION
          BCC PAR            CHECK OVRN BIT
          BR ERROR 4         OVERRUN ERROR - BRANCH TO ERROR ROUTINE
PAR       ASR A              SHIFT PE BIT TO C-BIT POSITION
          BCC R DATA         CHECK PE BIT
          BR ERROR 5         PARITY ERROR - BRANCH TO ERROR ROUTINE
R DATA    LDA B TXRX         LOAD B REGISTER WITH DATA
          RTS                RETURN FROM SUBROUTINE
```

Fig. 4-32: 6800 Receive Subroutine

Mechanically, the teletype appears complex but is really quite simple. To help understand the serial data format, an explanation of what happens internally will be presented.

When the start bit comes in, two things happen: the clutch engages all mechanical linkages so that a print cycle will occur and prepares the decoding selector magnet for the decoding process. The next eight bits come in, 9.09 milliseconds apart. They each trip the selector magnet, which stops eight notched wheels from spinning—one after the other. In turn, the print bars which select the character on the print head are raised, or lowered, due to the combination of notches on the wheels. The print head selects the proper character and the print hammer strikes the head onto the ribbon and paper. The stop bits are required to allow enough time to finish the present character before another comes along.

If the punch were on, the selection of the print bars would also send punches through the paper-tape, while printing the character.

When a key is pressed, the proper bit pattern is placed on eight contacts on the *distributor*. The distributor is like the spark distributor in an automobile. Fig. 4-33 illustrates the simplicity of this scheme. The motor is engaged to turn the commutator around once, which opens and closes the loop generating the 11-bit pattern for that key.

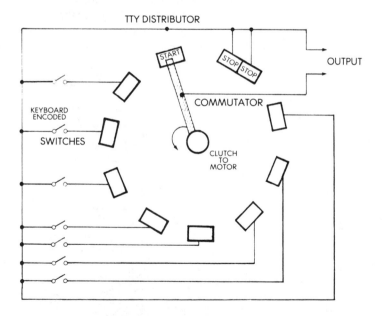

Fig. 4-33: Distributor in Teletype

Note that the synchronous motor is the timing source for the machine, and an accurate line frequency is necessary, or else the machine will lose due to old age, no oil, or mechanical problems.

A Teletype Output Subroutine

It is assumed here that the teletype is connected to bit 0 of port 2. This simple program will shift out the 11 bits necessary for representing the character in teletype format. The flow-chart appears in Fig. 4-34; the actual connection appears in Fig. 4-36. The program appears in Fig. 4-35. Register B is used as a counter. It is initially set to 11. The contents of register B will be decremented every time that the bit is shifted out, i.e. transmitted to port 2. It is important to remember that only bit 0 of the accumulator matters in this example. All other bits will be ignored. This is the right-most bit, or least significant bit (LSB) of the accumulator. Initially, the accumulator contains the 8 bits to be transmitted. In addition, both the start bit and the stop bit must be transmitted. This will be accomplished by using a feature of the rotation instruction of the 8080. The carry bit, which is in fact the ninth bit of the accumulator, in shift operations, will be set to 0. It will then be rotated into the accumulator in bit position 0. This will be the start bit. The crux of the operation is to use a *rotate* instruction. If the contents of the accumulator were simply *shifted* left-most bit would be lost. In this case the left-most bit is preserved in the carry, while a 0 gets writ-

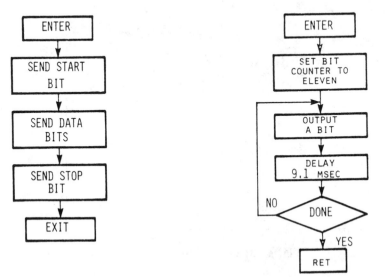

Fig. 4-34: Transmit Software

```
TELETYPE OUTPUT SUBROUTINE          (ASSUME TTY CONNECTED TO PORT 2 BIT
                                                                    0)
      ;
      ;   THIS SUBROUTINE ENTERED WITH CHARACTER TO BE OUTPUT IN THE
      ;                                                  C REGISTER
    TYOUT:    MVI     B,11    ;  SET COUNTER FOR 11 BITS
              MOV     A,C     ;  CHARACTER TO ACCUMULATOR
              ORA     A       ;  CLEAR CARRY-FOR START BIT
              RAL             ;  MOVE CARRY TO A(0)
    MORE:     OUT     2       ;  SEND TO TTY
              CALL    DELAY   ;  KILL TIME
              RAR             ;  POSITION NEXT BIT
              STC             ;  SET CARRY-FOR STOP BITS
              DCR     B       ;  DECREMENT BIT COUNTER
              JNZ     MORE    ;  DONE?
              RET             ;  YES
      ;
      ;   9 MSEC DELAY (ASSUME NO WAIT STATES)
      ;
    DELAY:    MVI     D,6
    DL0:      MVI     E,2000
    DL1:      DCR     E       ;   0.15MSEC
              JNZ     DL1     ;   INNER LOOP
              DCR     D
              JNZ     DL0
              RET
```

Fig. 4-35: 8080 TTY Output Program

ten in bit position 0. It will be noted in the program, that the next
operation in the accumulator will be a right rotation. It will re-install
the former bit 7, which had been preserved in the carry bit, in its correct position. Finally, once this has been done, successive rotations
will rotate into the left of the accumulator successive ones created in
the carry bit. This will guarantee that the stop bits get transmitted at
the end. The sequence of the program is straightforward:

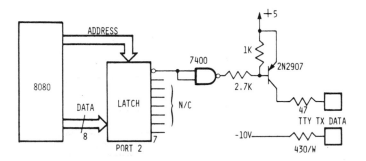

Fig. 4-36: Hardware TTY Interface

The counter register B is set at value 11, and the character which was preserved in register C is loaded into the accumulator A. The accumulator is ored with itself (third instruction). This does not change its contents, but guarantees that the carry is set to 0. This will be the start bit. A left rotate is performed: RAL. This moves the carry into bit position 0 of the accumulator. The output then occurs: OUT2. The bit is sent to the teletype. Everytime that the bit is sent to the teletype, a delay loop must be executed to guarantee a 9 ms delay. The delay routine is implemented as subroutine, and appears at the bottom of the program. Next, an RAR is executed to shift the correct next bit into bit position. The carry is set in anticipation of ulterior rotations to guarantee that eventually the start bits will be transmitted correctly. The bit-counter (register B) is then decremented and tested. If the counter reaches the value of 0, the program ends. If not, the program loops by going back to address MORE, where the next output occurs.

Software Example for ACIA

This subroutine sends a character to the teletype. If it is not ready to transmit, the subroutine *waits* until ready. It also checks the clear-to-send input (CTS) on the ACIA. This will be used with an EIA-RS232C interface system.

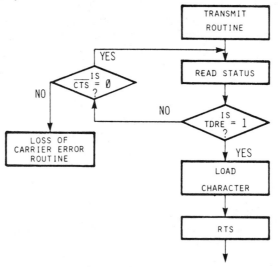

Fig. 4-37: ACIA Flowchart

The first instruction loads the status of the ACIA into accumulator A. The ready-to-transmit flag is in bit position 1, so it must be shifted twice to the right, into carry, to be tested. If we are ready to transmit, the program goes directly to DATA where the contents of accumulator B are sent to the ACIA.

If the ACIA were not ready to send, the CTS bit would be checked; if it were clear-to-send, a carrier loss would be indicated and the program would branch to an error routine. If the ACIA is clear-to-send, the transmit-ready flag would be checked until ready. This is a polling technique. Interrupts could also be used.

NEXT	LDA A STACON	LOAD STATUS
	ASR A	
	ASR A	SHIFT TDRE BIT TO C-BIT POSITION
	BCC TX DATA	CHECK TDRE BIT
	ASR A	
	ASR A	SHIFT $\overline{CTS}$ BIT TO C-BIT POSITION
	BCC NEXT	CHECK $\overline{CTS}$
	BR ERROR 1	CARRIER LOSS - BRANCH TO ERROR ROUTINE
TX DATA	STA B TXRX	STORE CHARACTER IN ACIA
	RTS	RETURN FROM SUBROUTINE

Fig. 4-38: ACIA Transmit Subroutine

PAPER-TAPE READER

The teletypewriters usually are slow for reading punched tapes. One helpful peripheral would be a high-speed paper-tape reader. Such a device would optically detect the code pattern on the paper-tape and advance to the next frame quickly. A typical reader has the schematic shown in Fig. 4-39.

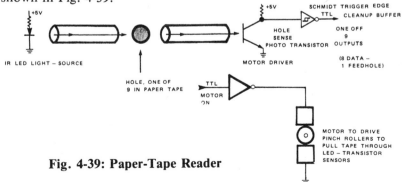

Fig. 4-39: Paper-Tape Reader

Our microcomputer must turn on the motor, sense a feedhold (which is smaller than the data, indicating the center of a bit frame), sense the frame-pattern and store the data before the next feedhole passes by. When an end-of-tape character is sensed, the reader motor should turn off.

8 LEVEL - PAPER TAPE

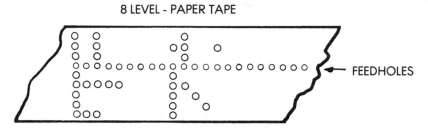

FEEDHOLES

Fig. 4-40: 8 Level Bit Frame

A bit frame for our 8-level tape appears in Fig. 4-40. A typical problem is caused by the ragged edges of the holes or by dirt on the tape. The hole data appears in Fig. 4-41. Due to this, the feedhole sensing might need some extra delay so that the middle of the feedhole will be the time at which the other holes are sampled. One must know the motor speed to do this.

Some systems can go forward and backward so that blocks of data with errors may be re-read.

The flowchart for this reader appears in Fig. 4-42.

Fig. 4-41: Hole Data

STEPPER MOTOR

Stepper motors are a popular means of implementing motion in many projects. Each time a stepper motor is actuated it moves its shaft by a precise angular amount. Popular large angle steppers move by 7.5, 15, 45, and 90 degrees each step. Small angle steppers come in 1.8-

and 5.0 degree standard step sizes. The advantage of such a discrete step output is that one always knows where the motor shaft is by counting how many steps the microcomputer has sent to the motor.

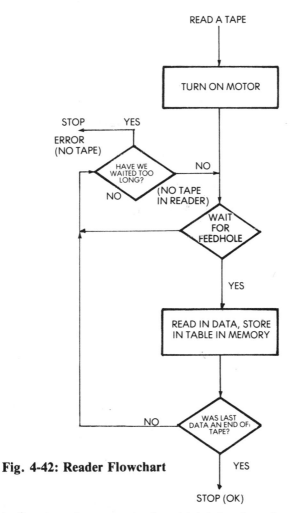

Fig. 4-42: Reader Flowchart

The interface to a stepper motor is not trivial and can be much more complex than the one that appears here. Use imagination to improve this design, as this one is the least energy efficient but most commonly used.

The motor itself has four windings: 1, 2, 3, and 4. By applying pulses of current in the proper sequence, the motor will step. There are three sequences.

— Low power sequence
— Normal sequence
— Half-step sequence

The low power sequence sends a pulse of current to 1, then 2, then 3, then 4, and then back to 1 again. No two windings are on at the same time and the motor will step one step.

The normal sequence activates two windings at once in the following sequence: 1 and 2, 2 and 3, 3 and 4, 4, and 1, and so on. This results in smoother operation but requires more power.

The half-step mode allows for a half angle step in between each angle step. The sequence here is: 1 and 2, 2, 2 and 3, 3, 3 and 4, 4, 4 and 1, 1.

The motor windings require a current source, as their resistance is rather low, typically .2 ohms. Also, due to the large inductance of the windings, special design techniques are required to prevent the inductive "kick-back" from destroying the switching transistors or filter capacitors. Fig. 4-43 shows the stepping motor interface circuit.

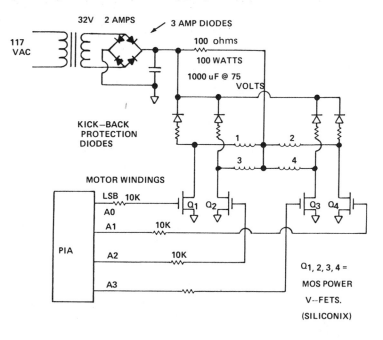

Fig. 4-43: Stepper Motor Interface

The time for mode 2 is in Figure 4-44.

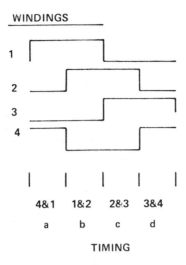

Fig. 4-44: Winding Timing

Note how in the truth table we are shifting a half byte of two 0's and two 1's around and around. The program then becomes quite trivial. All the programmer has to do is rotate the value 00110011 in an 8-bit around fashion, outputting it before each rotate to our PIA.

TIME	A0	A1	A2	A3
a	1	0	0	1
b	1	1	0	0
c	0	1	1	0
d	0	0	1	1

Fig. 4-45: Truth Table

In 6800 code we need to rotate 8 bits. Because the 6800 only rotates 9 bits, we must think about this problem. The solution lies in a simple programmer's trick. Instead of rotating, one can continually add the number to itself twice.

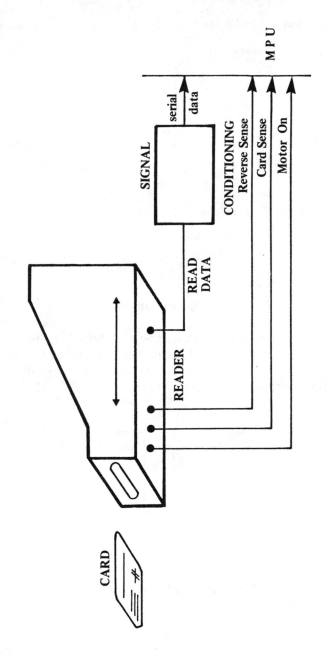

Fig. 4-46: Stripe Reader

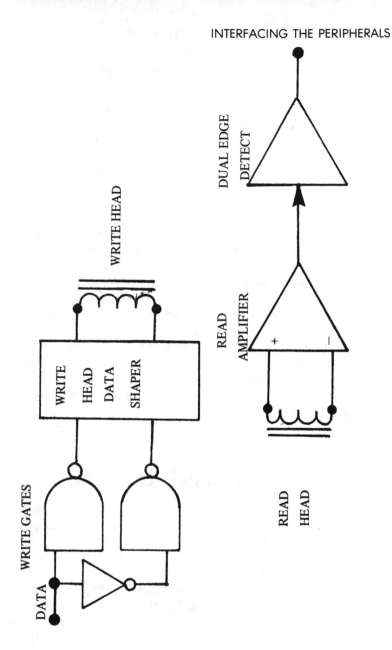

Fig. 4-47: Card Reader Block Diagram

The only thing we must remember is to add with carry so our byte will appear to rotate.

```
         LDAA @$CC      Load ACC A with 11001100
LOOP     STA A @$8000   Output ACC A to Stepper PIA
         ADC A          Add ACC A to ACC A twice
         ACD A
         JSR DELAY      Delay pulse step time
         BRA LOOP       Go back and loop again
```

To go in reverse, one needs another subroutine that has two SBC A instead of two ACD A instructions. To vary the speed, one changes the amount of time wasted in the delay subroutine. As a general rule, the faster the stepper must step, the higher the supply voltage must be. If one tries to step too fast, the stepper will "miss a step." This is serious, as the advantage of using a stepper motor is that one knows its position at all times. To lose a step means the software will have lost its place. Most mechanisms with stepper motors therefore have a limit switch which tells the controller that it has found a reference position. All measurements are then made from that reference point. This is why floppy disk drives seek track 0 so that the interface knows where to start seeking.

MAGNETIC-STRIPE-CREDIT-CARD CARD READER

One of the latest developments in the technology has been the use of encoded stripes on the backs of charge or bank-cards to carry information about the bearer's account. Described here is an interface for just such a stripe reader. Fig. 4-47 shows the block diagram of the interface.

The program will control the decoding of the information on the stripe and the movement of the card in the reader. In normal operation, the card will be sensed at the pressure roller, the drive will be turned on, and the card will be read. If the data is bad or represents a forgery, the card will be "eaten" by the reader. If valid, the card will be returned.

We will assume that the card has been recorded in F2F coding ("frequency-double frequency"), where each "1" bit is two transitions, and each "0" bit is one transition, per bit cell. Thus, the data off the head may appear as in Fig. 4-48, second trace down.

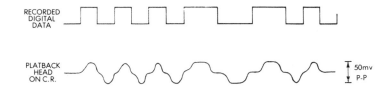

Fig. 4-48: Recorded Data

In order to use this signal, it must be conditioned. An analog pulse amplifier-detector will produce an output like the one in Fig. 4-49. The software, through timing loops, may then decode the waveform, back into serial bits, and then into characters. In order to insure proper data and security, data should be written *three times* in a scrambled form, with various parity checks and heading, and trailing blocks of ones or zeroes. (See synchronous formats and error-correction codes in Chapter 6.)

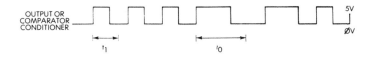

Fig. 4-49: Final Data

If it is necessary to write on the card, it can be read while going in and written while being returned. One must have a special software routine to reverse the sense of the data so that it can be read again upon reentry.

The control necessary will be three inputs: card-in sense, serial-data read, end-of-card sense (reverse motor to return); and two outputs: motor-on (automatically will reverse, unless turned-off), and serial-data-to-be-written. Thus, one half of a 6820 PIA or 8255 PPI will be sufficient input-out hardware!

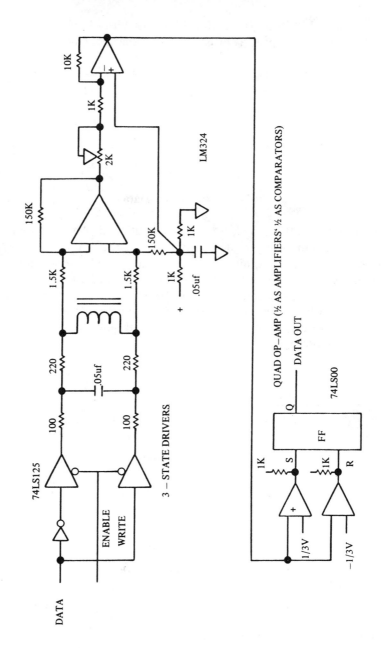

Fig. 4-50: The Read/Write Electronics

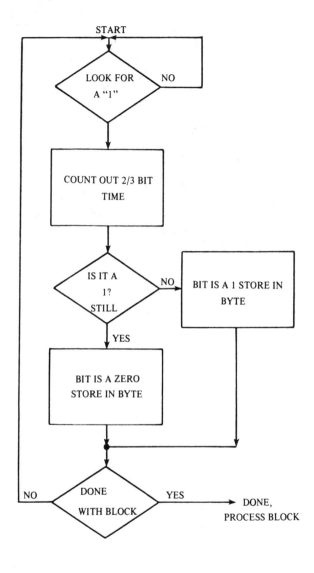

Fig. 4-51: Flowchart for Mag Stripe Read

Next the hardware for reading and writing on the card is examined. The write electronics will reverse the current through the write head, causing the magnetic field to change on the card stripe. Where illustrated in Fig. 4-50, the receive or read amplifier is also shown.

The read section detects both the positive and negative going signals to insure noise-free data recovery. Shown in Fig. 4-49 is the output waveform.

The read-write software can be aided by using a UART or USART for converting the data, but the UART in software allows the most versatility for reading and writing formats. The flowchart for the output data read decode is in Fig. 4-51.

THE KIM CASSETTE INTERFACE

In order to save programs and reload them when needed, some form of long-term storage is necessary. The inexpensive portable cassette tape recorder can be used without modification to store and load digital information. The interface required is simple to build and easy to program. Described here is the KIM-1® interface to a cassette recorder.(KIM-1 is a MOS Technology trademark.)

The format for transmission will need to convert the binary information in memory into a serial stream of bits that can be recorded on the tape. The logic conditions will be represented by the combination of two tones: 3700 hertz and 2400 hertz. The signals for a "1" or a "0" are illustrated in Fig. 4-52.

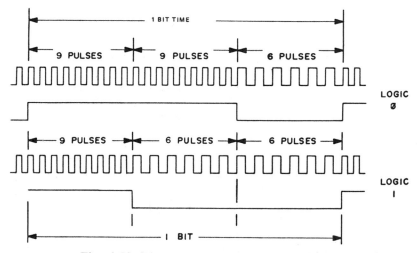

Fig. 4-52: Bit Format for KIM-1 Cassette

The program will generate these tones by counting loops that will generate either tone. This will use one output bit from the programmable interface and ROM chip on the board. This output bit will be buffered and filtered to conform to the input specifications of most tape recorders.

When a tone is sensed, the phase lock loop circuit on the board will differentiate between a 3700-hertz or 2400-hertz tone. By timing the duration of the tones, the data bits may be decoded. Fig. 4-53 is the complete tape recorder interface schematic.

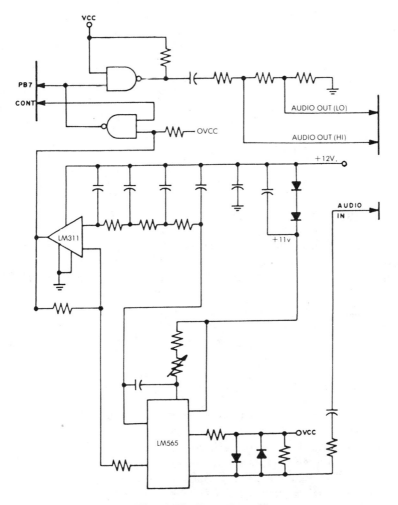

Fig. 4-53: Tape Interface

Note that different means of modulation exist that will result in higher densities. Because all timing for transmit and receive is done in software, different timing schemes may be implemented. However, the method described here is the most reliable, as the tape recorders are not well suited to any higher density recording, due to wow and flutter problems. A high quality tape deck may be used at higher densities if necessary.

The software breaks each byte of data into two 4-bit nibbles. Each nibble is then converted to a seven-bit ASCII character, plus parity. Two such ASCII characters now represent the original data byte. In order that the recorded block of data be identified, a header and trailer are added. The format appears in Fig. 4-54.

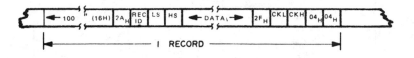

Fig. 4-54: Tape-Data Block Format

The long block of one hundred 16-hexadecimal bytes allows the software to synchronize to the data rate and find the first bit of each byte without any other timing information. Following the sync characters come the start-of-record character, and record-number bytes. After that, the starting address of the data block, and the block itself are written. At the end, a "2F" hexadecimal is written, as well as two check-characters. After that, two "04" hexadecimal are written, to indicate the end of the block.

This format is typical of many block-synchronous transmission schemes used. Other examples are the floppy disk, magnetic-stripe card reader, and inter-machine communications links (see Chapter 6 for the latter).

KANSAS CITY STANDARD

In order to use these inexpensive recorders in the hobby market, a standard was proposed and adopted by the hobbyists. Using frequency shift keying techniques, and frequency-double frequency modem techniques, this standard is easy to use. The drawback is the data rate of 30 characters per second.

The system takes standard serial RS232C data (see chapter 6) and converts each bit to either 8 cycles of 2400 hertz (a "1") or 4 cycles of

1200 hertz (a "0"). To generate this, only a few flip-flops are required along with a quad NAND gate. Shown in Fig. 4-55 is the modulator.

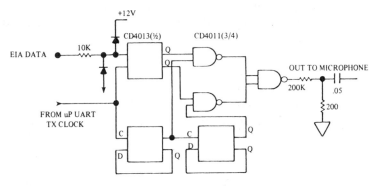

Fig. 4-55: Modulator

The condition of the input data will cause the multiplexer to choose from either 2400-hertz or 1200-hertz tones. The resistor network is used to reduce the output to 10 millivolts for the microphone input of the tape deck.

The demodulator must detect whether the 1200-hertz or 2400-hertz tones are present. There are many ways of doing this; however a common one is to detect zero crossings of the input signal. This will generate either 2400 or 4800 pulses per second. A one-shot is used, tuned so that if it is not kept triggered at the 4800 rate, it must be the other rate. The advantage of this method is that one generates the clock needed by the system's serial UART to untangle the data. This is why, in this case, the closk to the receiver UART is usually generated by this circuit rather than the transmitter clock.

The circuit for the demodulator appears in Fig. 4-56. The demodulator timing appears in Fig. 4-57. Note how one gets back what one started with, along with the necessary synchronizing clock information.

If the tape speed varies, the data may still be recovered, as the clock information will insure the UART receives the proper timing signal.

No special software is needed, as this interface makes the cassette look like a paper-tape, punch-reader combination to the computer.

TARBELL CASSETTE

The Tarbell cassette format is a cassette S100-compatible system which records at 187 bytes per second or 1500 bits per second. The technique used is biphase of F2F coding as in the credit-card reader. In fact, the circuitry shown will work well for building your own Tarbell-compatible interface. The only problem is that the home brew circuit does all decoding in software; whereas the Tarbell unit simplifies the interface by providing a board of ICs to perform the encoding and decoding of the bit stream as well as cassette-drive control.

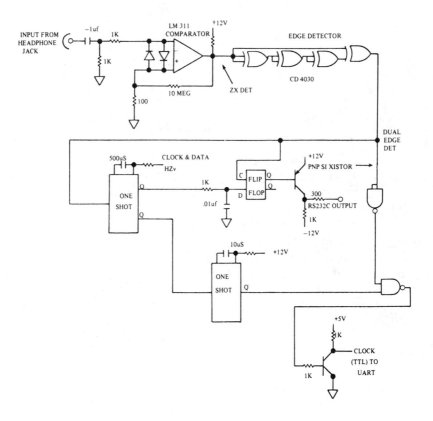

Fig. 4-56: Demodulator

The written data is a synchronous bit stream with a header byte, sync byte, data bytes, and check bytes.

One novel feature is that the interface may be adjusted to also read and write Kansas City Standard tapes using a software modification.

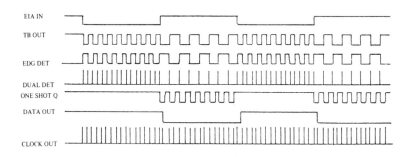

Fig. 4-57: Timing

In summary, this interface provides the basic circuitry for parallel-to-serial conversion, serial TTL data to NRZ (non-return to zero) data (see the floppy disk section for NRZ definition), and write-signal conditioning for the recorder. For playback, the read-signal conditioner, NRZ conversion, and serial-to-parallel converter are provided.

ONE-CHIP DIGITAL CASSETTE CONTROLLER

The NEC UPD371D provides in a single chip most of the functions required for interfacing a *digital* cassette transport. It uses the ISO format and performs:

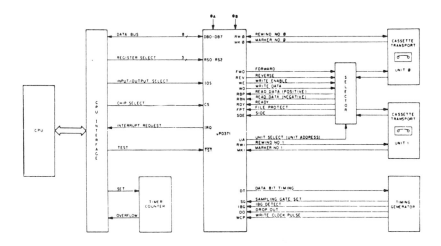

Fig. 4-58: NEC UPD371D Cassette Interface

— Parallel-to-serial and serial-to-parallel data conversion (functions normally accomplished by a UART)

— Error detection, including CRC (CRC will be explained in the disk section)

— Data-encoding two-phase encoding format

— It can control up to two cassette transports with read/write or rewind on one unit, or simultaneous rewind. It interfaces directly to the 8080A. The structure of the system is illustrated in 4-58, and its interface to the 8080 appears in Fig. 4-59.

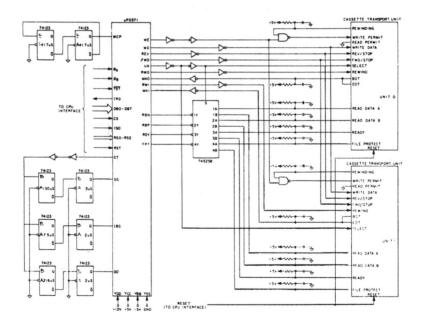

Fig. 4-59: 8080 with UPD371D

CRT DISPLAY INTERFACE

A number of CRTs displays have been created, to be used specifically as computer terminals. In the microprocessor world, the cost of peripherals is of critical importance. Therefore, the most-often-used CRT device, in the case of microprocessor systems, is the home television set. Higher quality CRT displays are used in the case of development systems, in order to permit the user to display more characters, more lines, or more dots per character. In addition, full graphics capability exists on specialized and expensive displays. We will concentrate here on the direct interface to a television-type display.

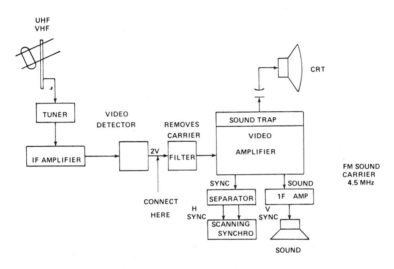

Fig. 4-60: A Television Block Diagram

The organization of a typical television appears in Fig. 4-60. The signal is fed from the antennae into the tuner, which outputs a video i-f frequency, at 4.5 MHz. The signal is fed into a filter amplifier, which is transformer-coupled to the video detector. The output of the detector is the video signal proper, with a 2-volt swing. It is fed to a filter, in order to remove the carrier frequency, and then to the video amplifier. The signal is then split three ways. The video signal is directed to the CRT through a sound trap which eliminates the sound-carrier frequency. The FM sound carrier is fed to a sound i-f amplifier (4.5 MHz), and the output is fed into the loud-speaker. Finally, the sync pulses are separated from the video signal, and identified as H (horizontal) sync and V (vertical) sync. The H sync and the V sync are

147

used to synchronize the display on the screen.

The microprocessor system can interface to the television at two points: it can be coupled directly to the television set antennae—this is the RF modulation method, or else the video signal can be fed directly at the output of the video detector. This is the direct-video-input method.* The advantage of the RF modulation method is that it does not require any connection inside the set. The output wires of the microprocessor system are simply connected to the antennae screws.

Besides requiring compliance with FCC regulations, the RF modulation method has a bandwidth limitation problem. Using standard television sets, the limit would be from 3 to 3.5 MHz. This limit could be, in fact, significantly lower with lesser quality sets. The bandwidth of the set will severely limit the definition on the screen as well as the total number of characters which can be displayed.

The disadvantage of the direct video input is naturally that it requires a connection within the television set itself. A few sets are equipped with an external connector for a direct video entry. This is often the case on color television sets in Europe, but not yet the case in the US.

In order to interface to the television set, we will review here briefly the principles of television operation, and then present the techniques used to display characters on a screen.

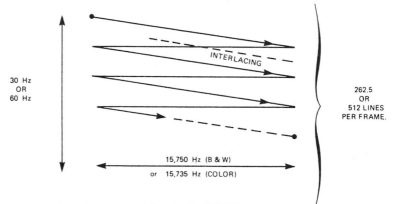

Fig. 4-61: TV Timing

A raster-scan television uses a beam of electrons which is deflected horizontally across the screen, with a varying intensity. When it reaches one end of the screen, the beam is blanked off and it flies back

---

* Warning: This method is highly dangerous in the case of a "hot chassis". It must not be used unless you have determined there is no risk.

to the other side of the screen, while going down one line. This is called the "horizontal-fly-back" phase. It is illustrated in Fig. 4-61. Two types of scan are used, called respectively the direct scan and the interlaced scan. In the interlaced scheme, the screen is scanned *twice*. The second scaning, or field, is made on lines between the previous ones. 262.5 lines are available in each field. An interlaced scheme therefore provides 525 lines per frame. In the case of a TV display connected to a microprocessor, the usual method is not to use interlace, and to use a straight single scan of the screen on 262 lines. The frame rate is then 60 Hz. Interlaced could be used to provide titles or to superimpose messages or titles on a TV broadcast. Two synchronization signals are used to synchronize the motion of the dot across the screen: the line sync supplies the flyback signal, and the vertical sync provides the vertical flyback signal to the beginning of the first line. Some limitations are imposed, which are illustrated in Fig. 4-62. The horizontal scan is usually longer than the screen size. The amount by which the dot deflects past the end of the screen is called the *screen overscan*. In addition, the message displayed on the screen is shorter than the screen itself. This is shown as the *display time* on the illustration. Whenever the dot reaches the end of the display time, it goes black. The time from the end of the display time to the line sync is called the *blank time*.

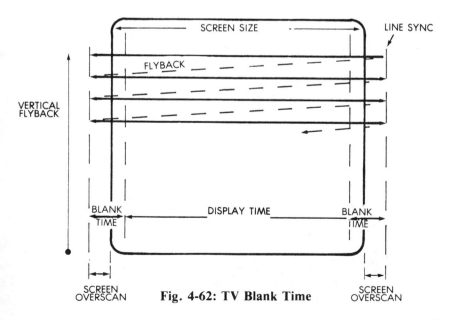

Fig. 4-62: TV Blank Time

Generating Characters

Characters are represented on the screen by a pattern of dots called a *dot matrix*. Two standard formats are used to represent characters. The most frequently used is the *5 × 7 dot matrix*. A lesser used system is the 7 × 9 dot matrix. The advantage of a 7 × 9 dot matrix is a better definition of characters, and a more pleasing representation of lower case letters. However, a 7 × 9 dot matrix requires the use of a high bandwidth, and, for this reason, is much less used. A 5 × 7 dot matrix represents each character with 35 dots. It uses 7 rows of 5 dots, and each character is represented by a sequence of dots and un-dots (blank dots or rather "black" dots). The representation of characters is illustrated in Fig. 4-63. Each scan of a TV line will present on the screen the five dots belonging to all the characters, and so on. At a minimum, a 5 × 7 dot matrix will require weight lines on the screen, since one blank line must be used between the characters. In practice, for good visual presentation, ten lines are used, and sometimes twelve, to present a line of characters.

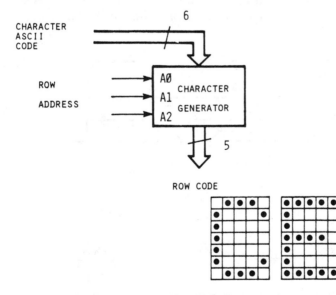

Fig. 4-63: 5X7-Dot Matrix

150

Each character is represented within the microprocessor system by its code, normally ASCII. The table of ASCII codes appears in Fig. 4-14. This seven bit ASCII code must be converted into the dot matrix representation. This can be accomplished simply by an ROM look-up mechanism. Or a specialized chip may be used, a *dot matrix character generator.* When using the generator, the first line of dots for each successive character will be output, then the next one, then the next one, up to the seventh one. A simple counter is used to keep track of the row of dots currently being output. It will be shown in the next sections how the dots are converted into video signals that will be fed to the television set.

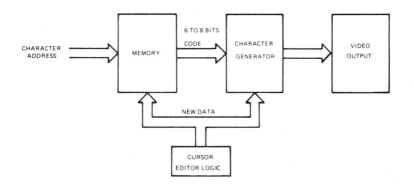

Fig. 4-64: Raster Generation

In addition, the whole picture, or frame, needs to be refreshed at a 60 Hz frequency, i.e., 60 times per second, to avoid flicker. This implies the necessity of a *refresh memory.* The timing for refreshing the screen is usually so fast that a standard microprocessor cannot be used. External circuits, such as a DMA, or other special circuits, must be used. The advantage of using a DMA is that the main memory of the microprocessor system can be shared with the screen refresh. However, it slows down the microprocessor's operation. In many cases, *dedicated memory* is used to refresh the screen. In this case, there is no slowdown of the microprocessor's operation.

Character generators are available from most semiconductor manufacturers, such as Fairchild, General Instruments, Monolithic Memories, MOS Technology, American Microsystems, Electronic Arrays, Signetics, and Texas Instruments.

The number of characters that can be displayed on the screen is limited by the bandwidth of the set being used. Assuming the use of a standard television without modifications, a 5 × 7 dot matrix will usually be selected, and the popular combination is to use 10 lines of 32 characters, or up to 16 lines of 32 characters, for a total of 512 characters. A complete scan line will require approximately 63.5 microseconds. The usable portion of the scan line will be perhaps 43 microseconds. Displaying 32 characters in 43 microseconds will leave us approximately 1.3 microseconds per character. This leaves plenty of time for using a relatively slow memory. If we were using 80 characters per line, an access time of less than 0.5 microsecond would be required for the memory.

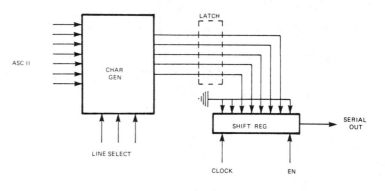

Fig. 4-65: Shift Register Serializes Characters

Converting to Serial Video

The dots coming out of the character generator must now be shifted out into serial form, to be presented as a video signal to the television. This is illustrated in Fig. 4-65. The character generator provides a row output for each character of the line. The 7-bit ASCII is presented on the left of the character generator on the illustration, and the three line-select lines, appearing at the bottom of the character generator, specify which one of the 7 rows of the dot matrix is being output on the right. The five dots corresponding to the row contents are then gated into the shift register, and are being clocked out in serial form to the video output.

152

Four kinds of data must be encoded into a composite video signal:

1. the dots representing the character
2. the eventual blinking signal (usually for the cursor)
3. the cursor
4. finally, the H and V sync signals.

A simple analog mixer will normally be used to form this composite video signal and the mechanism is illustrated in Fig. 4-66.

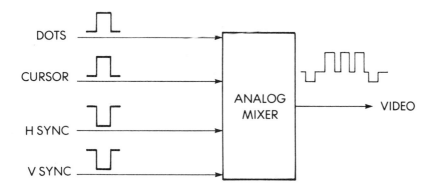

Fig. 4-66: Mixing to Produce Video with Sync

Typical video interface levels are 0 to 2.0 volts, .5 to .75 for the black level, and 1.5 to 2 volts for the white level. This is illustrated in Fig. 4-67. The sync signal is referred to as the sync tip. Its duration is 4.7 us. It is followed by the black and white dot signals encoded as a voltage swing between .5 and 2 volts. The timing appears in Fig. 4-68. On a standard television, white is 100% level, black is 25 to 30%, and sync is 0%. Typical voltage swing is 2 volts. Standard television line time is 45 us.

Finally, the composite video output can be connected to the television set either directly, at the level of video entry which has been presented, or through an RF modulator, for connection to the television antenna. This is illustrated in Fig. 4-69.

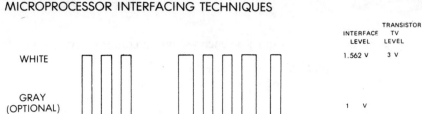

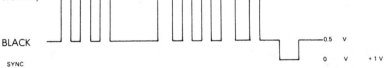

Fig. 4-67: Composite Video and Sync

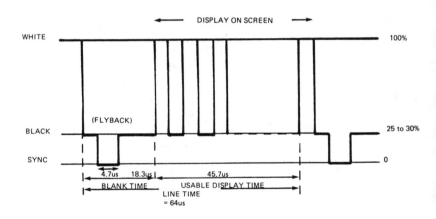

Fig. 4-68: TV Timing

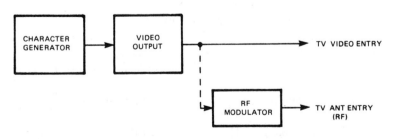

Fig. 4-69: Video vs RF Entry

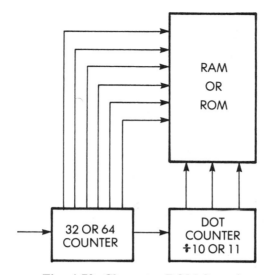

Fig. 4-70: Character ROM Scanning

Refresh Memory

For simplicity in design, the refresh is usually performed from a dedicated memory. However, a microprocessor system equipped with a DMA can be used to refresh a screen directly. In this case, dual-line buffers are used during the DMA transfers between the microprocessor's memory and the television display. This is illustrated in Fig. 4-71. The DMA will first fill line buffer 1. During this time, line buffer 2, which was presumed to be full, will empty itself into the output paths, on the right of the illustration. Typically, line buffer 2 will empty itself during time 2T or more, where T is the time necessary for the DMA to fill one of the buffers. Whenever line buffer 2 has finished emptying itself, line buffer 1, which was long-since full, will be switched on, and will start emptying itself through the multiplexer. As soon as line buffer 1 is switched on, the DMA will quickly refill line buffer 2. This dual buffering scheme guarantees continuous system operation. The only timing requirement is that the DMA be capable of filling one of the line buffers in less time than it takes the other to empty itself. Clearly the DMA should do better than this. The DMA should be capable of loading one of the line buffers much faster than the other empties itself. Otherwise, the memory and the DMA would be used almost exclusively for memory refresh, and no program could execute on the microprocessor itself.

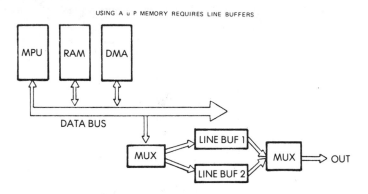

Fig. 4-71: MPU Requires Line Buffers

ONE-CHIP CRT CONTROLLERS

The new one-chip CRT controllers (CRTs) simplify the interfacing of a microprocessor system to a CRT. However, despite their name, they do not implement in a single chip all the functions required to interface to a CRT. They are intended for raster-scan CRT, and usually require a RAM page buffer. This RAM page buffer may have a size of 2K words or more (requiring 11 address outputs, at least). A 2K RAM is sufficient for 25 lines of 80 characters.

FUNCTIONS OF A CRT CONTROLLER

A CRT Controller generates four essential sets of signals:

1. *Refresh Address:* Address of the character which needs to be refreshed on the screen.
2. *Row Selects:* For each character, 7 or 9 rows (using a 5 × 7 or a 7 × 9 dot matrix) of dots must be displayed in sequence.
3. *Video Monitor Timing:* Proper horizontal and vertical synchronization signals must be generated: HSYNC and SYNC.
4. *Display Enable.*

In addition, two usual functions allocated to the CRTC are:

1. *Cursor Output:* The cursor is an independent character pointer, such as underline, square, arrow, or even reverse color. Its position is controlled by special keys or commands.

156

2. *Light-Pen Input:* A light pen is used as a convenient input device. It senses the spot of light when it passes by. The timing relationship to the beginning of a frame permits the calculation of its approximate position on the screen.

The CRTC provides the logic for cursor control, sync-pulse generation, and dot-row selection in an external character generator. All present CRTs require an external refresh, a ROM character generator, and the downstream logic which has been described, including essentially the shift register and video output. The use of such a typical CRTC is illustrated in Fig. 4-72.

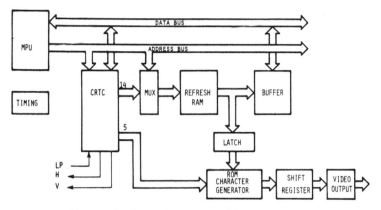

Fig. 4-72: CRT Controller Block Diagram

MOTOROLA 6845 CRT CONTROLLER

The chip pinout appears in Fig. 4-73. It generates the row count for the character generator, the V and H sync, the blanking signal, and a 14-bit refresh address for the RAM buffer. In addition, it provides scrolling and paging. *Scrolling* refers to the vertical shifting of lines across the screen. *Paging* refers to the automatic display of the next screen-full of characters. It is equipped with a cursor register, a light-pen register, and does not need a line buffer.
Programmable features are:

— Dot/rasters per character
— Characters per line
— Lines per sync
— Horizontal/vertical sync position
— Cursor appearance.

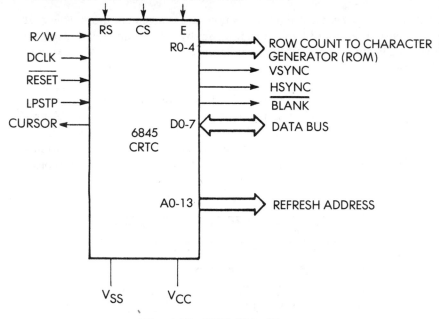

Fig. 4-73: CRT Chip Pinout

INTEL 8275 CRTC

Similarly, the Intel 8275 CRTC will interface to a 5 × 7 or 7 × 9 character generator, and generate all the usual video controls. The basic interconnect of the chip in a system appears in Fig. 4-74.

FAIRCHILD 9412 CRTC

As usual, the CRTC provides 11 address lines to address the buffer. It includes logic for cursor control (CM0/CM2 inputs in Fig. 4-75), and sync-pulse generation (COMP SYNC, VRT SYNC).
It is programmable:

— Display format (FS0-FS2 control inputs)
— Matrix size (5 × 7 or 7 × 9 dot matrix)
— Scroll mode (this is controlled by the scroll input)
— Auto feeding of new line
— Refresh rate (50 Hz/60 Hz - RR input)

Other output signals are:

— DLC0-3 is the dot-line counter: it provides the line address in a character.

158

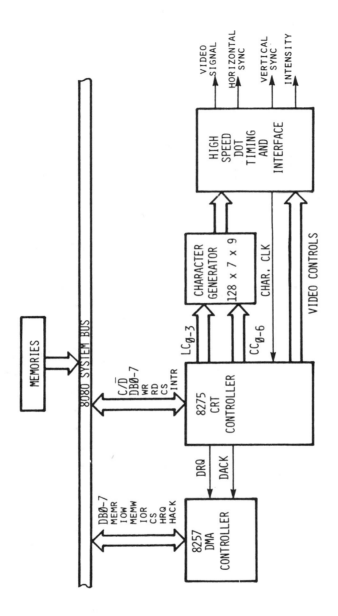

Fig. 4-74: Intel CRTC System

— LDV is "loaded video." It is the output dot into the external shift register.

— Blank is the blanking signal.

— Blink is for flashing the cursor or any other symbol on the screen.

As an example, the 8 code combinations allowed by CM0-CM1-CM2 for cursor motion-control appear in Fig. 4-76.

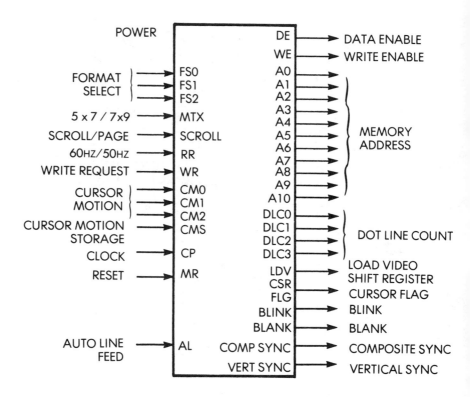

Fig. 4-75: Fairchild CRTC 9412 Chip

INTELLIGENT CRT

Now that the hardware interface of a microcomputer to our CRT system has been discussed, the software interface will be considered. For the CRT, this is one of the first opportunties to design what is considered an intelligent interface. The term *intelligent* implies that a substantial amount of processing is being done at the peripheral device itself, rather than in the Central Processing Unit. Such additions as editing, paging, and limited graphics are all desirable features to be added in an intelligent CRT controller.

CM2	CM1	CMØ	FUNCTION
L	L	L	UP
L	L	H	RETURN
L	H	L	LEFT
L	H	H	HOME
H	L	L	DOWN
H	L	H	NEW LINE
H	H	L	RIGHT
H	H	H	OUTPUT CURSOR ADDRESS (ADDRESS IS VALID WHEN DE OUTPUT IS LOW)

Fig. 4-76: 9412 CMX Codes

Devoting an entire microprocessor to performing the CRT interface function, with the aid of a CRT controller, implementation of all the functions can be done at relatively no cost. Typical terminals which are not intelligent will provide input and output facilities through the keyboard and CRT to the remote system. Here the new features can be added, specifically editing, paging, and graphics. After typing one or two paragraphs on the screen of our terminal, one may wish to edit the mistakes or change text. With the use of the *cursor controls, or light pen, or keyboard commands,* manipulation of the information on the screen can be accomplished so that text development is simplified. The microprocessor will take the commands from the input sensors, for example a light pen, and rearrange the characters in the memory so that they will be displayed in the order in which the operator wishes them to be displayed. Many advanced features of this type of editing system, such as moving blocks, searching for strings and formatting of text, are easy to add. All of these functions require fairly little program overhead in the microprocessor. However, it is reducing the program overhead in the overall system by quite a large amount, if one takes into account all of the other intelligent terminals in an entire network of terminals.

Since a CRT screen can usually hold no more than 24 lines of 80 characters per line, scrolling and paging our information in and out of the display is also a desired feature. This is not a difficult function, as with a large amount of memory a controller can usually store anywhere from four to ten pages of typewritten text. An interface could provide these functions in hardware; however, by the use of software algorithms, page-handling characteristics of our terminal are improved. Implementation of commands which will move text by any number of lines in and out of memory and onto the screen will simplify the editing or reading process.

In addition to normal text presentation, adding some form of limited graphics is simplified. The microprocessor will allow the interfaces to implement such functions as graph and display by using, perhaps, the characters *, —, and +. As an example, one can imagine the system where the beginning point and ending point of a line are specified, and the terminal automatically will graph to its best ability the line joining the two points on the screen. All these features are present in one degree or another in the new intelligent terminals being manufactured. In addition, there are some personal home computing products,such as the Commodore Business Machines PET computer, which also show the use of many of these intelligent functions. The general philosophy is: "Now that I have a microprocessor, how can I make it work to improve the interfacing function?"

THOMSON-CSF 96364 CRT CONTROLLER

In France, the appearance of the new CRT controller chip has pointed the way towards lower part count interface. The 96346 CRTC will interface with 19 other SSI and MSI circuits to provide a complete RS232C ASCII-compatible CRT terminal interface. Provisions also include direct connection to an ASCII keyboard. As such, it represents the lowest-cost terminal interface.

The basic CRT chip contains the timing and sync circuits for the television, cursor logic, display counters, and external display memory control logic, These are illustrated in Fig. 4-77. In Fig. 4-77 Concluded, the 96346 is connected to the memory, ROM character generator, serial-video 8-shift register, and UART.

Character data enters serially from the RS232C input to the UART. There the data are converted to parallel data. The parallel data are

entered into the screen memory. The small 32 by 4 control ROM determines whether the character should be displayed, or whether it is for
control i.e. line feed, carriage return, etc.

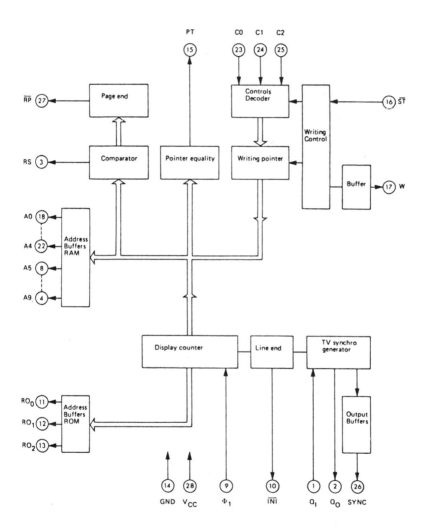

Fig. 4-77: Block Diagram

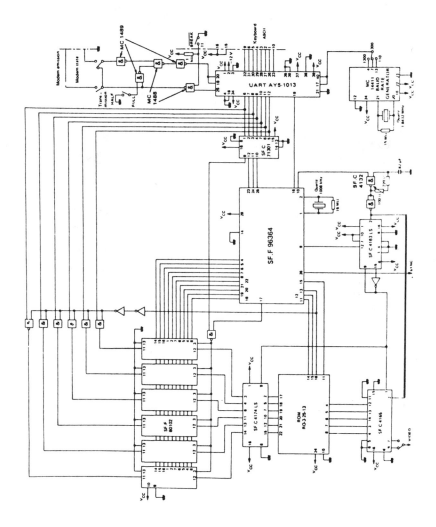

Fig. 4-77 Continued: Complete CRT Terminal

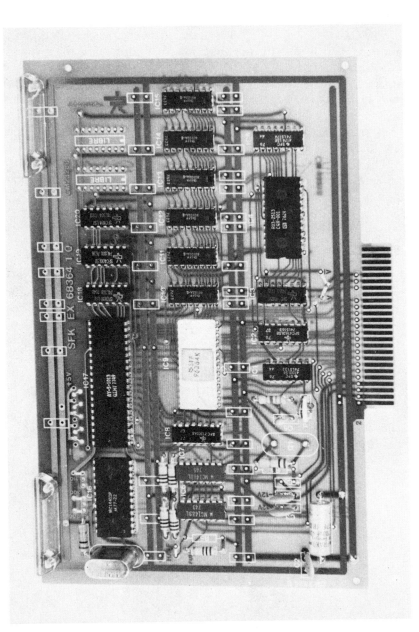

Fig. 4-77 Concluded: Thomson-CSF CRT Interface Board

The CRTC converts the ASCII data via the character ROM into the proper series of dots for the television. The format for the system is for European television of 625 lines at 50 frames per second with no interlace. Timing shown here will modify the circuit to drive a monitor in the U.S. with 625 lines at 60 frames per second. A regular television may be used, but an OEM television will operate far better. In addition, most OEM-terminal TV sections cost much less than a regular TV, because power supplies and the tuner are not implemented.

The circuit then is a complete terminal with 16 lines of 64 characters per line. The characters are displayed with a 5 by 7-dot matrix format. Lower case characters are possible by customizing the ROM.

FLOPPY DISK INTERFACING

SECTION I: *THEORY OF OPERATION*

A mini floppy disk appears in illustration 4-78. A *floppy disk* is simply a disk coded with a magnetic material, and divided into *sectors* and *tracks*, on which data is recorded. It provides a very low-cost storage medium with high-speed access and a large capacity. Two types of floppy disk exist today: the regular floppy disk and the mini floppy.

A regular floppy disk, such as the SHUGART SA800, provides the following facilities (It can be either single density or double density. We assume single density here):

— Total capacity per disk: 3.2 Megabits
— Capacity per track: 41.7 kilobits (unformatted).

Fig. 4-78: Shugart Mini-Floppy

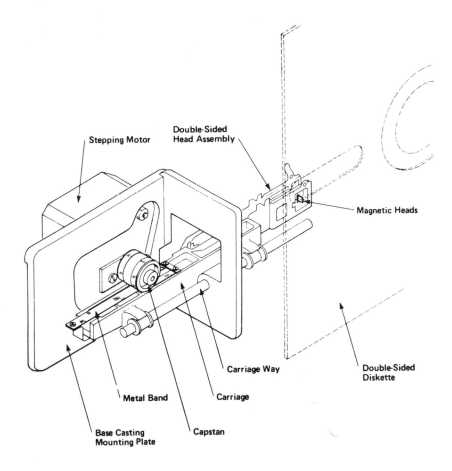

Fig. 4-78 Continued: Positioning Detail

Fig. 4-79: Floppy Diskette with Drive

Typical Floppy Specifications

Size: 8" diskette

Format: 76 tracks + index track (IBM 3740 format)
26 sectors/track

Capacity

128 bytes/sector
3.3 K bytes/track
253 K bytes/diskette

Density

tracks: 48 tpi
Bits: 3268 bpi (single density). Double density: 6536 pbi

Speed

Rotation: 360 rpm + 2%
Transfer: 250 K bps. Double density: 500 K bps

Timing

Track-to-track stepping: 10 to 18 ms (includes 8 to 15 ms head settling)
Maximum seek: 100 to 768 ms
Head engage: 40 ms
Average access: 136 to 476 ms

Reliability (Persci data)

Read error (soft):	less than 1 in 10^9 bits
Read error (hard):	less than 1 in 10^{12} bits
Positioning error:	less than 1 in 10^6 accesses
MTBF:	over 4000 hrs
MTTR:	less than 20 mn
Life:	1500 hours or 5 years

For example, the access times for a regular floppy such as the SHUGART SA800 are (single density is assumed):

— Track to track: 8 ms
— Average access time: 250 ms
— Settling time: 8 ms
— Head load time: 35 ms
— The rotational speed of the disk is 360 rpm and the recording density (inside track) is 3200 bpi for single density and 6400 bpi for double density.
— The track density is 48 tpi and the number of tracks is 77.

Mini Floppy Specifications

Size: 5.25'' mini diskettes
Format: 23 tracks
Capacity: 1/3 of standard floppy
89K Bytes/mini-diskette
Spool: 3 to 6 times slower than regular floppy

Diskette Formatting

Each diskette is usually formatted in IBM 3740 format, with 77 tracks, numbered from 00 (outermost) to 76 (innermost). One of the tracks is usually used as an index, leaving 76 tracks which can be used for data.

Each track is divided into sectors (like slices of a pie). Two techniques are used to define the sectors: hard sectoring, and soft sectoring.

In the *hard-sectoring* technique, 32 holes are punched in the diskette, defining 32 × 128-byte sectors. This results in highest data density.

In the *soft-sectoring* technique, only one hole is punched in the diskette, marking the beginning of sector zero. The number of sectors is then defined by the user. The IBM - compatible format defines 26 × 128-byte sectors. Since each sector must be clearly identified, sectors are separated by gaps, and preceded by a header containing their identification. This results in a lower data density than with hard sectoring. However, each sector is positively identified every time it is accessed, resulting in higher reliability.

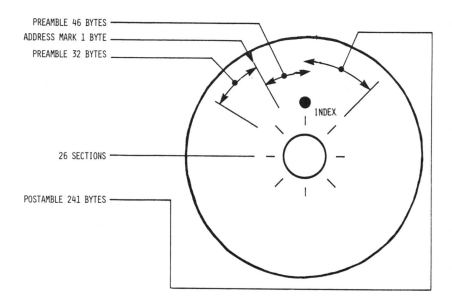

Fig. 4-80: Floppy Disk Format

Mini Floppy Characteristics

For a mini floppy, the characteristics are:

Capacity:
— Unformatted: 109.4 kilobytes per disk and 3125 bytes per track.
— Formatted: Two cases must be distinguished—soft format and hard format.

In a *hard format,* actual holes are punched on the disk, to mark the beginning of the new sector. In a *soft format,* only one hole is punched to indicate the beginning of every track, but the length of sector on the track is left up to the designer or the programmer.

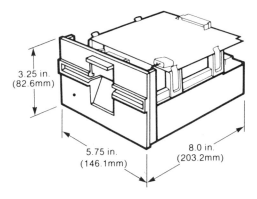

Fig. 4-81: Size of Mini Floppy

	Soft	Hard
Per disk:	80.6 Kbytes	72.03 Kbytes
Per track:	2304 bytes	2058 Kbytes
Per sector:	128 bytes	128 bytes
Sectors track:	18	16

Transfer rate: 125.0 kilobits per second
Access time:
   Track-to-track: 40 ms
   Average: 463 ms
Settling time: 10 ms
Head loading time: 75 ms
Rotational speed: 300 rpm
Density: 2581 bpi (for the inside track)
Total number of tracks: 35
Track density: 48 bpi

Basic Interface Signals for a Disk Drive

The interface signals include commands and data to the drive and status plus data from the drive to the controller. To the drive:

— step pulses to the head motor + direction
— load head
— read/write
— data + clock information
— reset error bit(s)

From the drive:

— index pulse
— sector pulses (if hard sectored)
— sense-error bit(s)
— write protect sensed (tab on diskette)
— data + clock
— track 00

The Floppy Disk Drive

The drive houses the mechanical functions and the electronics required to rotate the diskette and access data.

The diskette is a flexible ("floppy") milar disk coated with magnetic oxide and it rotates within a jacket. A long hole is cut in the jacket along a radius to provide access to the read/write head.

The same head is used for read/write and erase. The head is moved along a radius by a positioning motor, usually a step motor. Once it is positioned over the required track, the head is applied in direct contact with the surface of the diskette.

In addition, the jacket has an index hole. The index hole is punched in the diskette and marks the beginning of sector zero. It is detected by a photosense circuit in the drive.

The drive electronics perform four functions:

1. Move the head to the track
2. Load the head and either read or write
3. Generate or interpret control signals or status information (including index detection, track 0 detection)
4. Drive the spindle motor accurately.

Drive options are:

— Remote diskette eject
— Write protect

Typical Signals Between FDC and MPU

To the MPU:

— Interrupt request
— Transmission request
— 8-bit data

From the MPU:

— 8-bit data
— CLK
— RES
— R/W
— Select pulses (connected to address bus)
— Transmission acknowledge

Operation of the Floppy Drive

The principle of a read or write operation is to access the specified track and sector, and to then transfer a block of data. Three operations must therefore be performed: *head positioning, read-write control, and data transfer.*

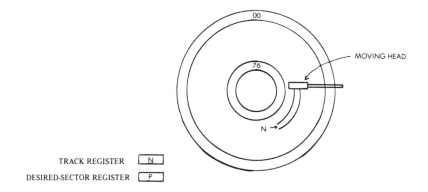

Fig. 4-82: The Formatter Accesses Sector p of Track n

1. Head positioning:
   The head is stepped with an incremental stepping motor (typically 3 to 10 ms per step). This implies the necessity of a programmable step delay in a general purpose formatter controller. Naturally, a line must specify the direction of the movement. A head settling delay of 8 to 15 ms must also be allowed for vibrations to die out. The head can then be loaded on the disk (10 ms settle). It is then necessary to verify proper positioning by reading the track number in the first ID

field on the diskette. It is compared to the track register. In addition, the ID field CRC is checked to verify the integrity of the information. The access may then proceed.

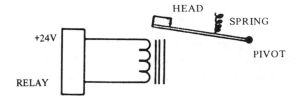

Fig. 4-83: Disk Drive: Head Load Assembly

2. R/W controls:
   Assuming that the device and the data are ready, the write gate is activated (for a write). The operation is inhibited by a write-protected diskette.
3. Data transfer:
   The transfer must occur at the specified speed. A typical clock is 1 MHz for single density (0.5 MHz for a mini floppy), 2 MHz for double density (1 MHz for a mini floppy).

A disk can be protected against accidental erasure simply by using a write-protect tab on the disk cardboard envelope. This is illustrated in Fig. 4-84.

The Disk Drive

The disk drive itself includes the following facilities:

1. Read/write control, plus control electronics (2 PC boards)
2. The drive mechanism
3. The read/write head positioning mechanism
4. The read/write head.

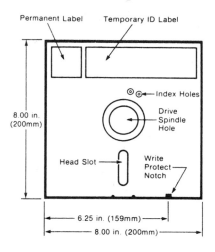

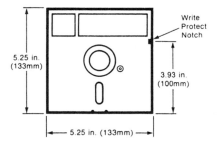

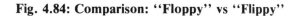

Fig. 4.84: Comparison: "Floppy" vs "Flippy"

The read-write facilities, mentioned in 1 above, include:

— Index and sector detection
— R/W head position actuator drivers
— R/W load actuator drivers
— Write drivers
— Read amplifier, plus transition detectors
— Write-protect detector
— Drive-select circuits
— Drive-motor control circuits.

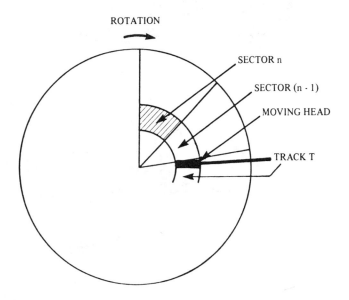

Fig. 4-85: Head Positioned Over Correct Track

Accessing a Track

The head moves over the disk surface from track to track. It is moved along a radius of the disk by a stepping motor. In order to access a track, the following sequence will occur.

1. The drive select must be activated. Usually a disk controller may control more than 1 unit and will enable the drive select of the mechanism which is selected for access.
2. The direction select will be set, resulting in a latching of the direction of the movement of the head. The head will move either towards the center of the disk or towards its periphery.
3. The write gate goes inactive. During head movement, no writing should occur.
4. The step line will be pulsed until the desired track is reached. Each pulse will result in a step of the head over to the next track, in the direction which has been latched.

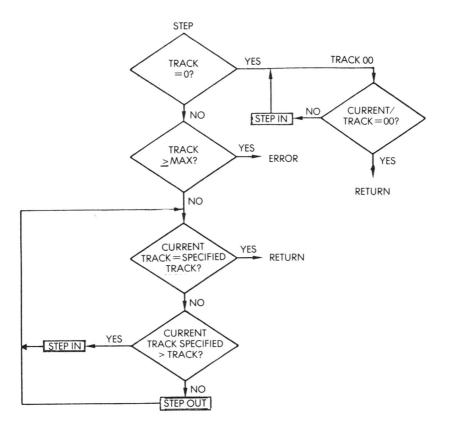

Fig. 4-86: Moving to a Specified Track

Reading and Writing

Reading is simply accomplished by:

— activate the drive select
— write gate inactive.

Writing is accomplished by:

— activate the drive select
— activate the write gate
— pulse data in on the write-data line.

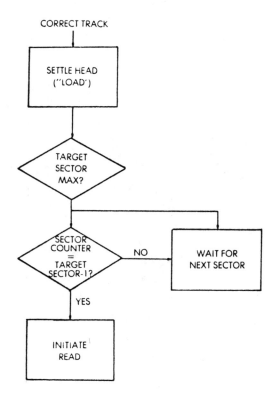

Fig. 4-87: Access Sector

A PRACTICAL READ SEQUENCE

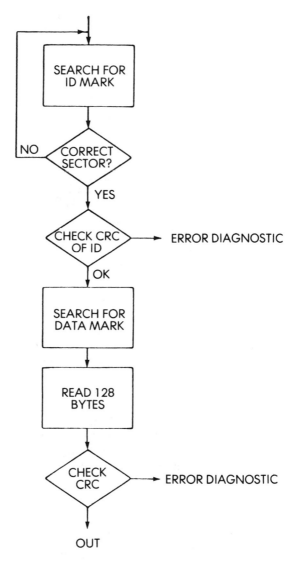

Fig. 4-88: A Practical Read Sequence

SIGNALS OF THE DISK DRIVE: AN EXAMPLE

The signals required by, or generated by, the SA 400 mini-floppy disk drive appear in illustration 4-89. Six essential signals are used to communicate with the disk drive:

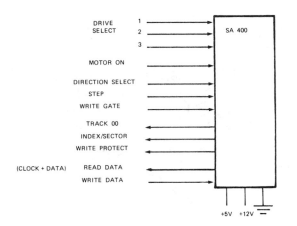

Fig. 4-89: SA 400 Floppy-Disk Drive

MOTOR ON

The signal will turn the motor on, or off. When turning the motor on, 1 second should be allowed after activation. Conversely, the disk drive should be deactivated after 2 seconds (or 10 revolutions), whenever no further commands are issued. This will extend the life of the drive.

DIRECTION SELECT

This input selects the direction in which the read/write head will be moved. The actual motion will be accomplished by pulsing the step line.

STEP

This moves the head by 1 track position towards the center or away from it. The movement occurs on the trailing edge of the pulse.

180

WRITE GATE

Write is enabled when this line is active. Read is specified when the line is inactive.

TRACK 00

The signal indicates that the head has reached the outside of the disk, i.e., its outermost track or track 0. The head will move no further even if additional step commands are issued.

INDEX/SECTOR

A signal is issued whenever a hole is sensed in the disk. Two types of holes may be used, index hole, and sector holes. Every disk will provide an *index hole* marking the beginning of the first sector on the disk.

A hard-formatted disk, which will be described below, has an additional number of holes marking the beginning of every sector. When soft sector is used, one pulse is issued per revolution at the beginning of a track. This is every 200 ms. When using a hard-sectored disk, 11 or 17 pulses are issued per revolution.

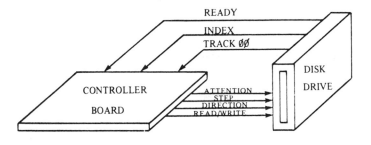

Fig. 4-90: Basic Floppy Drive Signals

The Disk STATUS Signals

The READY line is true when the diskette has been correctly inserted and is up to speed.

The INDEX line provides a pulse marking the beginning of sector 0. A hole is actually punched in the diskette and detected by a photosensitive circuit.

WRITE PROTECT (optional) tells the system that the user has cut out a notch in the diskette holder to prevent any accidental writing.

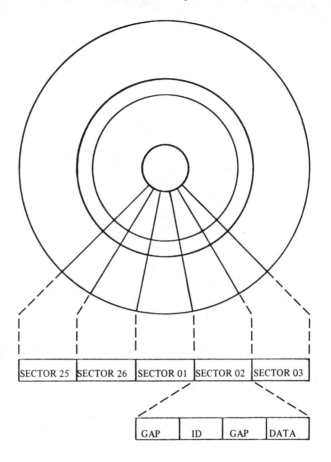

Fig. 4-91: Sector Layout

Other Disk Options

Some usual options are:

— WRITE PROTECT: a special tab can be removed from the diskette cover. An optical sensor in the drive will detect it at a notched position. This protects a diskette from accidental writing (not available on IBM equipment).

PHOTO-DARLINGTON XTOR

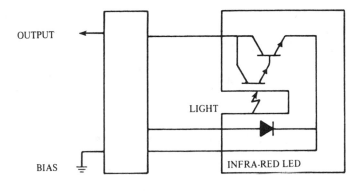

OUTPUT

LIGHT

BIAS

INFRA-RED LED

Fig. 4-92: Write Protect Module

— REMOTE EJECT: useful to insure that the diskette is out of the drive before turning the computer off, as the line transients could destroy the contents.
— STOP MOTOR: reduced motor wear, but increases the initial time needed to access the first sector.
— HIGH-SPEED SEEK: moves head directly to a given track, such as 44. It requires a seek-difference register on the drive.
— PHASE-LOCKED SEPARATOR (or PLO): usually part of the controller, rather than the drive. It removes the jitter due to peak shift from clock-data signals.

INFORMATION RECORDING

All information is recorded on the tracks of a disk in binary format. Usually, an NRZ technique is used (NRZ is "Non-Return to Zero"): each bit position is magnetized in one direction ("0"), or the other ("1"). There is no intermediate state (a true "zero"); this is called NRZ. In practice, FM encoding (Frequency Modulation) is used, as it is self-clocking: each data bit appears exactly in the middle of a "frame," i.e., between two successive clock pulses. In other words, every "frame" includes a clock bit (always "1"), and a data bit ("0" or "1"). Each "frame" is 4 microseconds and corresponds to a 250K bps transfer rate (the rotational speed of a diskette is a standard 360 rpm ± 2%, derived from the AC 60 Hz clock).

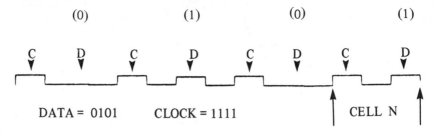

Fig. 4-93: Information Recording

Other recording methods are used to increase bit density. The basic principle is to eliminate as many "superfluous" clock or data bits as possible. Typically, MFM = Modified Frequency Modulation, or M2FM (Modified MFM) are used for double-density diskettes.

MFM has been used on high-performance disk drives such as the IBM 3330 and 3340.

The rules of MFM are:

1. The data bit still appears in the middle of a bit frame.
2. The clock bit is written at the beginning of the frame only if two conditions are met:

— No data bit will appear in the current frame
— There was no data bit in the previous frame.

In other words, a clock bit is inserted only if two consecutive frames would contain "00".

When reading data from the disk, FM must be converted to digital, with absolute accuracy. In addition, a separate detection is required for clock and data bits. Special problems may occur with some bit patterns. This is known as the "bit-shifting" problem, and a PLO (phase-locked oscillator) is normally used for precise bit detection.

All data on the disk is structured in bytes. Bytes (groups of 8 bits) must also be synchronized. This function is performed by starting every block of information with a special marker. When the diskette is first used, it must be initialized or "formatted" with these markers. Byte counts are initialized when these ID or data marks are read.

Finally, a serial-to-parallel conversion must be performed to assemble 8 bits into a byte. This is done by the disk controller.

The operations required by a "write" are naturally the reverse of those described above for a "read."

184

The Phase-Locked Oscillator (PLO)

A phase-locked loop (PLL) is used to synchronize read/write clocks. The data output of the PLL contains CLOCK + DATA from the disk in NRZ format. The clock output of the PLL generates the required clock edge in the middle of a bit cell.

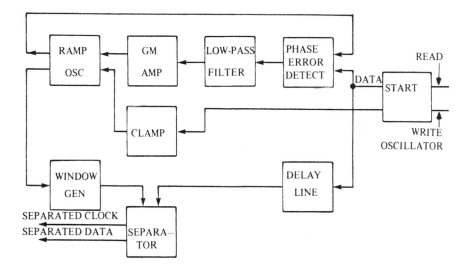

Fig. 4-94: A Discrete PLO

Basic FDC Program

The basic program follows a four-step sequence:

— Initialize FDC
— Seek track 0. Check for errors.
— Write a sector on a track. Check for errors.
— Read the same sector. Check for errors.

Head Load Philosophies

Two basic philosophies are used:

1. Load continuously. This results in continuous wear.
2. Load for minimum time. This results in frequent loading and unloading.

185

Applying Power

At power-on, the initialization program steps the head into track 00 (usually the index track, which must be accessed first). The sector counter automatically contains the sector number within less than one revolution after power is applied.

Updating a Sector

Once a diskette has been formatted, only the ID gap, data field, and first byte, or data gap, are altered.

Hard Sectoring vs. Soft Sectoring

A hard-sectored diskette has 32 sector holes which define 32 × 128-byte sectors. By eliminating the need for sector headers, it can store more information.

A soft-sectored diskette is IBM compatible, with 26 × 128-byte sectors. Sectors must be identified by a header. Less data can be stored, but reliability and flexibility are increased.

Double Density vs. Dual Sided vs. Dual Drive

Two techniques are used to increase the amount of information which can be stored on a floppy: double density and dual heads. Double density doubles the number of bits per track by using a "packed" recording technique, such as modified MFM (M2FM). It requires tight tolerances for reliable operation and is much less speed-tolerant than regular FM encoding.

Dual heads are required for using both sides of a floppy. The heads are positioned 180° apart. This increases the mechanical complexity and cost of the drive, as well as increases the wear.

Both techniques are currently used to double the number of bytes per diskette.

A dual drive uses two diskettes, but only one spindle motor and one positioner. It is much more economical than two separate drives, and somewhat slower.

186

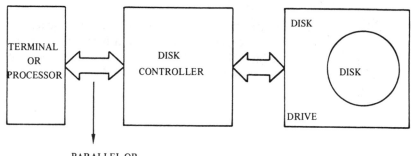

PARALLEL OR

SERIAL INTERFACE

Fig. 4-95: Disk Controller Interfaces Drive to Processor

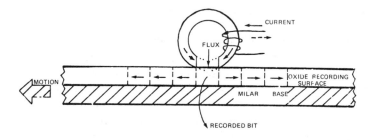

Fig. 4-96: Recording a Bit on a Disk

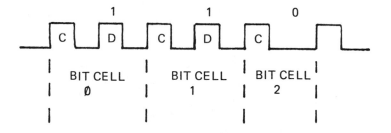

Fig. 4-97: Representing Clock and Data

187

Disk Formatting

Both clock and data information are encoded into the same signal. Clock pulses are issued for every bit. A "0" data is indicated by no further pulse during the bit cell time. This is illustrated in Fig. 4-97: A "1" is indicated by a data pulse occurring in the middle of the bit cell interval.

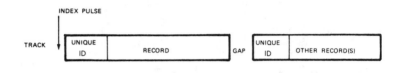

Fig. 4-98: Record Identifier

Soft sectoring refers to the fact that the division of the disk or track into sectors is performed by *software.* This is opposed to hard sectoring, where the beginning of each sector is physically delineated by a hole punched in the disk. In soft sectoring, each track is started by a physical *index pulse,* corresponding to the detection of the index hole on the disk. Every record is preceded by a *unique identifier.* See Fig. 4-98. Successive records are separated by *gaps.* Gaps are necessary in order to upgrade information without erasing the following or the preceding record. Because of minor speed variations in the disk-drive motor, whenever a record has all or part of its contents rewritten, the end of the record might extend beyond the previous record end.

	DATA	CLOCK
INDEX ADDRESS MARK	FC	D7
ID ADDRESS MARK	FE	C7
DATA ADDRESS MARK	FB	C7
DELETED DATA AM	F8	C7

Fig. 4-99: Address Marks

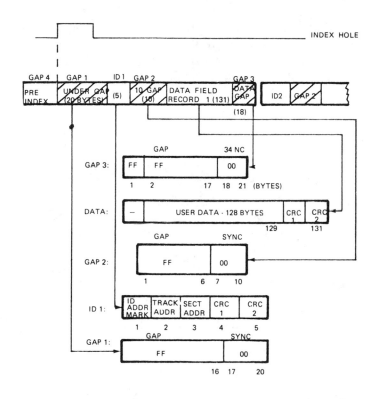

Fig. 4-100: IBM Floppy Disk Format

For this reason, a blank gap must be provided between the end of one record and the beginning of the next one. In fact, a gap must be provided between any two zones which might be updated separately. Most often, the IBM disk-track format is used, sometimes with minor variations. This format is illustrated in Fig. 4-100. Four kinds of gaps are used:

Gap 4 is used only once on the track. It is free-index gap. It appears at the end of the track just before the index hole position.

Gap 1 is called the index gap and is used at the beginning of every track. It contains 20 bytes: the first 16 bytes contain the hexadecimal pattern "FF" followed by 4 bytes containing "00". These four bytes of 0's are the classic way of providing the synchronization for the data separator. The length of gap 1 may never vary in length. The index gap is followed by the identification of the first record.

189

ID 1 is the identification field of the first record. It uses 5 bytes: the ID address mark, the track address, the sector address, and two CRC check-sum bytes to verify the integrity of the field. The track address and the sector address provide a verification that the right track and sector have indeed been accessed.

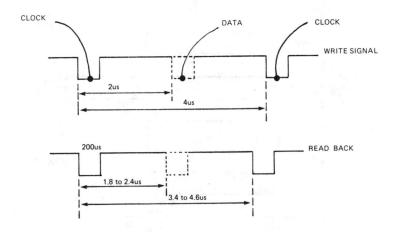

Fig. 4-101: Timing

Gap 2 is called the ID gap and separates each successive identification field from its data field. It uses 10 bytes. The first 6 bytes contain the hexadecimal pattern "FF". They are followed by the four usual synchronization bytes containing "00". The length of gap 2 may vary after file updating.

The first *record,* or data field, follows. It uses 131 bytes (see Fig. 4-100). The first byte contains a data or deleted address mark and is followed by the actual 128 bytes of user data. It is terminated by the two usual CRC check-sum bytes.

Finally, *gap 3* terminates the first record. It is called the data gap and uses 21 bytes. The first 17 bytes are set to the pattern "FF", and the four last bytes contain "00", for the sync. Every successive record on the disk, or sector, will start with ID, gap 2, and so on.

Hard-sectoring

When using hard sectoring, a special diskette and drive are used. A hole is punched at the beginning of every sector on the disk. Each sector is then started by a physical sector pulse. In the case of the mini floppy disk, two configurations are used: 16 sectors of 128 bytes or 10 sectors of 256 bytes per track. The track is started by the index pulse. This is illustrated in Fig. 4-102.

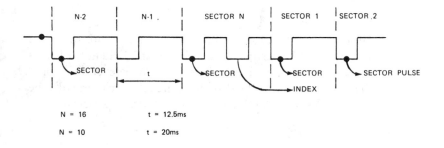

N = 16   t = 12.5ms

N = 10   t = 20ms

Fig. 4-102: Hard-Sectored Disk Timing

Error Detection and Correction

Three types of errors are distinguished:

Write Error

This corresponds to the case in which the data being written on the disk is not written correctly. The way to verify whether data has been correctly written is to use a "write-check" procedure, where the data is read again during the next revolution of the disk. Normally, the user will simply write again data which has not been correctly written on the disk, and attempt to do so repeatedly (up to 10 times). If this effort fails continuously, the sector or the track must be considered as damaged and not usable.

Read Error

Two types of read errors must be distinguished:

1. Soft: This corresponds to the case in which the error has been transient and is corrected by simple rereading (up to 10 times) or by moving the head back and forth once. Typically, the head is moved

191

one more step in its previous direction, then moved back. Usually this corrects most reading errors. If this procedure fails, we have a hard error.

2. Hard: Whenever usual correction procedures fail to read data from the disk, it must be deemed unrecoverable. This is a fatal error. Data is lost.

SEEK ERROR

This corresponds to the case in which the head does not reach the correct track. This can be verified by reading the ID field at the beginning of the track. It contains the track address. Whenever an error is detected, the track counter of the disk drive must be recalibrated. The head is moved back to track 00 and a new seek order is issued.

DETECTING ERRORS

Universally, the error detection for any data written on a disk is accomplished by using a *checksum* method. Cyclic-redundance-check (CRC) is used for this purpose. Each field is terminated with two CRC bytes. The data bits are divided by a generator polynomial G(X) such as $G(X) = X^{16} + X^{12} + X^3 + 1$. The remainder of this division is called the CRC. It is written in the two bytes that follow the data. When reading back data from the diskette, everything is read, including data in the CRC bytes. If the remainder of the division by the G(X) polynomial is not 0, an error has been detected.

Single-chip CRCs exist, such as the Fairchild 9401 and the Motorola 8501, that will detect such failures in a single chip. One-chip floppy disk controllers (FDC) also accomplish the CRC generation and checking, within the single chip.

Cyclic Redundancy Check

CRC is the favorite method for verifying the integrity of memory areas with a minimal waste of bits. Parity will detect a single-bit error within a word. Whenever parity is not available, or would be too costly to provide, CRC is used to detect errors in a block of words. In particular, CRC is almost always used in the case of floppy disks, and tape cassettes. In addition, it is often used to verify the integrity of a ROM. The principle of a CRC technique is the following: the eight bits of the word are treated as coefficients of a polynomial of degree 7.

The bit pattern $B_7\ B_6\ B_5\ B_4\ B_3\ B_2\ B_1\ B_0$ is interpreted as $B_7\ X^7 + B_6$

$X^6 + B_5 X^5 + B_4 X^4 + B_3 X^3 + B_2 X^2 + B_1 X^1 + B_0 X^0$.

X is called here a dummy variable.

Fig. 4-103: Picture of Double-Sided Floppy Drive

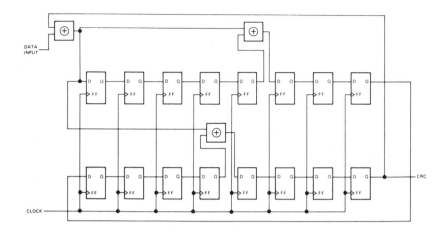

Fig. 4-104: CRC Check Hardware Detail

For example, the binary word: "10000011" will represent:

$$B(X) = 1\,X^7 + 0\,X^6 + 0\,X^5 + 0\,X^4 + 0\,X^3 + 0\,X^2 + 1\,X^1 + 1\,X^0 = X^7 + X^1 + X^0$$

A generator polynomial $G(X)$ will be used. The polynomial $B(X)$ corresponding to the binary word is divided by this generator $G(X)$. The result is the quotient $Q(X)$ and a remainder $R(X)$.

$$B(X) = G(X)\,Q(R) + R(X)$$

The value of CRC-redundancy-checking is to append to a bit string an extra byte (or bytes), equal to $R(X)$, so that the total string will be exactly divisible by the generator polynomial. The above equation can be rewritten: $B(X) - R(X) = Q(X) \times G(X)$. The string formed by B and the remainder R is exactly divisible by $G(X)$. The extra bits appended to the string B are called the CRC bits (or bytes). When receiving a string B, for the first time, the CRC generator will compute the remainder R, which will be appended to the string. When the string is retrieved another time, the complete sequence of bits, including the CRC bits, will be read. They should then be exactly divisible by the generator polynomial $G(X)$. If they are not, an error has been detected. If they are divisible, no error has occurred, or else a non-detectable error has occurred.

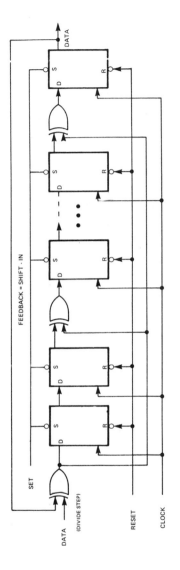

Fig. 4-105: CRC-Generation Hardware Detail

As usual, the CRC algorithm can be implemented either in hardware or in software. One-chip CRC generators are available. An example of hardware for the CRC, *if not done in software,* is shown in Fig. 4-105. Software for the CRC, using the Signetics 2650, appears in Fig. 4-106. The hardware division is accomplished there by the shift register with feedback. The CRC generator corresponding to the illustration is $G(X) = X^{16} + X^{15} + X^2 + 1$. The exclusive-OR feedback accomplishes the division during the successive shifts through the flip-flops of the register.

SUMMARY OF DISK OPERATION

The complete principles of floppy-disk operation have now been presented: The signals necessary to drive the disk; its operation; the formatting of data; as well as the error-checking mechanisms that must be implemented. We will now describe the implementation of a disk-drive controller to be interfaced to a microprocessor system.

SECTION II: *SHUGARD SA 4400 CONTROLLER*

This controller board is implemented with the SMS/Signetics 300 bipolar controller chip. It is designed to control 1, 2, or 3 SA 400 mini floppies. It will be briefly described here, in order to show the capabilities of a full mini floppy controller. Then other compact designs will be presented, using the new FDC chips.

This controller is compatible with the IBM 3740 format, but uses a modified gap structure (the pre-index gap, gap 4, is shorter). It provides a 128-byte buffer for the data. Eight control functions are supplied:

— INIT: resets the controller in the disk
— SEEK: steps ahead to the specified track
— READ: reads a sector (128 bytes)
— READ ID: reads the next sector identification
— WRITE: writes a sector of data (128 bytes) with data AM

The previous three commands will read or write data between the host processor and the disk buffer, or between the buffer and the disk.

— WRITE - DDL: accomplishes the same as the WRITE command but with deleted data AM (address mark)
— FORMAT: writes address marks, gaps, data on the entire track in 3740 format

```
* CYCLIC REDUNDANCY CHECK SUBROUTINE (SIGNETICS 2650)
*
* THIS ROUTINE GENERATES A 16-BIT CHECK CHARACTER FOR
*    THE DATA CHARACTER IN RØ; VARIOUS POLYNOMIALS
*    CAN BE ACCOMODATED BY CHANGING THE CONSTANTS
*    SPECIFIED AT PROGRAM LOCATIONS CKØ AND CK1 AS PRR
*    THE TABLE BELOW
*
* DEFINITION OF SYMBOLS
*
RØ      EQU     Ø          PROCESSOR REGISTERS
R1      EQU     1
R2      EQU     2
WC      EQU     H'Ø8'      PSL:  1=WITH,Ø=WITHOUT CARRY
C       EQU     H'Ø1'            CARRY/BORROW
UN      EQU     3          BRANCH CONDITION  UNCONDITIONAL
EQ      EQU     Ø                            EQUAL
*
* TABLE OF POLYNOMIALS
*
CRCFØ   EQU     H'4Ø'      CRC16 FORWARD
CRCF1   EQU     H'Ø2'
CHCRØ   EQU     H'2Ø'      CRC16 REVERSE
CRCR1   EQU     H'Ø1'
CCIFØ   EQU     H'Ø8'      CCITT FORWARD
CCIF1   EQU     H'1Ø'
CCIRØ   EQU     H'Ø4'      CCITT REVERSE
CCIR1   EQU     H'Ø8'
*
* BEGINNING OF SUBROUTINE
*
        ORG     Ø
*                          INITIALIZATION
CRCGEN  PPSL    WC         OPERATIONS WITH CARRY
        LODI,R2 8          INITIALIZE BIT COUNTER
        LODA,R1 CRC+1      GET OLD REMAINDER LSB
        EORA,RØ CRC        EX-OR OLD REMAINDER MSB WITH DATA
*
TEST    CPSL    C          CLEAR CARRY
        TMI,RØ  H'8Ø'      TEST MS-BIT OF RØ
        BCFR,EQ SHIFT      BRANCH IF NOT A '1'
        PPSL    C          PRESET CARRY
CKØ     EORI,RØ CRCFØ      APPLY 'FEEDBACK'
CK1     EORI,R1 CRCF1
*
SHIFT   RRL,R1             SHIFT THE DOUBLE CHARACTER
        RRL,RØ
        BDRR,R2 TEST       CHECK IF DONE
        STRA,RØ CRC        SAVE THE NEW REMAINDER
        STRA,R1 CRC+1
        RETC,UN
*
* RAM AREA
*
        ORG     H'5ØØ'
CRC     RES     2          REMAINDER MSB IN CRC
        END     CRCGEN
```

Fig. 4-106: 2650 CRC Program

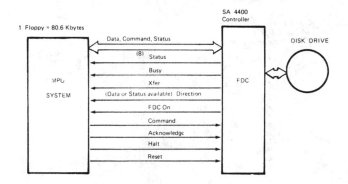

Fig. 4-107: Interface Signals

— STATUS: gets status for the drive

The signals used by the 4400 interface to communicate with the host microprocessor system appear in illustration 4-107. The basic sequence of events implemented by the controller is simply:

1. Seek track.
2. Find sector.
3. Shift and transfer the desired number of sectors.
4. Check the CRC.

Few commands are necessary for the controller's operation and most controllers provide six to ten commands only.

The SHUGART SA 4400 FDC Board

It accommodates 1 to 3 drives with overlapped head positioning, and provides eight commands.
It uses bipolar logic. The eight commands are:

INIT	system reset
SEEK	position head on track
READ	read disk sector
READID	read next ID
WRITE	write disk sector

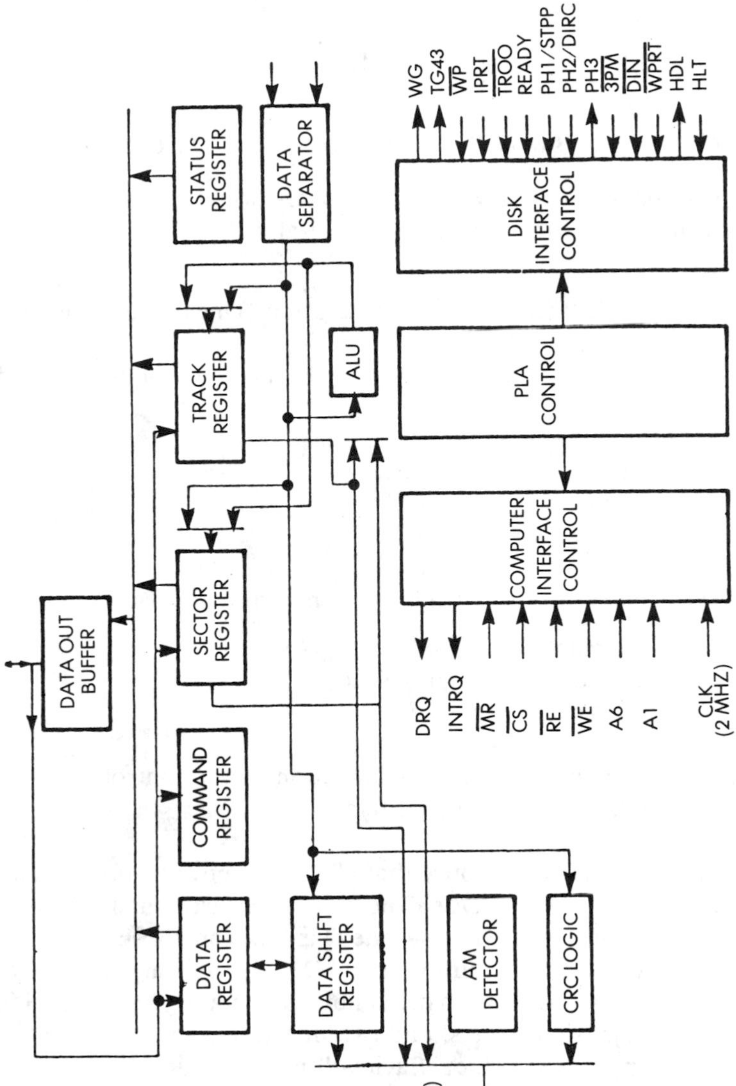

Fig. 4-108: FDC Chip: Western Digital

WRDEL	write sector of deleted data
FORMAT	write address marks, gaps, and data on entire track
STATUS	return status for addressed drive

SECTION III: *WD 1771 FLOPPY DISK CONTROLLER CHIP*

This one-chip floppy disk controller-formatter will interface to most *drive manufacturers* and is naturally IBM-3740 compatible. It provides:

— automatic track seek with verification. This feature must be provided on all FDCs.
— soft-sector format compatibility. This feature should be standard on an FDC.
— read or write with:
  — single or multiple records
  — automatic sector search
  — entire-track read or write.

Again, these features should be standard in an FDC.

— programmable controls:
  — track-to-track stepping time
  — head-settling time
  — head-engage time
  — three-phase or step-plus-direction motor control
  — DMA or program transfers.

The alert reader will notice that all of the above features are essentially standard for all FDCs. The differences are usually the level of the number of disk drives that one chip will control simultaneously.

The internal architecture of the FD1771B appears in illustration 4-108. It will be described in detail now. It contains *five* essential functional circuits, six registers, and two interfaces: a processor interface and a floppy disk interface. Each will now be examined.

The Four Functional Circuits

The *four essential* circuits, which appear on the illustration, are:

— The CRC logic which generates the check character
— the ALU (Arithmetic-Logical-Unit), which was used for the ob-

vious arithmetic functions, in particular to compare characters for incrementing or decrementing contents.
— the disk-interface control
— the computer-interface control.

Both interfaces will be described below.

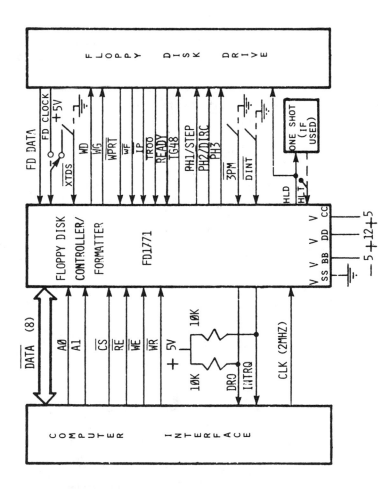

Fig. 4-109: Floppy Disk Interface Using FD1771

The Six Internal Registers

From left to right in illustration 4-108 one can distinguish:

1. The *data shift register* assembles 8 bits from the floppy disk data, or serializes 8 bits received from the microprocessor data bus into the floppy disk data line.

2. The *data register* is a simple holding register for a byte during read and write operations. It communicates with the data-out buffer, and may receive data directly from the microprocessor data bus.

3. The *command-register* is used to hold the 8-bit command being executed. This register is loaded by the programmer and specifies the mode of operation of the disk.

4. The *sector register* holds the address of the desired sector position.

5. The *track register* holds the track number of the current head position. It is incremented towards the inside (up to track 76 on the regular-size disk), and decremented otherwise.

6. The *status register* simply holds the status information of the controller.

Processor Interface

The processor interface and the floppy disk interface are illustrated in Fig. 4-109. The FDC communicates with the processor via 8 bi-directional data lines labelled DAL (Data-Access-Lines). An input is

(COMMAND WORD)		PERIOD (MS)	RATE (STEPS/S)
BIT 1	BIT 0		
0	0	6	166
0	1	6	166
1	0	8	125
1	1	10	100

Fig. 4-110: Command Word Bits

specified when CS and RE (read-enable) are active. The internal destination is specified by A1-A0 according to the table below.

The data-request-output (DRO) is used for the DMA. The interrupt -request (INTRT) is activated by various conditions.

A1	A0	RE	WE
0	0	STATUS REG.	COMMAND REG.
0	1	TRACK REG.	TRACK REG.
1	0	SECTOR REG.	SECTOR REG.
1	1	DATA REG.	DATA REG.

Fig. 4-111: Register Addressing

Floppy Disk Interface

The signals appear on the right of illustration 4-109. They provide head-positioning controls, write controls, and data transfers. The clock is a 2MHz square-wave clock, internally divided by 4, yielding 500KHz. It provides three programmable stepping rates, controlled by bit 0 and bit 1 of the command word according to the table in Fig. 4-110.

The head-settling time is additional and involves 10 milliseconds.

Disk Operation

A *read operation* on the disk is performed in five steps:

1. Load the track register.
2. Give the seek command.
3. Wait for verification.
4. Transfer data to the microprocessor under interrupt control.
5. Check for interrupt after the correct number of transfers.

Conversely, a *write operation* is performed in seven steps:

1. Load the track register.
2. Give the seek command.
3. Wait for verification.
4. Give the write command.
5. Load the first data after the data request is received.

6. Load the remaining data.

7. Check BUSY and CRC-error flag.

Summary

The FD1771D illustrates how it is possible to integrate most of the functions required for the control of a regular floppy disk into a single chip. It provides essentially all the facilities needed to control and format the disk.

SECTION IV: *WD 1781 FLOPPY DISK CONTROLLER CHIP*

This one-chip FDC is the double-density version of the 1771, and is second-sourced by National Semiconductor. It provides both single-and-double-density format. In the double-density mode, the encoding/decoding must be provided by the user's data-recovery circuits. In this way, the 1781 accommodates both MFM and M2FM.

FD 1781 Command Summary:

1. Restore
2. Seek
3. Step
4. Step in
5. Step out
6. Read Command
7. Write Command
8. Read Address
9. Read Track
10. Write Track
11. Force Interrupt

The Hardware Errors

Typical disk errors can be classified as follows:

1. READ
   1.1 Data not accessible
   It may not be possible to retrieve data, due to a bad recording, noise, surface defects, or dirt. This is detected by a checksum or CRC character(s). The formatter/controller must compute its own checksum or CRC during a READ operation. It then reads the character(s) recorded on the disk, and compares it to the computed value. A discrepancy indicates an error.

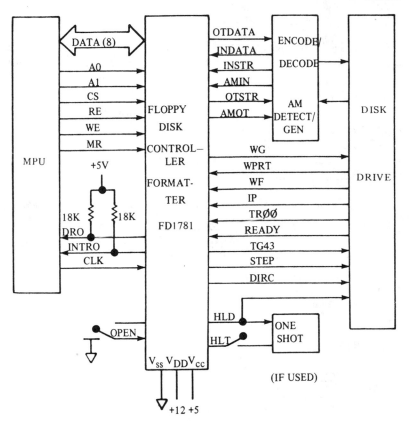

Fig. 4-112: WD 1781 System Block Diagram

1.2 Wrong sector or wrong track

This is a positioning error of the head. It may be due to a wrong step-pulse frequency or noise on the counter. In the case of a track error, the head will be repositioned to track 00 (equipped with a special sensor), then moved again.

Naturally, detecting this error implies that the sector and track ID's are stored at the beginning of every sector. This information is always read and checked by the controller, prior to using the sector.

2. WRITE

The essential error is denoted by a FILE UNSAFE flag. It occurs when an attempt to write is made, on a write-protected diskette, with a drive door open, during a drive-electronics malfunction.

PERSCI CONTROLLER BOARD

The PerSci Controller uses the WD 1771 and an 8080 to perform the intelligent floppy disk control functions. The board contains the data separator PLO, the 1771 interface chip, a 1K static RAM buffer, 4K ROM memory, 8080 CPU, and miscellaneous circuitry.

Physically, the system consists of one small printed circuit board. In order to adapt the controller to the S100 bus, a "piggy back" arrangement can be made by placing this controller on a standard S100 bus board. The data are recorded in the standard IBM format and up to 4 drives may be accommodated.

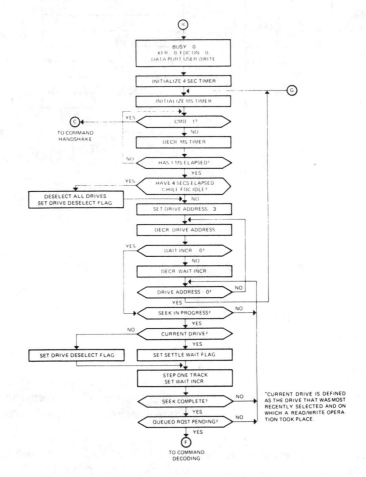

Fig. 4-113: PerSci Software Flowchart

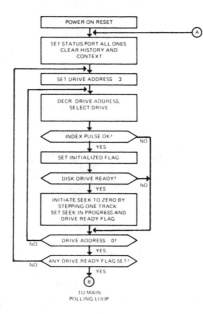

Fig. 4-114: Software Flowchart Continued

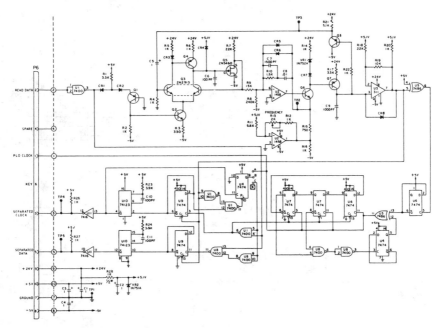

Fig. 4-115: Data Separator PLO

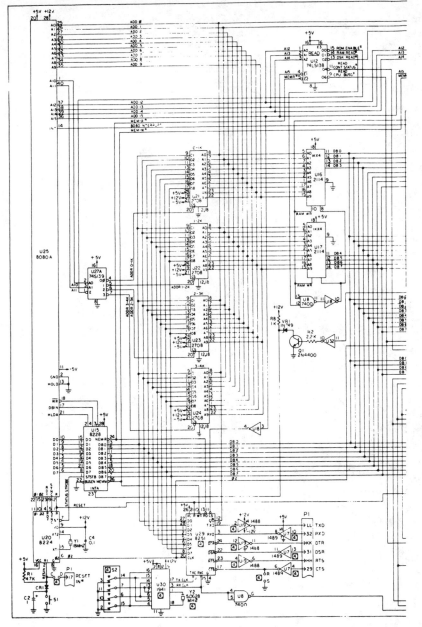

Fig. 4-116: PROMs, CPU

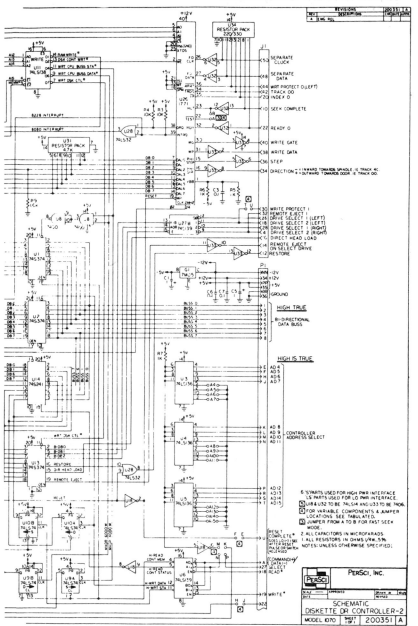

Fig. 4-117: Controller, Buffers

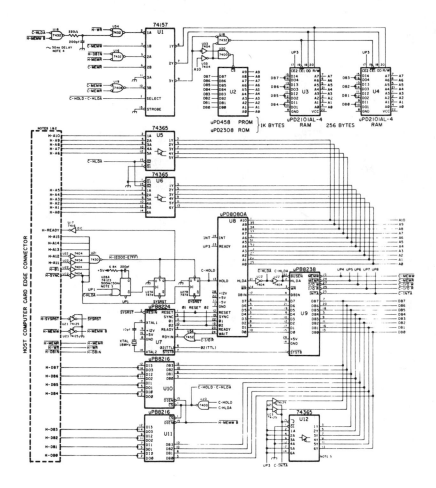

Fig. 4-118: NEC 8080 Disk Controller

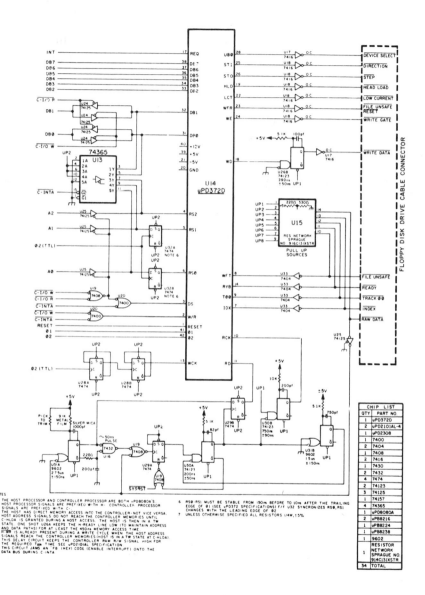

Fig. 4-119: NEC 8080 Disk Controller

SECTION V: NEC FLOPPY DISK CONTROLLER

The NEC FDC is called the UPD372D. It is compatible with the IBM 3740 as well as the SHUGART mini floppy. It provides the usual facilities, such as CRC generation, programmable step pulse, track-stepping rate, sector size, data-transfer rate. In addition, it controls up to 4 disk drives, but with read/write limited to one drive, with simultaneous track seek on the others.

Other disk drives are: CAL COMP 140, CDC BR 803, GSI 050 and 110, INNOVEX 210, ORBIS 74, PERSCI 75, PERTEC FD400, POTTER DD4740, SYCOR 145.

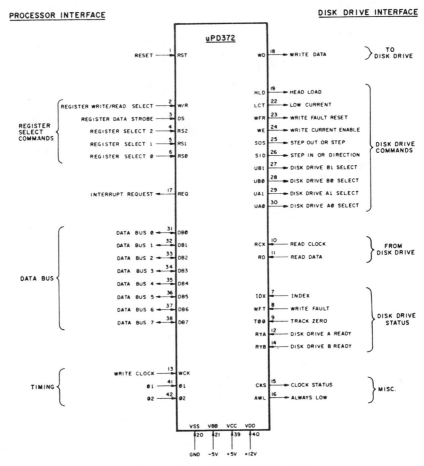

Fig. 4-120: NEC UPD372 FDC

SECTION VI: MOTOROLA 6843 FDC

This FDC is designed for direct interface to the 6800. It provides 10 macrocommands:

1. Seek track 0 (STZ)
2. Seek (SEK)
3. Single-sector-write (SSW)
4. SSW with selected address mark (SWD)
5. Single-sector read (SSR)
6. Read CRC (RCR)
7. Multiple-sector-write (MSW)
8. Multiple-sector-read (MSR)
9. Free-format-write (FFW)
10. Free-format-read (FFR)

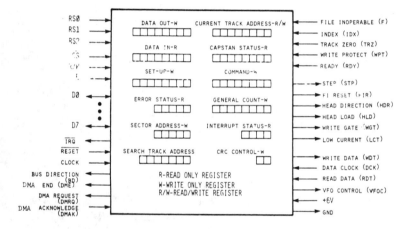

Fig. 4-121: Register Format

The 6843 assembly-language program driver for the 6800 processor appears in Fig. 4-122. The system requires the use of a DMA controller. The routines will read and write on the floppy disk through the 6843 by utilizing the previous registers. Note the declarations of where these registers are and their addresses in the I/O space. Additional error routines and file handling must be added to this program to form a complete software floppy-disk-drive package.

ROUTINE TO WRITE TO, AND READ FROM
ONE SECTOR OF THE FLOPPY DISK
USING THE MMC 6843 FDC
ORG $0000

FDC REGISTERS

DORREC	EQU	$DFF0	W/O WRITE TO FLOPPY
DIRREQ	EQU	$DFF0	R/O READ FROM FLOPPY
CTAREQ	EQU	$DFF1	R/W CURRENT TRACK
CMRREQ	EQU	$DFF2	W/O MACRO COMND & IRQ MASK STRB MASK; WRT CLK CNTRL; DMA ENABLE
ISRREG	EQU	$DFF2	R/O IRQ REG. B3 = I FROM STRB, B2 = STAT SEN. REQ., B1 = STC., B0 = MAC COM END.
SURREG	EQU	$DFF3	W/O B0-3 = ST TM; B4-7 = SEK TM
STAREG	EQU	$DFF3	R/O STRA 0-DTR; 1-DEL DATA DETECT: 2-READY; 3-TRZ; 4-WPT; 5-TRK NOT EQUAL; 6-INDEX; 7-BUSY;
SARREG	EQU	$DFF4	W/O START SEC ADD DB, 0-4
STBREG	EQU	$DFF4	R/O STAT B; 0-DTE; 1-CRC; 2-DTA MK NO DET; 3-NO SEC ADD; 4-SEEK ERROR; 5-FILE INOP; 6-WRITE ERROR; 7-HARD ERROR;
GCRREG	EQU	$DFF5	W/O GEN CNT REG; TRK FOR SEK; ALSO SECT CNT FOR MULTI SECT R/W
CCREG	EQU	$DFF6	W/O SET CRC CONTROL DB0 = CRC SHIFT DBI = CRC ENBLE THIS IS FOR FREE FORMAT R/W

Fig. 4-122: 6843 Assembly-Language Driver

LTAREG	EQU	$DFF7	W/O TRK NO FOR TRK ADD SRCH
			TO COMPARE TO ID FLD ON DSK
FDSELI	EQU	$DFF8	FL DSK SELECT ADD

ADDITIONAL EQUATE STATEMENTS USED

XBPRNT	EQU	$F728	X-BUG LOC TO START PRINTING
BEGADD	EQU	$FFOR	X-BUG BEGIN PRINT VECTOR
ENADD	EQU	$FFOC	X-BUG END PRINT VECTOR
ERQVEC	EQU	$FFF3	X-BUG IRQ VECTOR

IMAGE STORAGE FOR FDC RESISTERS

DORIMG	RMB	1	W/FLOP GETS DATA TO WRT HR
DIRIMG	RMB	1	R/FROM FLOPPY
CMRIMG	RMB	1	MACRO COMM REG IMAGE
ISRIMG	RMB	1	INTERRUPT IMG
SURIMG	RMB	1	SETUP REG IMAGE
SARIMG	RMB	1	SECTO ADD IMG
STBIMG	RMB	1	STATUS REG B IMG
GCRIGM	RMB	1	GEN COUNT REG IMAGE
CCRIMG	RMB	1	CRC CONTROL REG IMAGE
SELIMG	RMB	1	DISK SELECT IMAGE

STATUS FLAG BUFFERS

RSTKPR	RMB	2	STR RCV DATA BUFF PTR
STKPTR	RMB	2	STR STK PTR IF DO PSH OR PULL
INXSTR	RMB	2	STORE THE INDEX REG HERE
SSRFLG	RMB	1	FLAG IF WE FIND STATUS SENSE
TRKNUM	RMB	1	TRACK NUMBER FOR LTAR & GCR
SECNUM	RMB	1	SECTOR NUMBER FOR SAR

Fig. 4-122 Continued: 6843 Driver

```
TOTSEC  RMB   1       TOTAL SEC TO BE R/W
STRPRT  RMB   2       START ADD TO PRINT A BUFFER
ENDPRT  RMB   2       END ADD OF BUFFER FOR PRINT


              ORG $0000
         DATA BUFFER FOR READ DATA


REDBUF  RMB   80          SAVE DEC 128 LOC FOR 1 SEC
                   OF READ STORAGE BUFFER


              ORG              $100
         PROGRAM AND FLOPPY DISK INITIALIZE


           SEI            SET THE INTERRUPT MASK
FLZERO  CLR    X
           DEX
           BNE    FLZERO  LOOP UNTIL DONE

CLRMEM LDX    #$00FF    CLR RD DATA STORAGE BUFF
           STX    RSTKPR  USE AS RECV DATA PTR
MEZERO CLR    X          CLEAR THE RECV BUFFER
           DEX
           CPX    #$0080  ARE WE TO ADDRESS 80
           BNE    MEZERO  IF = 0 GO ON
NXTVEC NDX    #$0080  SETUP BEG PRINTOUT VECTOR
           STX    STRPRT  FOR EXBUG PRINT
           LDX    #$00FF  SETUP END PRINTOUT VECTOR
           STX    ENDPRT  FOR EXBUG PRINT
           LDAA  #$80    LOAD DATA FOR DOPREG
           STAA  DORIMG  SO WE HAVE DATA TO WORK
                          WITH

           LDAA  #$03    SELECT FD #0
           STAA  FDSELI
           STAA  SELIMG
           LDAA  #$30    SET FOR TRACK 30
           STAA  TRKNUM  WE WILL START WITH THIS
                          TRACK
           LDAA  #$64    SETUP SEEK & SET TIMES
```

Fig. 4-122 Continued: 6843 Driver

```
STAA   SURREG   SEEK = 6MS = IM6
STAA   SURIMG   SETL = 16MS = 4X4
LDAA   #$5
STAA   TOTSEC   TOTAL SEC IN MULSEC R/W
STAA   SECNUM   ADD OF FIRST SECT TO BE
                READ
LDS    #$0FFF   SET STACK POINTER FOR LOTS
                OF STORAGE AREA IF NEEDED

LDAA   STAREG
BITA   #$04     IS DRIVE READY?
BNE    STZAGN   GO TO STZ IF WE ARE READY
SWI             READY NOT THERE RETURN
```

ORG $0400
SUBROUTINE TO REMOVE DATA TRANSFER
ERRORS OF PREVIOUS OPERATION FROM REGISTERS

```
CLRERR   INC    DIRREG   REMOVE DIR FROM STRA
         TST    STBREG   REMOVE DTE FROM STRB
         TST    ISPREG   CLEAR ISR
         TST    STBREG
         BEQ    DONEOO
         SWI             LEAVE IS STRB WILL NOT CLR
DONEDO   RTS             RETURN NO ERRORS FOUND
         END
```

Fig. 4-122 Concluded: 6843 Driver

It is naturally equipped with two programmable delays for seek time and for settling time. The chip signals are illustrated in 4-65. This FDC requires three DMA channels. It uses an average of three percent MPU time. Assuming 256 KPS transfer rate, the maximum MPU load is 12.5%.

SECTION VII: *ROCKWELL FLOPPY DISK CONTROLLER*

The basic interconnect of this FDC in a Rockwell system appears in Fig. 4-123. It uses three DMA channels (see Fig. 4-124), where channel 7 refreshes channel 1. The FDC I/O instructions appear in Fig. 4-125. Typical floppy disk routines for the Rockwell PPS-8 are shown on Fig. 4-126.

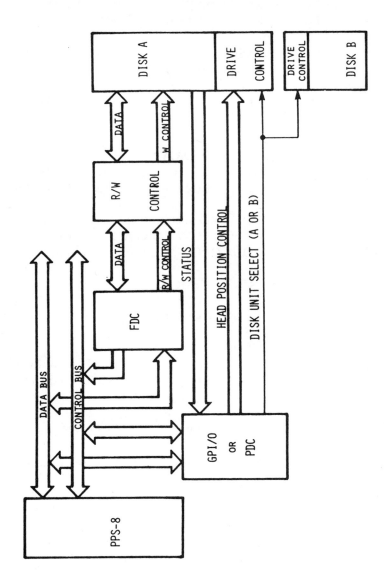

Fig. 4-123: PPS FDC

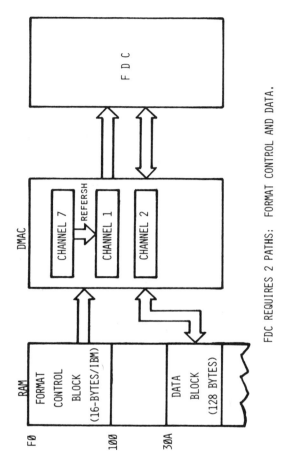

Fig. 4-124: PPS-8 FDC DMAC Block Diagram

0	1	S	S	0	0	0	0	NOOP
0	1	S	S	0	0	0	1	START
0	1	S	S	0	0	1	0	LOAD
0	1	S	S	0	0	1	1	CLEAR
0	1	S	S	1	0	1	0	READ DATA
0	1	S	S	1	1	0	0	READ STATUS
0	1	S	S	1	1	0	1	READ STATUS
0	1	S	S	0	1	0	0	NOOP
0	1	S	S	1	1	1	0	NOOP
0	1	S	S	1	0	0	-	UNDEFINED READ
0	0	0	0	1	0	0	0	READ INTERRUPT STATUS

Fig. 4-125: Commands

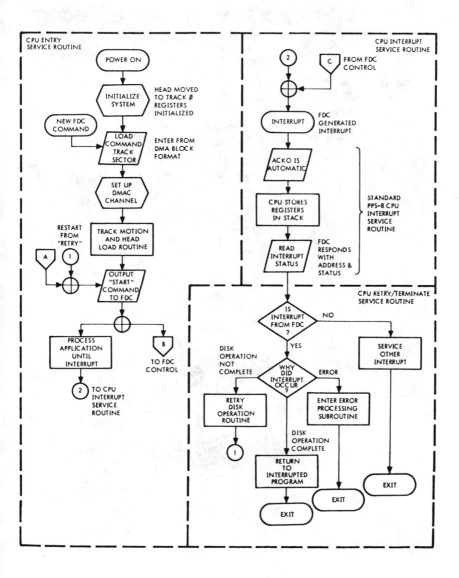

Fig. 4-126: Software Flowchart

Fig. 4-127: Double-Sided Head Detail (Shugart)

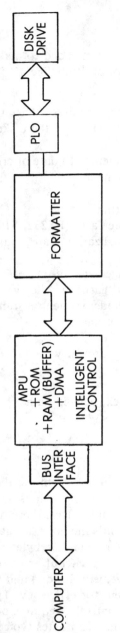

Fig. 4-128: An Intelligent Floppy Controller

Intelligent FDC

An "intelligent FDC" is intended to make the disk transparent to the user. The facilities of an "intelligent" floppy disk controller can include:

— symbolic file naming (requires a Disk Operating System)
— automatic space allocation on the diskette (requires a File Management System)
— file header management with date of creation, date last modified
— index track management
— file editing
— input-output buffering
— various optional interfaces (RS232, S100, 8-bit parallel)
— diskette format initialization (gaps, marks, ID fields, data fields)
— sector interleave
— file directory management
— space reclamation ("garbage collection")
— various access methods: sequential, random, direct, stream
— renaming/deletion of names
— file copying
— error detection and auto-retry on soft errors
— diagnostics
— code specification
   — write ASCII, Hex, deleted data
   — read ASCII, Hex
— display buffer
— enter into buffer.

In practice, an intelligent FDC achieves these functions by software and includes an on-board MPU, such as an 8080 or a 6800.

In order to provide a data buffer, thereby minimizing the interference with the main system's memory, a dual-port memory is usually available. A typical buffer size is 256 bytes per disk drive. In a typical configuration there will be a 1K buffer for up to 4 drives.

The FMS (File Management System) and the DOS (Disk Operating System) are ROM-resident for efficiency. Typical size is 4K bytes. A complete "intelligent" controller requires only a *minimal* I/O driver for the host CPU (less than 256 bytes typical).

The index track of the disk *(track 00)* is used to contain file index references (100 typical). It is essentially used as a table of contents. Its first section is a volume ID. The other sectors contain file index references. Typical information contained in an *index reference* includes:

— name of the file and version number
— drive number
— type of file
— start address and length
— position of file EOF mark
— date when created (= age of file)
— date of last update.

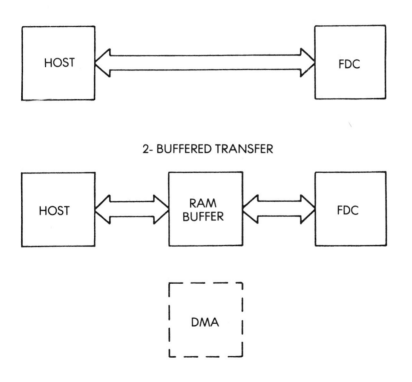

Fig. 4-129: Communicating with an Intelligent FDC

Storage Management

Files are usually granted contiguous sectors so that they can be read or written at full disk speed. However, when a file is deleted, the de-allocation process will leave gaps on the disk. Unused gaps waste storage by fragmenting it. Periodically, or whenever a storage request cannot be granted, it becomes necessary to compact the gaps. The process is known as "garbage collection," or compaction.

The File Management System

An FMS is in charge of making the actual storage management invisible to the user. A typical FMS will provide the following functions, or commands:

— allocate n-sector file to - name -
— delete file
— open/close file
— copy
— R/W in various formats
— change name to - name -
— read/modify descriptor
— diagnostic test.

Intelligent Controller Interface

An intelligent controller requires a minimal interface to the host computer and none to the disk drive. The hardware interface to the host interface is typically RS232, S100, or 8-bit parallel (through memory, for the processor indepedence). (See Chapter 6 for description of RS232 and S100.)

File Access Methods

1. Sequential, or stream
   The complete file is stored/accessed continuously. This implies the use of contiguous sectors. The method is simple and efficient if all the data need be stored/accessed.
2. Variable length, or punctuated
   A file is handled as a sequence of variable-length records. Used when portions of a file will be modified.
3. Random access or relative
   Any byte (or number of bytes) may be read/written, even across sector boundaries.

4. Direct access

Any sector on any track may be directly specified, bypassing the File Management System.

Ref on Diskette Formatting:

IBM Diskette for Standard Data Interchange, CA 21-9182-0, File No. GENL 03180.

THE MUSIC SYNTHESIZER

One of the most important considerations in this interface is the design of the music synthesizer hardware. A brief description of the synthesizer follows. This music synthesizer consists of two channels: right and left. Each channel covers a slightly different pitch range corresponding roughly to those covered by the right and left hands on a piano. All the pitches attainable on a piano, except for the 7 lowest keys, are attainable on this synthesizer.

The hardware will be examined carefully in subsections as follows: the DCO, the harmonic generator, the voicing circuit, the articulator, and the tempo generator. With the exception of the differences in the ranges, the two channels are identical. Only one channel is described here.

The DCO

The heart of any music synthesizer is the oscillator that determines the frequency or pitch of the note heard.

In this music synthesizer, the controlling entity is a microprocessor-based microcomputer, whose inputs and outputs are strictly digital in nature. A digital approach to generating the needed frequencies is used in this example. Using a timing program, the microcomputer could generate these frequencies itself; however, this would severely limit the number of other operations the micro could perform and would not utilize its potential power as a computing machine. Consequently, an external digital *Data Controlled Oscillator,* or DCO, was developed. As the name connotes, the frequency of its output is determined by the digital data supplied to its input.

The DCO is basically a cascade of three 4-bit presetable binary up counters. It operates as follows: a 12-bit number is supplied to the DCO from the microprocessor. The binary counter is preset to this 12-bit number, and then counts up at the rate of the OSC input. When

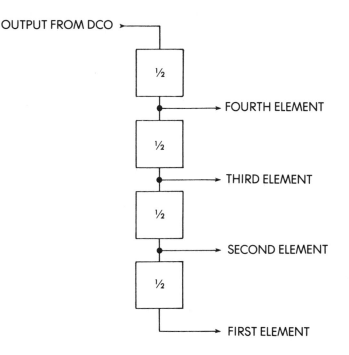

OUTPUT FROM DCO

½ — FOURTH ELEMENT

½ — THIRD ELEMENT

½ — SECOND ELEMENT

½ — FIRST ELEMENT

Fig. 4-130: Divider Chain

the counter reaches its maximum count, a carry pulse is produced. This pulse is used as the output and also to preset the counter back to the 12-bit number. Thus, the larger this 12-bit number is, the sooner the counter reaches its maximum count and the more often an output pulse is produced; hence, the higher the output frequency. if N represents the two's complement of the 12-bit number, then the output frequency is:

$$f_{out} = OSC/N$$

Note that N can only have integer values. This limits the accuracy with which a certain frequency can be approximated. An analysis was performed to determine if 12 bits provided enough accuracy for the music synthesis. For a 5 MHz oscillator, it was found that for a 4-octave range, the maximum possible error is 2.25 cent, where a cent is 1/100 of the logarithmic distance between any 2 adjacent notes (half step).

This is quite acceptable. Consequently, this 12-bit DCO was used for generating the basic frequencies of this synthesizer.

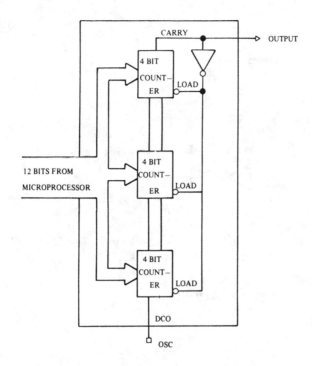

Fig. 4-131: The DCO

The Harmonic Generator

If the output of the DCO were played through a speaker, it would have a very unappealing quality or timbre. This is due to its poor harmonic structure. Harmonics of a note are the frequencies that are integer multiples of the fundamental. What gives a particular musical instrument its characteristic sound is the harmonic structure. To vary the harmonic content, a set of square waves whose period is always half that of the previous member, starting at the fundamental frequency, is used.

To produce these functions, the output of the DCO was successivly divided by 2 using D flip-flops.

Using the first four members of this basis, any wave form can be approximated, though its error may be large. After examining the wave forms of a harpsichord and piano, it was decided that the easiest approximations for these would be that of a sawtooth wave and a distorted square wave.

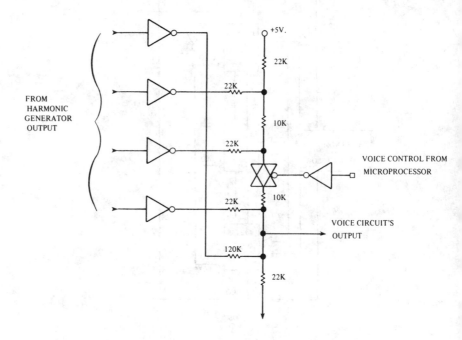

Fig. 4-132: Voicing

The outputs of the harmonic generator were not suitable for mixing directly to produce these wave forms, since the output levels varied anywhere from 2.2 volts to 3.8 volts. Thus, these outputs were buffered using CMOS since the CMOS logic family's output levels differ from that of the supply voltages by only several millivolts. The unusual element that appears in the resistor ladder is a member of the CMOS logic family, called a bilateral analogue switch. When its input control voltage is high, the analogue switch appears to be a 200-ohm resistor for all voltages bracketed by the supply voltages. When the input control voltage is low, the analogue switch appears to be a 200 Meg-ohm resistor. This analogue switch is used to select one of the two voices.

Articulator

Another factor which colors the characteristic of a particular musical instrument is the rate of decay of the sound. For example, when a key of a harpsichord is depressed, a string is plucked and its loudness quickly dies out. Whereas with a piano, if the key is held down, the loudness of the note dies out very slowly. But by releasing the key, the note is quenched. The equivalent of these functions is accomplished in this synthesizer by the articulation circuit, or articulator.

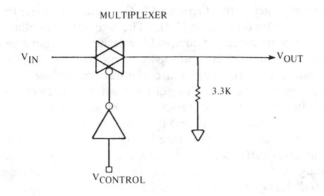

Fig. 4-133: Articulator Multiplier Detail

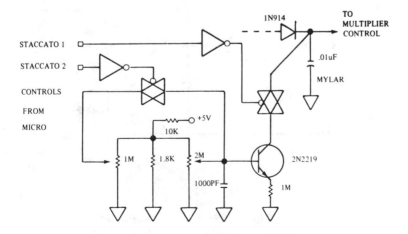

Fig. 4-134: Articulator—Complete

231

The articulator is basically an analog multiplier; one of its inputs is the output of the voicing circuit, and the other input is the decay envelope. The multiplying function is actually performed by controlling a CMOS bilateral analog switch in an analog manner. In order to accommodate different decay envelopes, additional discharge paths are provided for the capacitor. The insertion of these paths are controlled by the microprocessor. The rates of discharge are determined by potentiometer settings and can be adjusted by the user to suit his taste.

Tempo Generator

In the tempo generator, there is a CMOS oscillator whose frequency is adjustable from 0.25 Hz to 15 Hz. The rate of this oscillator determines the rate at which the composition is stepped from one note to the next. The oscillator is connected to a mono-stable multivibrator, or one-shot, which produces a pulse of duration 3 milliseconds on the negative edge of the clock. This pulse is then buffered and connected to a test line of the microprocessor. This pulse signals the microprocessor that the next note is about to be played. This pulse is also delayed for 1.5 milliseconds before it is applied to the articulator circuit. This gives sufficient time for the microprocessor to update the data being sent to the music synthesizer. Hence, the correct pitch, voice, and decay rate are communicated to the synthesizer for the playing of each note.

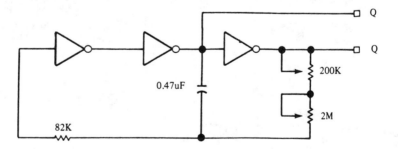

Fig. 4-135: Tempo Oscillator

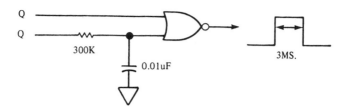

Fig. 4-136: Tempo One-Shot

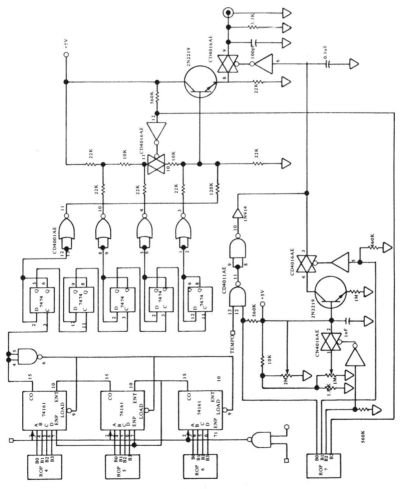

Fig. 4-137: Left-Hand Circuit

The Software

For this music synthesizer, the microprocessor plays the roles of controller, sequencer and data processor. A brief functional description follows: one word of a list of music code in memory, as identified by a pointer, is retrieved. This word may be the code for a rest, for one

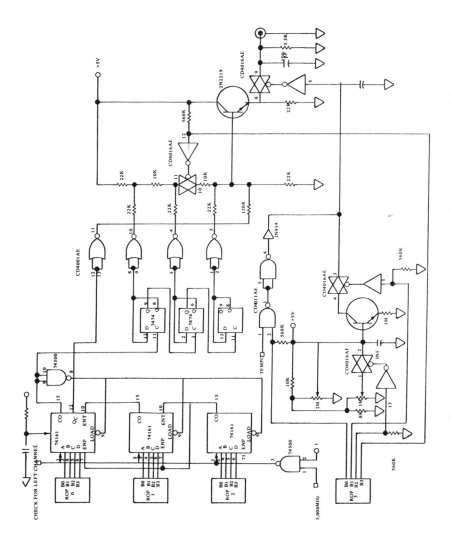

Fig. 4-138: Right-Hand Circuit

of 12 possible notes, for a range change, or for a voice and articulation change. If the code corresponds to a range change or a voice and articulation change, then the next word in the list is retrieved and placed in the range or voice control memory cell. If the code corresponds to a note, it is decoded into the particular note, and is scaled according to the previously assigned range. Upon reaching a note or rest, the information needed for playing the next note in one channel is complete. The same procedure is repeated for the other channel. The microprocessor then waits for a signal from the music synthesizer

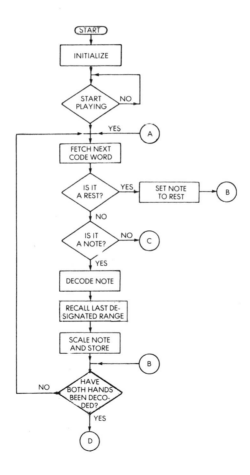

Fig. 4-139: Main Loop Flowchart

hardware (the tempo-generator pulse) to tell it when to send this decoded information. This procedure is continued throughout the playing of a composition.

The steps enumerated above are carried out by the microprocessor through an execution of a program and a set of sub-programs or sub-routines. The following is a list of these: Main Program, Fetch sub-routine, Rest subroutine, Note Decoder subroutine, Note Scaler sub-routine, Sync suroutine, Send subroutine and Refresh subroutine.

The Main Program performs the function of decoding words and coordinating the subroutines with the decoded words. It also determines which hand is being decoded presently, and, consequently, which set of memory cells is active. Because of its extensive use of sub-routines, the behavior of the Main Program can best be understood by examining the structure of the subroutines.

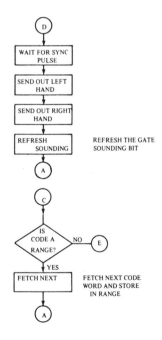

Fig. 4-140: Sounding and Fetch Flowchart

When the retrieved code word specifies a rest, the Main Program places the number 4095_{10} into the DCO memory cells. This would be interpreted by the DCO as asking for infinite frequency. However, because of the idiosyncrasies of the DCO, this number will cause the DCO to stop oscillating. The Main Program then calls the Rest subroutine, which clears the Gate Sounding bit of the voice control memory cell.

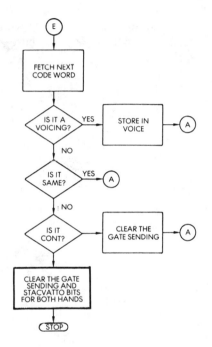

Fig. 4-141: Fetch, Voice, Sound Flowchart: Detail

Before discussing the Note Decoder and Note Scaler subroutines, let us review the DCO. Recall that the output frequency of the DCO is given by:

$$f_{out} = 5.000 \text{ MHz}/N$$

Therefore, all that need be done to generate any note is to store a table of values, N, which correspond to the frequencies of all possible notes. Although this method is certainly straightforward, it isn't very viable, for the list of all possible notes is rather long. Another property of music from which we can now benefit is the fact that notes occur in octaves; e.g., the frequency of middle C (261.81 Hz) is twice of that C-below-middle-C (130.81 Hz). Consequently, if the number N is known for one octave of notes, then all other octaves of a note can be derived by multiplying or dividing N by 2, which is a trivial task in a binary machine. This is precisely what the Note Decoder and Note Scaler subroutines do. When the Main Program retrieves a code word specifying a note, those subroutines are called, and the resulting number, N, is placed in the DCO memory cells.

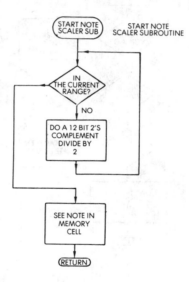

Fig. 4-142: Note Scaler Subroutine Flowchart

After both channels, or hands, have been deciphered, the Main Program calls the Sync subroutine, which waits for the tempo-generator pulse. This pulse signals the software that it's time to send the next group of information to the music synthesizer hardware. The Main Program then calls the Send subroutine, which sends the contents of

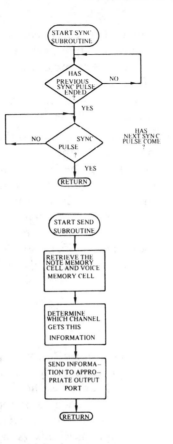

Fig. 4-143: Sync and Send Subroutine Flowchart

the DCO memory cells and the voice control memory cell to the correct channel. This is done for each channel. Lastly, the main program calls the Refresh subroutine, which resets the Gate Sounding bit in the voice control memory cell, and then returns to the beginning of the program for the next cycle.

Coding Music for the Music Synthesizer

The software for this music synthesizer was designed so that the entry and debugging of a musical composition would be relatively simple and straightforward. The coded music is entered one hand at a time.

For each note, the desired range, voice, and articulation changes, when applicable, are specified first, followed by the note, rest or system-command code. If there are no changes in the range or voice or articulation, then this field is deleted.

The two pages following those contain the coded music for the First Two Part Inventions by J.S. Bach.

The system commands are treated in the same way as notes, for they can only result in small changes in the previous note played. The commands are to continue playing the same note, play the same note again, and stop playing for the composition is finished. The command for continue playing the same note means that the note should remain audible, but should not be "struck" again. This is accomplished by clearing the Gate Sounding bit in the voice control memory cell. The command to play the same note again means that nothing at all should be changed; the note should be exactly like the previous note.

DYNAMIC RAM REFRESH

Dynamic MOS RAMs store bits of information as charges on MOS capacitors. One capacitor is required for each bit. A read operation discharges the capacitor and compares the voltage to a reference voltage. A subsequent rewrite is needed to preserve the contents of the RAM. Unfortunately, leakage within the MOS circuit will discharge such capacitors within a few milliseconds. As a result, the charge must be restored, generally every 2 milliseconds. This is called *refreshing* the RAM. It implies the need to refresh *all locations* within the RAM within 2 ms.

This can be contrasted to the operation of a static RAM. A static RAM stores a bit in a flip-flop. It requires no clock and will conserve information as long as power is applied (no refresh). However, a dynamic RAM cell can be implemented with a single MOS transistor, resulting in a higher density. Typically, a dynamic RAM is 4 times as dense as a static RAM, resulting in a significantly lower cost. Dynamic RAMs are also characterized by a lower power consumption. Their disadvantage is that they require a refresh controller, which is often complex. Dynamic RAMs are usually used for larger memories (say over 8K or 16K), while static RAMs tend to be used in smaller systems.

In order to reduce the number of refresh cycles required for a RAM memory array, a typical 4K RAM is structured in 64 rows by 64 col-

Inventio 1   J. S. Bach

Coded music for Right Hand

```
9:00,FF 09 BD 11 2D 0B D1 1D 09 D1 4F 49 F4 3F F4
9:10,B4 68 96 84 BF 4D 24 F4 2F 44 F4 16 42 14 42
9:20,1D 13 9D 21 D1 BD 1D 4B 1D 98 8B 93 69 64 48
9:30,6F 4D 0B F4 D1 9F 4F 46 36 43 36 48 14 69 9D
9:40,21 D1 38 ED 24 D1 3F 93 44 F4 00 00 00 84 96
9:50,34 3F 40 00 00 00 63 D2 89 68 00 00 00 24 98
9:60,69 8B 9F 43 00 00 00 D2 1D 1D BA D2 1D 00 F4
9:70,AF 43 F4 D2 1F 42 F4 D1 6F 43 4F 4D D2 1D 45
9:80,F4 6F 48 F4 9F 43 F4 F4 F4 F4 56 35 4F F4 D1
9:90,39 D2 1D 1B 93 39 D2 65 36 12 4F D2 21 21 B9
9:A0,F4 36 6D 26 42 14 26 4F 4F 4F 4F 4F 4F D1 22
9:B0,24 62 41 2F 4F 4F 4F 4F 4F 4F 44 21 41 4F 1B
9:C0,14 2F 4F 4F 4F 4F 4F 4F 4F 4D 1B 2D 1D 4F D2
9:D0,D2 1F 4F 4F 4F 4F 4D 19 63 96 D2 21 41 D1 D2
9:E0,1D 19 3D 21 62 62 41 24 96 84 BD 2D F4 1F 4D
9:F0,1D 99 76 42 64 76 89 1D 0B D1 92 89 36 3F CC
```

Fig. 4-144: Music for Right Hand

Coded Music for Left Hand

```
8.00,FF 00 00 00 00 0D 19 BD 21 2D 1B D2 1D 19 D2 4F
8.10,4D 14 00 06 00 0D 24 68 96 84 9F 43 F4 9F 43 F4
8.20,D3 1F F4 24 F4 6F 48 F4 9F 41 F4 3F 44 F4 6F 48
8.30,F4 9F 4B 4F 4F 4D 1B D2 13 41 3D 1B D2 4F 4D 18
8.40,F4 9F F4 F4 D2 1F 43 F4 4F 41 F4 D1 8F 4F 49 BF
8.50,4D 0B 13 0D 14 68 96 84 BF 4D 24 F4 3F 44 F4 6D
8.60,1B D2 32 41 3D 1B D2 6F 4B F4 9F 4B F4 4D 34 21
8.70,D2 BD F4 4F 2F 41 F4 64 4D 2B F4 D3 16 42 14 26
8.80,4F 42 B9 9F 41 F4 27 B9 26 47 64 21 D2 BD 32 14
8.90,21 31 D2 93 9D 31 D2 69 86 58 69 8F 41 F4 4F 4F
8.A0,4D F4 D3 1F 64 36 58 8B 8B 9D 31 D2 BD F4 BF 4D
8.B0,26 D3 AD D2 D2 21 F4 6F 4D 16 F4 00 00 32 1F D2
8.C0,B9 8F 4F 4F 4F BF 4F 4F 4F 4F 4F 4F 4F D3 01 B8
8.D0,96 4F 4F 4F 4F 4F 4F 4F 74 43 93 69 83 46 39 4F
8.E0,4F 4F 4F 4F 4F 44 67 96 F4 6F 47 F4 6F 9F F4 2F
8.F0,4B F4 9F 47 F4 6F 4D 32 F4 1F 4D 2B F4 3F 36 CC

A.00,D3 1D 1B D2 12 41 2D 1B D2 1F 4D 19 F4 BF 4D 21
A.10,F4 2D 1B D2 12 4F 4D 14 F4 D0 9F 4F 4F C0
```

Fig. 4-145: Music for Left Hand

umns, requiring only 64 refresh cycles. The 2116, a recent 16K RAM, is structured in two arrays and organized in 64 rows by 128 columns. Because both arrays may be accessed simultaneously, only 64 refresh cycles are required.

Refresh Control

The refresh controller is in charge of refreshing the whole RAM within 2 milliseconds. Two basic techniques are used to access the memory:

1. *Burst Mode:* The refresh controller refreshes all rows "at once," i.e. in sequence. This is conceptually simple, but makes the RAM unavailable to the processor for 64 cycles. The worst case overhead can be computed easily. Assuming a 500-nanosecond clock cycle, and 64 refresh cycles within 2 milliseconds, $64 \times 500 = 32$ microseconds will be lost to refresh. 32 microseconds every 2 milliseconds represent a loss of: $32/200 = 1.6\%$.
2. *Distributed* or *Single-Cycle Mode:* The refresh controller accesses the memory every n microseconds to refresh the next row. This technique has a potential for less delay to the processor, provided that the overhead per memory access be kept small.

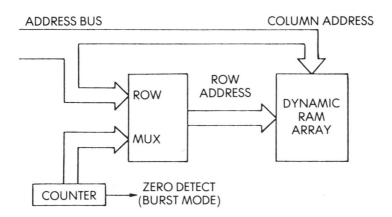

Fig. 4-146: Basic Refresh Logic

Memory Contention

Both techniques require getting access to the memory when it is not busy, and at a higher priority than the processor. Two main techniques are used to achieve such synchronization:

Asynchronous Access

Requests are generated at a fixed rate, such as every 31 microseconds (i.e. 64 times every 2 milliseconds), independently of the microprocessor state. This method is microprocessor-independent, but requires complex controller design and results in access delay. The controller may have to wait for the completion of an RAM cycle in progress; however, this is a refresh delay, not a delay of the MPU. Request priorities must be resolved, and propagation delays through the controller logic must be allowed for.

Hidden Refresh

The principle of this method is to refresh the RAM while the MPU does not need it. Hidden refresh is also known as *Transparent Refresh,* or *Synchronous Access.* For every MPU, situations normally exist in which it can be guaranteed that it will not require the use of the memory for one or more cycles. If such states can be identified externally, a refresh cycle can be started

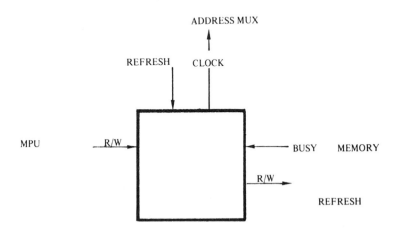

Fig. 4-147: Asynchronous Controller

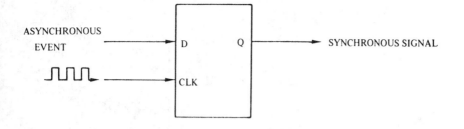

Fig. 4-148: Flip-Flop Is Synchronizing Device

without any arbitration or multiplexer delay (no overhead). The MPU incurs no overhead and is thus completely unaware of the refresh, hence the name of *"hidden"* or *"transparent"* refresh

The speed advantage of this method is obvious. However, the design of the refresh controller becomes completely specific to the microprocessor utilized. In addition, one must guard against "unusual" situations by providing an override to guarantee the 2-millisecond refresh. Such "unusual" events are, for example, in the case of an 8080: Halt, Reset applied too long, long Wait caused by a slow memory or a single step facility during debugging, and finally the Hold state used for DMA cycles.

As an example, state T4 of machine cycle M1 of the 8080A can be used for refresh; the 8080 decodes and executes an internal instruction during T4 and does not require the memory. A simple counter by 4 can be used to detect the end of T3 and start the refresh authorization (see Fig. 4-150).

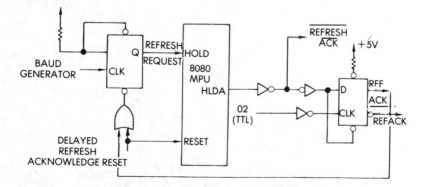

Fig. 4-149: Using Hold to Steal Memory Cycle

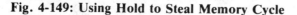

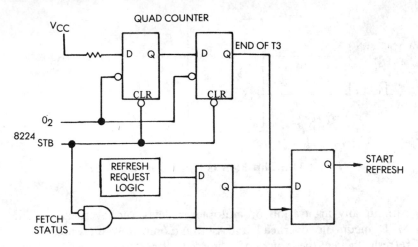

Fig. 4-150: Basic Synchronous Refresh Control for 8080

Similarly, for any processor, a RAM refresh authorization can be granted, giving any ROM access. An example of a simplified synchronous design appears in Fig. 4-149, where HOLD is used to obtain bus control. (This cannot be used with RESET or WAIT.)

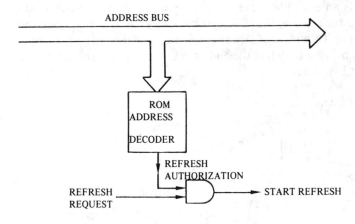

Fig. 4-151: Refresh During ROM Access

Other Methods

A number of other methods can be used. They are combinations of the above techniques, often taking advantage of the idiosyncrasies of the specific microprocessor. For example, an asynchronous refresh can be clocked by the low-to-high transition of Φ2 (phase 2 of the clock). This guarantees that there will be no simultaneous memory request from the 8080 and somewhat simplifies the design of the arbitration unit.

Refresh Logic

A complete refresh controller may include several elements, depending on the efficiency required and the cost limitations. The usual elements are:

— refresh counter: a 6 or 7-bit counter, used to generate sequentially the 64 or 128 row addresses.
— address multiplexer: supplies the RAM chips with a row address originating either from the refresh counter (during a refresh cycle), or from the address bus (during a regular memory cycle).
— the "first-in" request arbitration unit: grants a memory cycle to the refresh-request unit or to the MPU memory request (Fig. 4-152).
— the priority resolver: systematically grants memory access to a refresh request, sometimes depending on specific conditions.
— baud-rate generator: timing circuit in charge of supplying pulses at the required rate, such as 64 times every 2 milliseconds.
— latches: in charge of memorizing the previous status.

Refresh-Controller Chips

Refresh-controller chips have been introduced to facilitate the design of dynamic RAM controllers. The Intel 3222 is used with the 2107B to implement an asynchronous technique. The 3222 requires external timing for its signals, but supplies in a single chip latches, oscillator (requires external R-C circuit), address multiplexer, refresh counter, priority resolver. It supplies a 6-bit row address (Fig. 4-153).

The 3242 is a simple controller used with the 2104A (4K) and the 2116 (16K). It supplies 6 or 7 bits, and integrates address multiplexer and refresh counter (see Fig. 4-154). The next section will present the actual design of a dynamic memory board for the S100 bus.

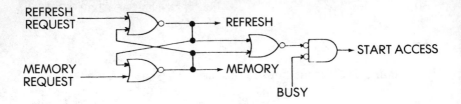

Fig. 4-152: Request Arbiter

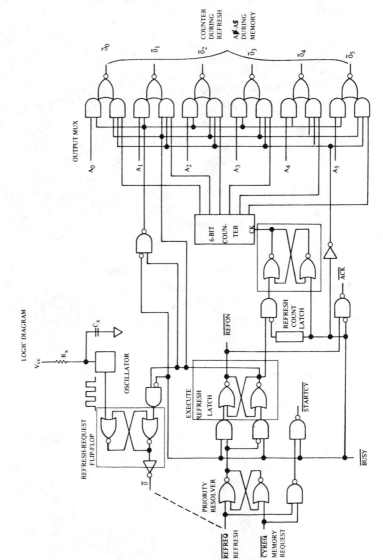

Fig. 4-153: 6-Line Refresh-Control Chip (Intel)

248

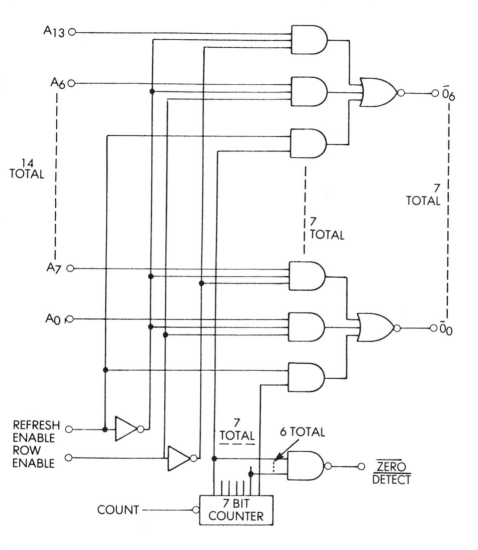

Fig. 4-154: 7-Line Refresh-Control Chip (Intel)

DYNAMIC MEMORIES

In review, three methods can be used for refresh: *group refresh,* i.e. all thirty-two rows every two milliseconds, *dedicated refresh* for one

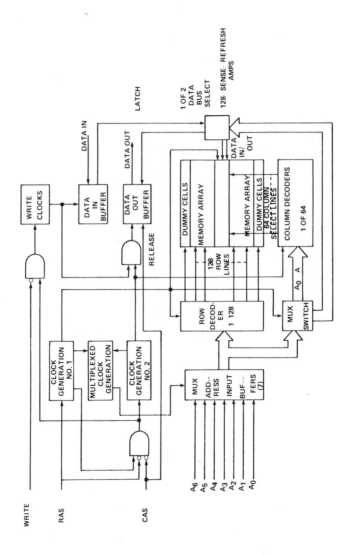

Fig. 4-155: 4116 RAM Internal Diagram

column every few microseconds (which takes up memory bandwidth), and *transparent refresh* (hidden refresh) where the refresh cycle are done during unused portions of the system instruction.

Designing a Dynamic Memory for the S100 Bus

The problem here can be divided into two parts: the first is studying the specifications of the particular dynamic memory chip used; the second is studying the S100 bus interface requirements and memory timing. Unfortunately, DMA cycles, front panel access cycles, and other special hardware considerations having little or nothing to do with the original 8080 system timing must be considered. The chips used in this case are the Mostek 16,384-by-one-bit dynamic RAM chips.

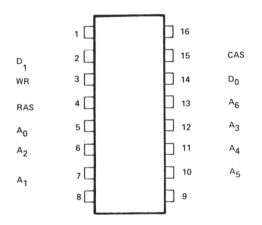

Fig. 4-156: 4116 Pin Layout

The 16,384-bit dynamic RAM chip, the MK4116P, comes in a 16-pin RAM package. Because it has 16 pins, 14 address bits are needed to address a single cell, thus the address must be multiplexed in two groups of seven. Fig. 4-157 shows the timing diagram for a Read cycle in the system. Fig. 4-158 shows the timing diagram for the Write cycle in the system. The address multiplexing is accomplished by the RAS, CAS signals. The only information needed is when a memory Read or Write cycle is going to begin. As soon as this information is known, it is very easy to generate the timing signals shown in Fig. 4-159 by using a synchronous-state counter.

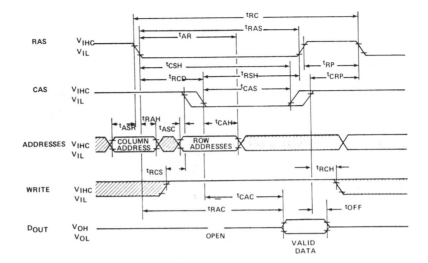

Fig. 4-157: Read Cycle Timing

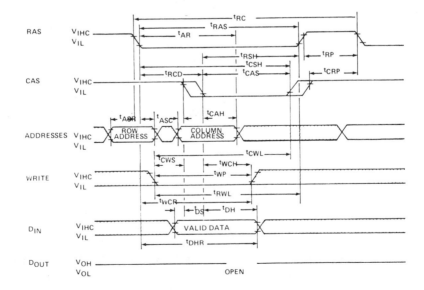

Fig. 4-158: Write Cycle Timing

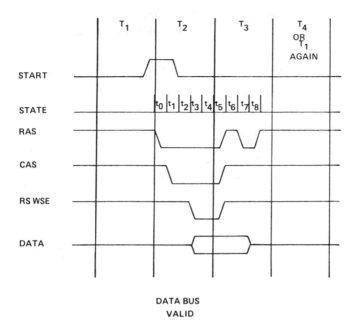

DATA BUS
VALID

Fig. 4-159: State Controller Timing

The synchronous-state counter will deliver eight 100-nanosecond pulses one after the other. Each state, labelled t0 through t7, is used to generate the strobe and control signals for the dynamic memories. Referring to the system schematic diagram in Fig. 4-160, the eight chips for the memory, a data-output latch, a data-input buffer, the address multiplexing, and the refresh counter are illustrated. All of the control signals indicated are generated by the timing control in Fig. 4-161. Fig. 4-161 has the state counter, which is triggered by any memory Read or Write cycle.

The design proceeds in a simple fashion. The synchronous-state counter gives the designer flexibility in timing control without the problems with the use of asynchronous timing devices. The proper number of cycles together generates the RAS and CAS signals, as well as the others. As an example, the RAS signal is false for t0, t1, t2, t3, t4, t5, and t6. The CAS signal is false for t1, t2, t3, t4, t5, and t6. Note how the RAS signal is false for t0 and the CAS signal is true for t0. According to the timing diagram in Fig. 4-159, this will allow multiplexing the address for the row first, and then the column, into the chip's internal address registers. Thus, the t0 timing signal becomes the strobe for the address multiplexer from the address bus.

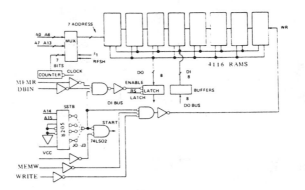

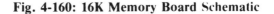

Fig. 4-160: 16K Memory Board Schematic

Now the choice of method of refresh must be made. In this case, hidden refresh would obviously be the best, since it would be completely transparent to the processor. To achieve transparent refresh, the memory is refreshed within every Read or Write cycle. Referring to the memory Read cycle timing and memory Write cycle timing in Chapter 6, Figures 6-3 and 6-4, in the worst case a Read or Write must be performed within 650 nanoseconds and then complete a refresh before the beginning of the next M cycle. Referring to the timing in Figure 4-159, there are exactly 400 nanoseconds, assuming there are no Wait states, in which to perform the transparent refresh. These particular dynamic memories are fast enough so that within that 400 nanoseconds, a hidden refresh can be performed. To do this, after every Read or Write cycle is complete, the refresh counter is incremented and the RAS signal for 200 nanoseconds is activated, to perform a row refresh. In the worst case, only 50 nanoseconds are left before the beginning of a possible new memory cycle.

254

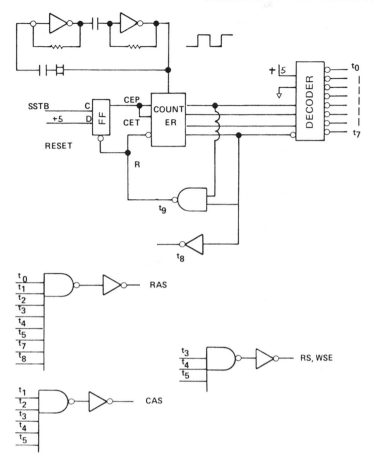

Fig. 4-161: 16K-Memory-Board Control Section

The basic Read and the basic Write cycle requirements for the S100 bus are now satisfied. The status strobe signal has been used. This one signal is the key to our entire dynamic refresh system. If any other processor besides the 8080 is used, this status strobe signal must be identical to the timing requirements that are necessary in the 8080 base system. Besides this, any other operation, such as the front panel, or DMA cycles, must also follow through this same state sequence. Unfortunately, there is no agreement among the S100 bus manufacturers as to the actual Read and Write cycle requirements under these alternative conditions.

255

"RAS ONLY" REFRESH CYCLE

NOTE: CAS=V$_{IHC}$, WRITE=DON'T CARE

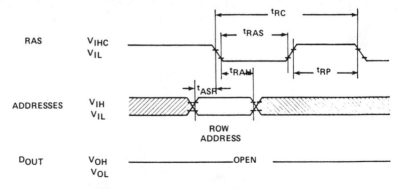

RAS   V$_{IHC}$
     V$_{IL}$

ADDRESSES   V$_{IH}$
     V$_{IL}$

ROW ADDRESS

D$_{OUT}$ V$_{OH}$
     V$_{OL}$ OPEN

Fig. 4-162: Refresh Timing

PARAMETER	SYMBOL	MK 4116-2 MIN	MAX	UNITS
RANDOM READ OR WRITE CYCLE TIME	t_{RC}	375		ns
READ–WRITE CYCLE TIME	t_{RWC}	375		ns
PAGE MODE CYCLE TIME	t_{PC}	170		ns
ACCESS TIME FROM RAS	t_{RAC}		150	ns
ACCESS TIME FROM CAS	t_{CAC}		100	ns
OUTPUT BUFFER TURN-OFF DELAY	t_{OFF}	0	40	ns
TRANSITION TIME (RISE AND FALL)	t_T	3	35	ns
RAS PRECHARGE TIME	t_{RP}	100		ns
RAS PULSE WIDTH	t_{RAS}	150	10,000	ns
RAS HOLD TIME	t_{RSH}	100		ns
CAS HOLD TIME	t_{CSH}	150		ns
CAS PULSE WIDTH	t_{CAS}	100	10,000	ns
RAS TO CAS DELAY TIME	t_{RCD}	20	50	ns
CAS TO RAS PRECHARGE TIME	t_{CRP}	-20		ns
ROW ADDRESS SET-UP TIME	t_{ASR}	0		ns
ROW ADDRESS HOLD TIME	t_{RAH}	20		ns
COLUMN ADDRESS SET-UP TIME	t_{ASC}	-10		ns
COLUMN ADDRESS HOLD TIME	t_{CAH}	45		ns
COLUMN ADDRESS HOLD TIME REFERENCED TO RAS	t_{AR}	95		ns
READ COMMAND SET-UP TIME	t_{RCS}	0		ns
READ COMMAND HOLD TIME	t_{RCH}	0		ns
WRITE COMMAND HOLD TIME	t_{WCH}	45		ns
WRITE COMMAND HOLD TIME REFERENCED TO RAS	t_{WCR}	95		ns
WRITE COMMAND PULSE WIDTH	t_{WP}	45		ns
WRITE COMMAND TO RAS LEAD TIME	t_{RWL}	60		ns
WRITE COMMAND TO CAS LEAD TIME	t_{CWL}	60		ns
DATA–IN SET-UP TIME	t_{DS}	0		ns
DATA–IN HOLD TIME	t_{DH}	45		ns
DATA–IN HOLD TIME REFERENCED TO RAS	t_{DHR}	95		ns
CAS PRECHARGE TIME (FOR PAGE-MODE CYCLE ONLY)	t_{CP}	60		ns
REFRESH PERIOD	t_{REF}		2	ms
WRITE COMMAND SET-UP TIME	t_{WCS}	-20		ns
CAS TO WRITE DELAY	t_{CWD}	70		ns
RAS TO WRITE DELAY	t_{RWD}	120		ns

Fig. 4-163: 4116 Timing Definitions

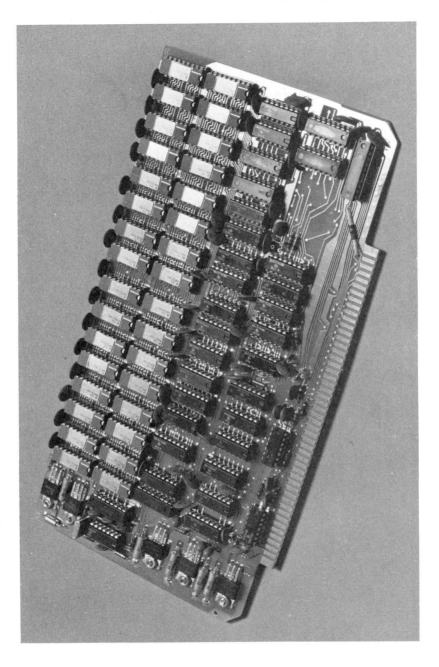

Fig. 4-164: Dynabyte 16K RAM Board

Because of these timing incompatibilities, certain dynamic memory boards cannot be used in all systems. As an example of a board which uses this same method of synchronous-state hidden-refresh timing, there is the Dynabyte 16K memory board. This board uses 4K dynamic RAM chips. It has the capability of adjusting the timing so that it will interface to most other S100 bus memory applications, including other processors. Appearing in Figure 4-164 is the photograph

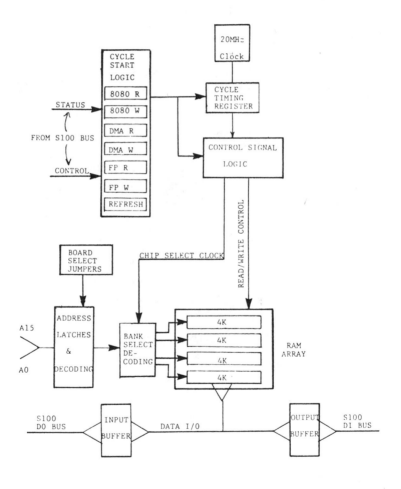

16K RAM MODULE

Fig. 4-165: Block Diagram of Dynabyte Board

of the board. A block diagram of the control scheme for this board appears in Fig. 4-165. Note how in order to determine the present cycle of operation that many status signals are used from the bus. This means that any DMA device must also generate these same signals.

In summary, a dynamic memory system was built by looking at the timing requirements of the chips and at the timing requirements of the system. The use of a synchonous-state system simplifies and defines the system timing. As an example, it was assumed here the designer had access to the system clocks, so that under all conditions it was known what the system processor was doing. The use of asynchronous one-shots, RC time delays, and delay lines may also lead to a working design; however, these designs suffer seriously from timing problems related to tolerance of components, change of temperature, etc. The added complication of Wait states, different system clocks, and the lack of complete status signals on some buses and the lack of agreement on these same signals, brings abut the practical result of there being no general-purpose dynamic RAM boards which can be universally used on any S100 bus. The more valuable boards, such as the Dynabyte product, can be configured to work in particular systems through the use of hardware jumpers, although there are some systems where even this amount of flexibility is not adequate. In contrast, if we look at the 6800 bus for the Altair 680B, we see that the system timing is so well-defined as to highly simplify the interfacing problem.

The design of a dynamic memory board is quite often made even more complex by the triple power supply and noise bypassing problems. In fact, such a design quite often results in a memory which cannot reliably Read and Write information. Therefore, the design of a dynamic memory system should be considered carefully from the various points presented, including the difficult area of high-frequency noise spikes induced by normal chip operation. The best reference for the design of a dynamic memory system is the manufacturer's memory handbook. Since memories are the bread and butter of the semiconductor manufacturers, they are more than happy to help memory board designers in using their product.

SUMMARY

The progress from PIOs, UARTs, and other simple LSI chips to FDCs and CRTCs points towards the trend of the technology. More peripheral controllers will be fully integrated onto a single chip, and more controllers will be "intelligent." Local editing, file libraries, text processing will become standard features on the peripherals of tomorrow.

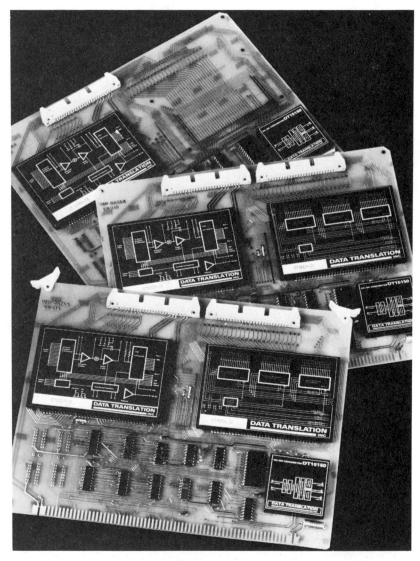

Fig. 5-0: A/D, D/A Boards

5

ANALOG TO DIGITAL
AND DIGITAL TO ANALOG
CONVERSION

INTRODUCTION

In any system, two basic kinds of signals must be measured, or generated. They are *analog* and *digital* signals. *Analog signals* assume a *continuous* range of values, whereas *digital signals* assume only a *finite number* of values. As an example, a binary signal is a digital signal which assumes one of two values, either "on" or "off" ("1" or "0"). A typical example of an analog signal is the value of the temperature in an oven. The temperature, being an analog variable, can assume an infinite number of intermediate values.

In view of the finite precision and limited storage of a computer, a digital representation will be used. The precision of the measurement is said to be limited to n significant digits. In addition, *sampling* will be used to reduce the overall storage required. The concept of sampling will be presented below.

The chapter will explain how to perform analog-to-digital conversion (A/D) and digital-to-analog conversion (D/A). In addition, the specific components required for building a complete data collection system will be introduced. We will consider successively:

— a real D/A converter (or DAC)
— a real A/D converter (or ADC)
— the sampling process
— analog multiplexing.

Finally, all these techniques will be used to design a complete data collection system.

A CONCEPTUAL D/A

Let us consider the problem of converting a binary number into an analog voltage. This is the typical problem of digital-to-analog conversion. A simple solution is the following: a voltage is generated for each bit-position of the binary number. The value of the voltage is proportional to the binary weight of the bit.

For example, bit 0 will generate a voltage $V(2^0)$; bit 1 will generate a voltage $2V(2^1)$; bit 2 will generate a voltage $4V(2^2)$; and bit n will generate a voltage $2^n \times V$. The resulting voltages are simply added. The result is proportional to the original binary number.

A simple 4-bit D/A appears in Fig. 5-1. This D/A consists of: four switches, four proportional summing resistors, an operational amplifier, and a proportional feedback-resistor. The values of the resistors are in the proportion 1, 2, 4, 8. This results in gains of: $-\frac{1}{8}$, $-\frac{1}{4}$, $-\frac{1}{2}$, and -1. Let us examine the function of this circuit.

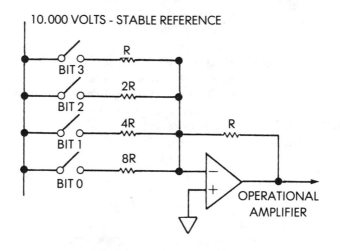

Fig. 5-1: A Simple 4-Bit D/A

Let us begin with all the switches in the *open* position. Since there is no input to the operational amplifier, the output will be "0". Closing the bit switch numbered "0" will apply the − 10V reference to the input of the operational amplifier, through the resistor marked 8R. This will result in an output voltage of 1.25V (due to the gain of − ⅛ at this point). Closing the switch marked "bit 1" will then add 2.5V to the previous value (1.25V) (due to the gain of − ¼ at this point). The resulting output is 3.75V. If all switches are *closed,* the resulting output voltage is 10.0 + 5.0 + 2.5 + 1.25 or 18.75 volts. Here, we have converted a 4-bit binary number, represented by the four switches, into a voltage. It is the analog representation of one of the 16 possible digital values.

We will now examine the structure of a practical D/A converter.

A Practical D/A

The practical design in Fig. 5-2 illustrates the typical design for a monolithic D/A converter. This device has four bits of resolution. Practically, currents are summed instead of voltages, due to the fact that currents are easier to switch on and off accurately. To provide a voltage output, the last stage of the converter becomes a *current-to-voltage converter.* This is easily done by an operational amplifier. Typical converters have eight bits of resolution.

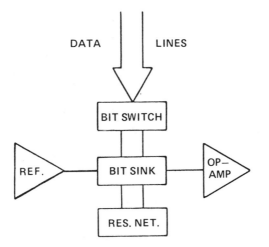

Fig. 5-2: A Practical Converter Diagram

Fig. 5-3 illustrates the functional elements of our converter. They are: the reference-current source, the bit-sink transistors, the ladder-resistor network, the bit-sink switches, and the voltage-current converter.

The bit-sink current reference establishes a stable reference current. The bit-sink current sources will be proprotional to this reference current. The current in each bit-sink transistor is established by its position on the R-2R ladder-resistor network. The R-2R resistor network produces a 2^{-n} series of currents flowing through each bit-sink collector. The switches will route the current either to the bit-sink bus, which connects to the current-to-voltage converter—or to ground. In our example, these currents are $1/20$ ampere, $1/40$ ampere, $1/80$ ampere, and $1/160$ ampere. These elements combine to perform the conversion from a 4-bit binary number into an analog voltage.

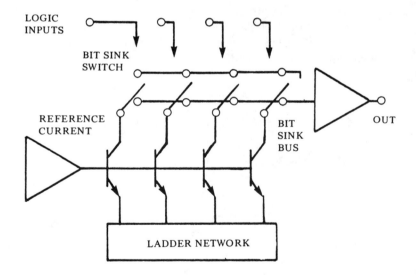

Fig. 5-3: Monolithic Converter Functional Elements

An actual monolithic converter uses transistors as switches to route the current between the bit-sink bus to the amplifier and ground. Fig. 5-4 shows the logic-signal to bit-current-sink switches interface cir-

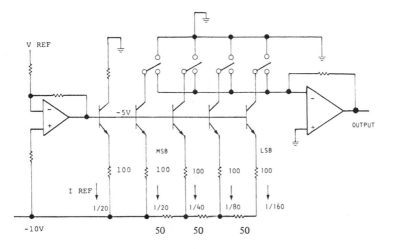

Fig. 5-4: Completed Monolithic Converter

cuitry. When the input is a logic "0", which corresponds to 0V, the bit sink will draw current through Q4 to the bit-sink bus. When the input is a logic "1", which corresponds to an input voltage greater than 2V, the bit sink will draw current through Q3, instead of Q4, disconnecting the bit-sink bus from this sink bit. The four binary signals will switch the four bit sinks on and off the bit-sink bus. The resulting current is converted to the output voltage.

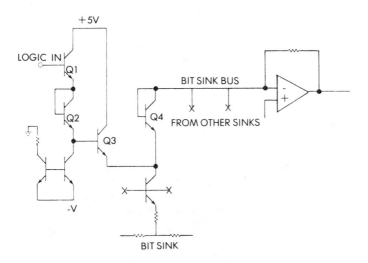

Fig. 5-5: Detail—The Bit Switches

By extending the R-2R ladder network and adding more bit-sink transistors, we can increase the resolution of our converter to more than 10 bits. Using any more than 14 bits results in stability problems that this simple circuit cannot overcome. In fact, 16-bit converters are usually certified to be calibrated against a national standard. (One must remember that using 16 bits results in an accuracy of 1 part in 65,000!)

Real Products

Table 5-1 represents a sampling of some real products that perform D/A conversion. Cost increases with speed.

Manufacturer	Type #	Resolution	Speed
Motorola	MC1408	8	300ns
PMI	DAC-08	8	100ns
PMI	DAC-03	10	250ns
Analog Devices	AD7520	10	500ns
Datel	DAC-4Z12D	12	1us
Burr-Brown	DAC70/CSB	16	75us

Table 5-1: D/A Converters

THE A/D

Now that we have converted the binary representation of a number into an analog signal, we must solve the reverse problem. We must measure an analog signal and convert it into a binary number. There are three methods of conversion: successive approximation, integration, and direct comparison. Before discussing these, we must first examine the concept of sampling.

Sampling

The binary number representing our analog signal represents a value at one point in time. This is known as a *sample*. In the following waveform, in Fig. 5-6, we have sampled where indicated. The sample values will not give us any information as to the true shape of the analog signal. We must collect samples which will accurately represent the signal. The frequency at which we sample is known as the *sampling rate*. In order to represent accurately we must sample more frequently. How often must we sample?

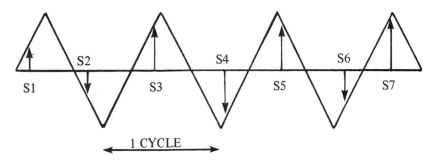

Fig. 5-6: Infrequent Sampling

The Sampling Theorem

The answer lies in the sampling theorem: *We must sample at least twice as fast as the fastest occurring signal in our system.* As a rough rule, in order to represent our signal, we must sample at least 10 times as fast as our average frequency. Fig. 5-7 illustrates the results of more frequent sampling.

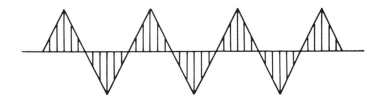

Fig. 5-7: Frequent Sampling

Sample and Hold

The analog input to a converter must be stable for the duration of the time it takes to complete the conversion. This may be accomplished by using a *sample and hold* circuit. This device will sample the analog input and hold it constant until the next sample of the input. The device holds the sample in a high-quality capacitor, buffered by an operational amplifier. Sample-and-holds are available in both monolithic and hybrid forms.

267

Fig. 5-8: 12 Bit A/D and D/A Converters

ANALOG TO DIGITAL CONVERSION TECHNIQUES

Several conversion techniques have been devised to perform analog to digital conversion. Each one has advantages and disadvantages. The main parameters used to evaluate the merits of each technique are usually speed, cost, and accuracy.

Four basic conversion techniques are used. They are: successive approximations, integration (single, dual, and quad slope), counter comparator and servo, and parallel. Each of these methods will now be examined and explained.

After a presentation of the four basic conversion techniques, single chip implementations of these conversion techniques will be presented. Then, the techniques and components required for data acquisition will be examined.

Successive approximations A/D

The successive approximations technique is probably the technique most frequently used with microprocessors, as it is characterized by high speed, high resolution and low cost.

268

The principle of the method is to generate an initial guess of the input value, convert it to analog, and then compare it to the actual input. Depending on the result of the comparison, this initial guess will then be increased or decreased. The required hardware is shown on Fig. 5-9:

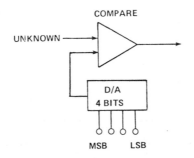

Fig. 5-9: Successive Approximation Hardware

For example, assuming an 8-bit approximation, the initial guess could be "10000000". If the actual input is greater than the analog equivalent of "10000000", the next bit (the second one from the left) is turned on.

The next guess is then "11000000". If it is too small again, the next guess is "11100000".

If the actual input is now smaller than the current approximation the bit most recently set to "1" will be turned off, and the next bit is tried. The next guess will be "11010000", and so on:

	Too low	Exact	Too high
Guess 1: 10000000	✔	—	—
Guess 2: 11000000	✔	—	—
Guess 3: 11100000	—	—	✔
Guess 4: 11010000	—	—	—

In other words, whenever the actual input is greater than the approximation, the current bit is left on and the next bit is "tried".

Whenever it is not greater, the current bit is turned off and the next bit is tried. The algorithm is presented formally on Fig. 5-10. The corresponding hardware is shown on Fig. 5-11.

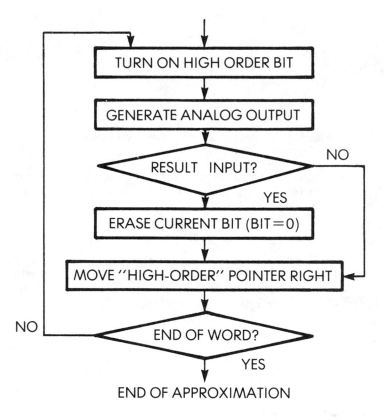

Fig. 5-10: Successive Approximation ADC

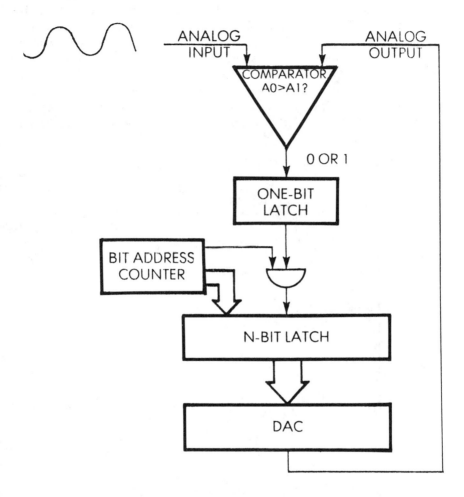

Fig. 5-11: Detailed Successive Approximation Hardware

Let us follow a sample approximation on an example, as shown on Fig. 5-12.

The most significant bit (bit n) is first turned on. The resulting value V_1 is smaller than the input signal. The bit stays on the next one is turned on. This is shown on Fig. 5-12. However, this time, the resulting approximation V_2 is larger than the input value. Bit n-1, which had been set initially to the value "1" is now reset to the value "0". This is shown at the bottom of Fig. 5-12 where the successive bits of the approximation are shown. The next approximation to be tried is therefore "101", followed by zeroes. This is V_3. It is smaller than the input, and bit n-2 is left at the value "1" while the next bit is turned on.

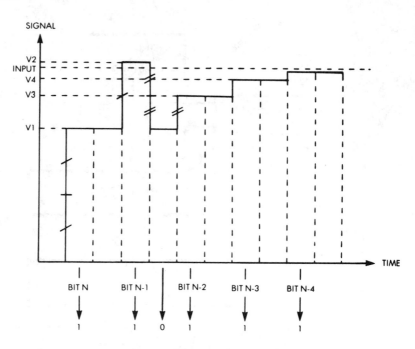

Fig. 5-12: A Sample Approximation

The next approximation is "1011" followed by zeroes. This results in the approximation V_4, and so on. By inspecting Fig. 5-12 it can be seen that the first 5 bits of the approximation are "10111". Depending on the precision required, and the hardware, the final result might have 8, 10, or more bits.

Connecting a microprocessor

Instead of implementing the control logic in hardware, a microprocessor may be used to test the result of the comparison and generate the next digital approximation. The resulting diagram is shown on Fig. 5-13. The corresponding hardware logic is replaced by a simple program.

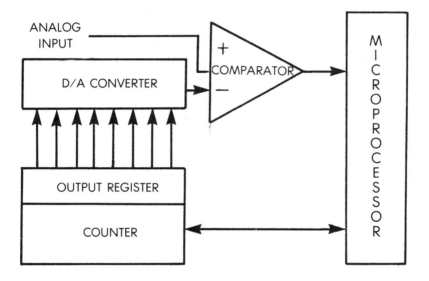

Fig. 5-13: Connecting a MPU

Fluctuating input

It has been assumed so far that the input value does not change during the conversion. If it did change, the conversion might no longer be accurate. A simple solution to this problem is to use a *sample-and-hold* circuit (S/H) to freeze the value being approximated. The operation of a sample-and-hold circuit is shown on Fig. 5-14. The resulting system interconnect is shown on Fig. 5-15. A sample-and-hold circuit will normally be used unless the input signal varies slowly and is noise-free during the conversion process.

273

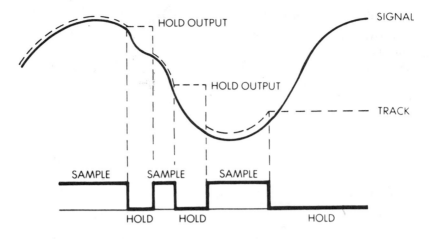

Fig. 5-14: Sample and Hold

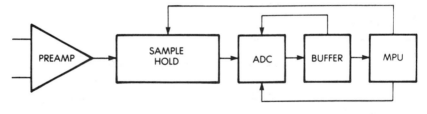

SAMPLE-HOLD ESTABLISHES PRECISE TIMING FOR SAMPLING

Fig. 5-15: Adding Sample-Hold Speeds ADC

An example of the error introduced by a fast rising input, using the successive approximation technique, is shown on Fig. 5-16. Looking at the left of the picture, it can be seen that the first 5-bit approximation "01111" achieves a correct approximation. However, the second one, still "01111", is incorrect. This is because the value of the input kept rising while the approximation was going on. It is a typical case of the possible error introduced by the variation of an input and requires a sample and hold circuit.

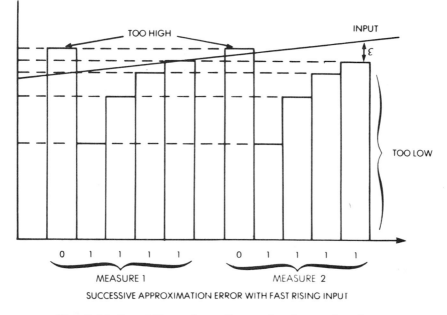

SUCCESSIVE APPROXIMATION ERROR WITH FAST RISING INPUT

Fig. 5-16: Input Error from Successive Approximation

Summary of successive approximations

The successive approximations technique is analogous to the "logarithmic search" technique used in programming a search on an interval. The concept is to jump to the middle of the interval, then jump to the middle of either the bottom or the top remaining halves, depending on the value of the comparison. This guarantees that the final value will be reached in $\log_2 n$ operations, where n is the number of elements. The logarithmic search is used in programming to retrieve an element within a file. A simpler comparison consists in opening a book in the middle, then jumping to the middle of the first section or else the middle of the next section depending on whether the item one is looking for was before or after the middle of the book, and so on. This is also called *binary search*. The intent is to reduce the amount of time required for the search process.

The successive approximations technique is conceptually simple, and lends itself well to single-chip implementation. As a result, it is widely used with microprocessors and results in low-cost LSI ADC chips performing conversions with a good precision.

Integration techniques

The principle used by integration techniques is to let an integrator (a capacitor) be charged by the input volgage, and measure the corresponding time required. Using a reference voltage for comparison, it is then possible to determine the value of the input voltage.

The main integration techniques are *dual or quad slope*, and single ramp or V/F. They will be examined now.

Dual slope integration

The basis of the method is to measure the time it takes for a capacitor to charge to the unknown voltage, and to discharge under a known reference voltage. The ratio between the known and unknown voltages is equal to the ratio of the values of the two time measurements.

This technique offers the advantage of noise reduction through signal averaging. It can yield excellent precision but is slower than the successive approximations technique. However, it is inexpensive and extensively used in DVM's.

The principle of the method is illustrated on Fig. 5-17. the corresponding hardware is shown on Fig. 5-18. Two phases can be distinguished.

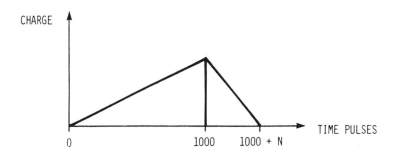

Fig. 5-17: Integration Timing

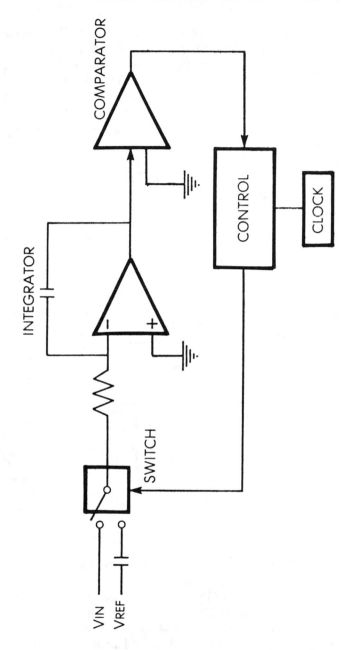

Fig. 5-18: Dual Slope Converter

In the first phase, the capacitor is charged under the (positive) input voltage during n pulses (1000 for example). A capacitor charges at a rate proportional to the input voltage, or more exactly to the average input value over the time "T". T is a predefined period of time.

In the second phase, the capacitor is discharged by a calibrated (negative) reference current. V_{ref} (of opposite polarity to V_{in}) is applied. The time required to discharge the capacitor is measured. It is "t".

When used in conjunction with a microprocessor, the input is generally scaled and offset by V_{ref} divided by 2, so that:

$$\frac{t - T}{T} = \frac{1}{2} \left(\frac{V_{in}}{V_{ref}} + 1 \right)$$

In other words, the value of the counter essentially provides the digital value of V_{in}. The complete diagram of a bipolar dual slope ADC is shown on Fig. 5-19.

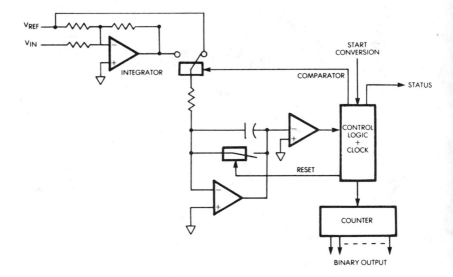

Fig. 5-19: A Bipolar Dual Slope ADC Circuit

The linearity of the method as well as its resolution are excellent. However, its speed is limited. The maximum number of conversions per second (the throughput) is limited to $1/T$ conversions per second.

The choice of T is determined by the fundamental frequency to be rejected. For example, assuming that the AC frequency of 60 hertz is to be rejected, and its harmonics (in Europe this would be 50 hertz), the minimum time for a conversion will be 16.666 ms.

The maximum throughput is therefore less than 30 conversions per second.

As a result, the integration technique is too slow for data acquisition and is mostly used for DVMs, thermocouples and other slow-varying inputs.

Quad slope

Quad slope is directly derived from the dual slope technique. An extra charge and discharge are performed initially in order to reduce some potential errors. The technique integrates inaccuracies caused by offset and ground errors that may be present. The corresponding waveform is shown in Fig. 5-20. The method derives its name from the four slopes.

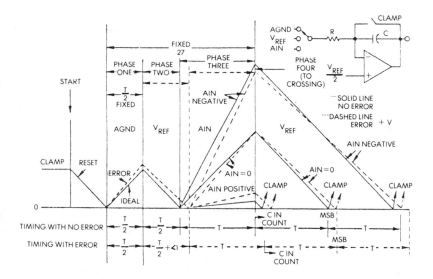

Fig. 5-20: Quad-Slope Principle

SINGLE RAMP AND V/F

In the single ramp technique a reference voltage of opposite polarity to the input voltage is used. It is integrated until it is found to be equal to the input. As in the previous technique, a timer is used to count the number of pulses used to achieve equality. The accuracy of this method depends both on the capacitor (since no offsetting discharge is used), and on the clock frequency used. However, it has a potential for being somewhat faster than the previous one since a single charge is used.

In the V/F method, the input voltage is converted into a frequency proportional to it. A counter is then used to measure the frequency and provide a digital output.

This technique is sometimes used for transmitting information over communication lines and saves the cost of an ADC, when a limited precision is sufficient.

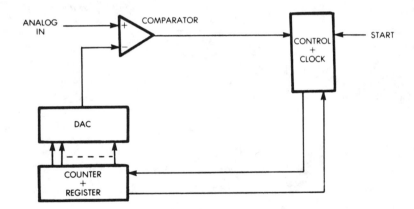

Fig. 5-21: Counter-Comparator is like Single Ramp, but Time Scale Independent

THE COUNTER-COMPARATOR TECHNIQUE

This technique is basically analogous to the single ramp technique, but it is independent from the time scale. It is illustrated on Fig. 5–21, and the resulting approximation is shown on Fig. 5–22.

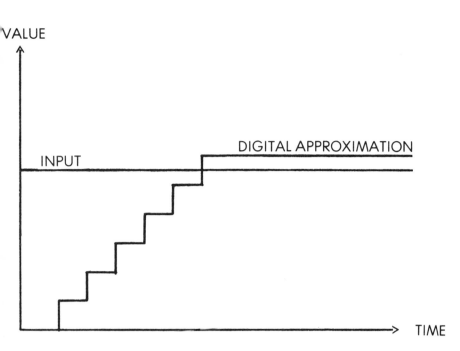

Fig. 5-22: Approximation with Counter-Comparator

The input is compared to the DAC output, and the counter counts up until the approximation becomes larger than the input.

The technique is very simple, but has limited speed. It may take a long time for the approximation to finally reach the value of the input. This is because no specific technique is used to reduce the length of time necessary to search the possible interval. In some cases (low input values) the approximation will be obtained quickly. However, in the general case, the method will require n/2 counts, where n is the maximum value which can be achieved with the counter (n = 2p where p is the number of bits in the counter).

THE SERVO TECHNIQUE

This technique is essentially like the counter comparator technique, except it uses an up-down counter so that it can track a *varying* input signal. Whenever the input signal is reached, it will generally jump back and forth over the input signal, seeking to home in on its value.

It will follow small changes rapidly, and can provide the function of a sample and hold circuit.

The basic tracking circuit is shown on Fig. 5-23 and the resulting approximation is shown on Fig. 5-24.

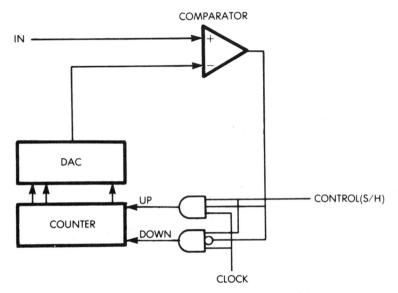

Fig. 5-23: The Basic Tracking S/H

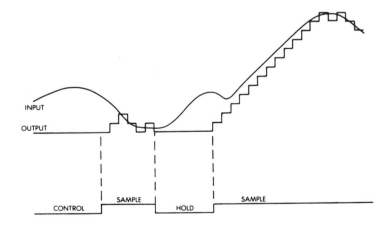

Fig. 5-24: Approximation with Tracking S/H

PARALLEL CONVERSION

The principle of *parallel conversion* or *direct comparison* technique is to convert *simultaneously* all possible digital values into their analog form and to compare them to the input signal. This way, during the time necessary for a single conversion, equality can be detected. This is illustrated by Fig. 5-25. This method has the advantage of very high speed, but requires a large number of components. The circuit of Fig. 5-26 shows the gates required for just 3-bits of precision. The number of components required increases geometrically with the number of bits. 2^{n-1} comparators are required. They are biased 1 LSB apart.

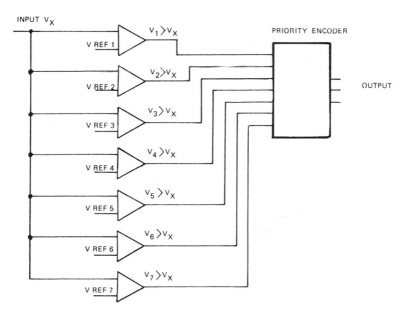

Fig. 5-25: Direct Comparison Converter

Let us examine how this works. We will consider a 3-bit direct comparison converter. Our input can be measured in terms of eight levels. Figure 5-25 illustrates the structure of our converter.

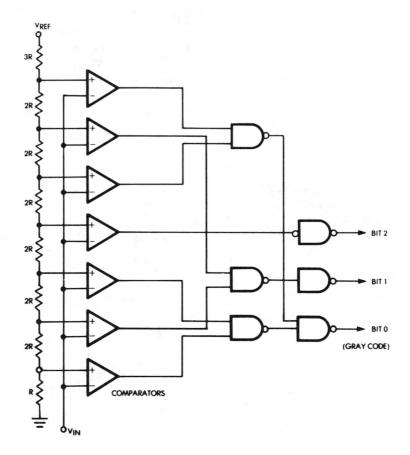

Fig. 5-26: Parallel A/D Example

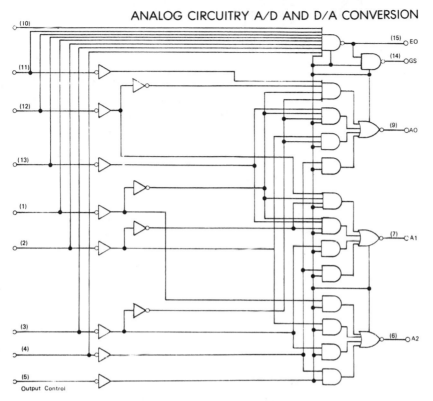

Fig. 5-27: 8 to 3 Priority Encoder

The seven comparators will establish if our input voltage is greater than, or less than, each of the possible eight reference values. For example, if all comparators below the fifth one are on, and all above it are off, then the priority encoder will encode the eight inputs into a 3-bit binary number, 100_2. Other inputs will be encoded into other 3-bit representations.

Such systems provide a resolution of five bits in less than 100ns per conversion. The need for many comparators and reference voltages, and a complex priority scheme, results in this method being the most expensive for anything beyond 3-bits of resolution.

However, monolithic devices are being introduced to provide high speed direct conversion.

MULTIPLYING DAC

The term "multiplying DAC" is frequently encountered and simply refers to a DAC which accepts multiple references. It may operate in 1, 2 or 4 quadrants.

285

Summary of conversion techniques

The main conversion techniques have been presented above. Combination of these techniques may also be used. The characteristics of any ADC must be evaluated in function of its accuracy, linearity, speed, price, stability, resolution, input ranges and other specific criteria (such as size).

Using a microprocessor may reduce the component count. The microprocessor can also control the gain, and the bias setting for both inputs and output, as well as refine the precision by program.

MONOLITHIC ADCs

It has become possible to integrate all of the circuitry required by an ADC into a single chip. Some typical single chip ADCs will be described here. A table summary appears below:

Manufacturer	Type #	Resolution	Speed	Type of Conversion	Cost
National	MM5357	8	40us	SA	$10
PMI	AD-02	8	8us	SA	
Analog Devices	AD7570	10	18us	SA	$70
Datel	ADC-EK12B	12	24ms	Integrating	
Analog Devices	AD7550	13	40ms	Integrating	$25
National	ADC 0816	8	114ms	SA	$20

The three techniques of A/D conversion, successive approximation, integration, and direct comparison, are all available as monolithic LSI modules. The trade-offs among the three techniques are simple. The direct converter is of medium speed, and average resolution. Dual-slope integration conversion has the highest accuracy, but requires the most time to perform this conversion. The time the analog signal must be held stable, and the time it takes to convert, determine the maximum sampling frequency and the need for a sample-and-hold circuit.

Connecting the ADC to the microprocessor

When interfacing an ADC to a microprocessor, at least two control signals are required (see Fig. 5-28).

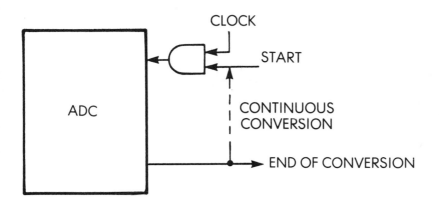

Fig. 5-28: ADC Control Signals

SC is the *start-conversion* signal used by the microprocessor to order the ADC to start conversion. *EOC* is the *end-of-conversion* signal, or a *busy* signal, which tells the microprocessor that the conversion has been completed.

Additionally, an *overrange* signal is usually desirable to indicate an overflow situation. Also, whenever the number of bits used in the approximation is larger than 8, two signals are required to enable the first 8 bits of the approximation onto the data bus, then the next n bits. They may be called for example, LBEN and HBEN (low byte enable and high byte enable).

For the direct connection of the ADC to the bus, tri-state outputs and a buffer are required within the ADC.

A successive-approximations converter (Analog Devices 7570)

This is a monolithic CMOS converter, providing 10-bit resolution with a 28-pin ceramic DIP. It requires 40 microseconds. It is equipped with tri-state outputs. Its pinout and internal diagram are shown on

Fig. 5-29. The corresponding timing sequence is shown on Fig. 5-30.

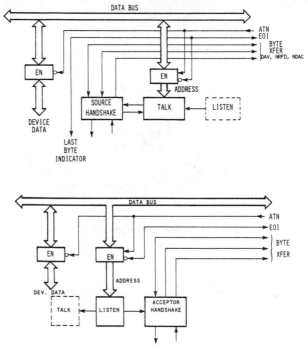

Fig. 5-29: AD7570 Monolithic CMOS ADC

A possible connection of the AD7570 to a microprocessor system is shown on Fig. 5-31. In a typical conversion, the conversion start signal is given by enabling STRT.

BSEN (Bus Enable) will then be enabled, and BUSY goes on the data bus (D0 here). Assuming that the microprocessor monitors BUSY, the conversion will be complete whenever BUSY equals 0. BSEN may then be disabled, and BUSY will float. At this point, the results are ready to be read by the microprocessor from the internal register.

LBEN (Low Byte Enable) will then be enabled, and the least significant byte becomes available on the data lines D0 through D7. LBEN may be disabled after the transfer has taken place.

HBEN (High Byte Enable) will then be enabled, and bits DB8 and DB9 will become available on lines D0 and D1 of the data bus. Similarly, HBEN can then be disabled after the transfer.

Similarly, multiple 7570's can be directly connected to a microprocessor system, as shown on Fig. 5-30.

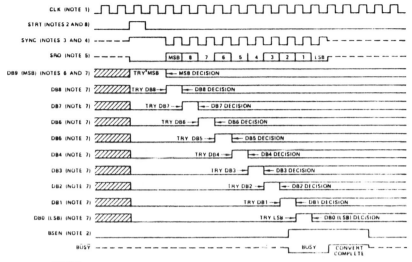

NOTES:
1. Internal Clock Runs Only During Conversion Cycle (External Clock Shown).
2. Externally Initiated.
3. Serial Sync Lags Clock by ≈ 200 ns.
4. Dotted Lines Indicate "Floating" State.
5. For Illustrative Purposes, Serial Out Shown as 1101001110.
6. Cross Hatching Indicates "Don't Care" State.
7. Set and Reset of Output Data Bits Lags Clock Positive Edge by ≈ 200 ns.
8. Trailing edge of STRT Should be Externally Synchronized to Leading Edge of CLK
9. Shown for SC8 = 1.

Fig. 5-30: AD7570 Conversion Timing Sequence

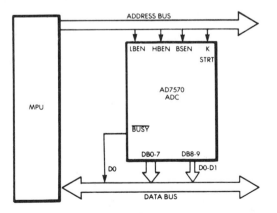

Fig. 5-31: Connecting the 7570

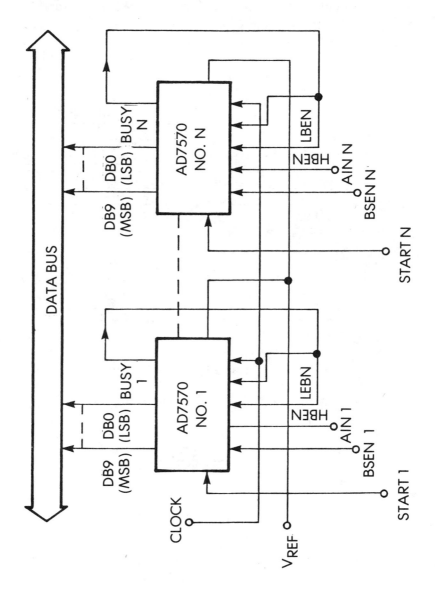

Fig. 5-32: Bussing Multiple AD7570's

A multiplying DAC (Analog Devices 7522)

It is a ten bit converter on a 28-bit DIP, using thin-film-on-CMOS, and an R-2R ladder. It has a double-buffered input structure and allows either serial or parallel output. Its internal organization is shown on Fig. 5-33.

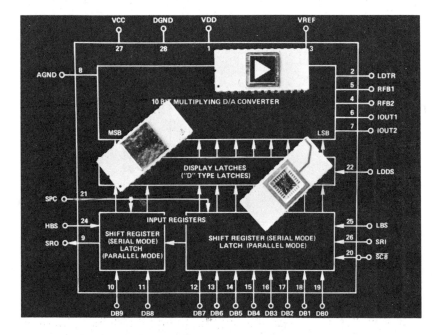

Fig. 5-33: AD7522: Double Buffered ADC

The connection of the AD7522 to a microprocessor system is shown on Fig. 5-34. It can also be connected serially, in case a serial output of the data is preferred. The corresponding serial diagram is shown on Fig. 5-36, and the interface timing diagram on Fig. 5-37.

Just as in the previous case, multiple 7522's can be easily connected to a microprocessor bus as shown on Fig. 5-38.

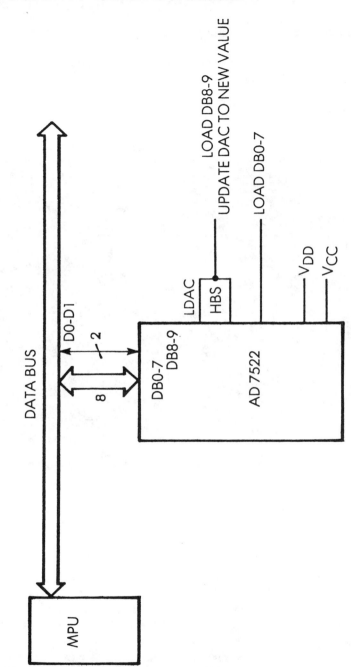

Fig. 5-34: Connecting the AD7522 for Byte-Serial Updating

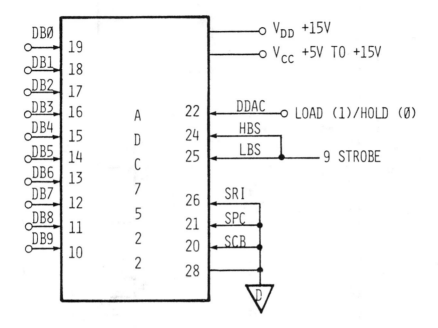

Fig. 5-35: AD7522 Connection for 10-Bit Parallel Operation

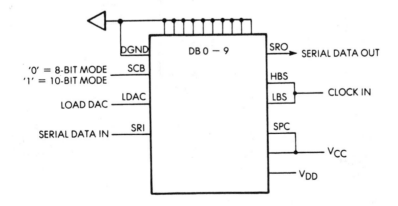

Fig. 5-36: Serial Operation

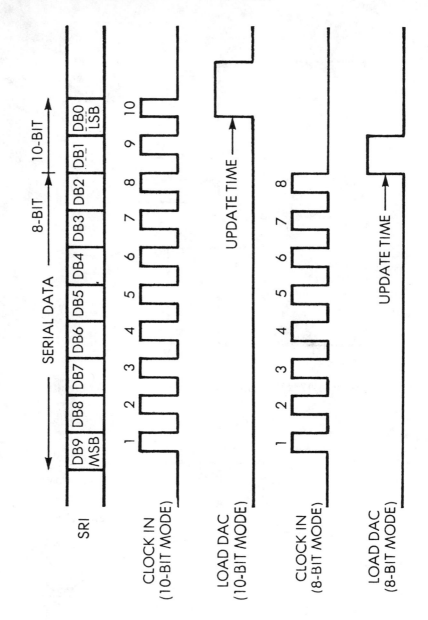

Fig. 5-37: Serial Timing Diagram

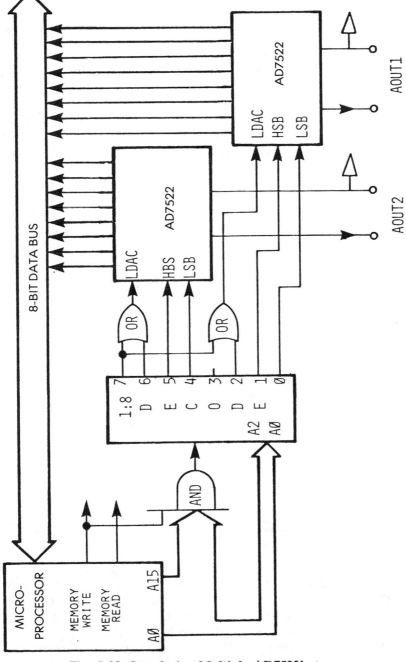

Fig. 5-38: Interfacing Multiple AD7522's to Microprocessor

A quad slope converter (AD 7550)

It is a 13-bit integrating converter implemented as a monolithic CMOS device. It presents a digital value in two's-complement format, requires a 40 pin ceramic DIP. The conversion is 40 ms with a 1 MHz clock. It provides tristate logic output.

Interfacing the AD 7550 to an 8-bit microprocessor bus is as simple as usual and shown on Fig. 5-39. The control signals are essentially analogous to those that were discussed for the 7570. Additionally it is equipped with an overange signal.

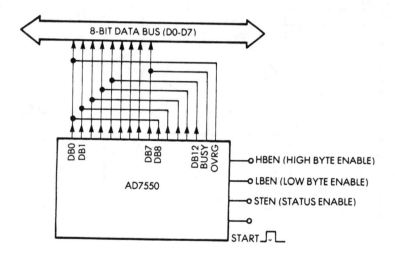

Fig. 5-39: Interfacing AD7550 to 8-Bit Data Path

By inspecting Fig. 5-39, it will be noticed that "BUSY" and "OVRG" are respectively connected to bits 0 and 7. This is because these two bits are the easiest to test for the microprocessor (additional shifts are usually required for all other bits).

Connecting multiple AD 7550's is also simple and is shown on Fig. 5-40.

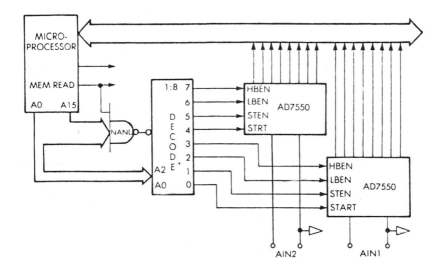

Fig. 5-40: Interfacing Multiple AD7550's to Microprocessor

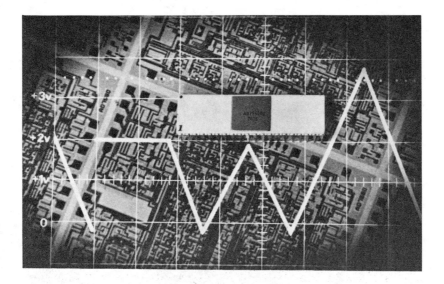

A Quad-Slope Monolithic Converter (AD 7550)

A simple successive approximation ADC (The MM4357 of National Semiconductor)

This is a low cost, fast (20 us), successive approximations device which provides 8-bit resolution. Its pinout is shown on Fig. 5-41. The control signals are straightfoward and respond to the definitions given above.

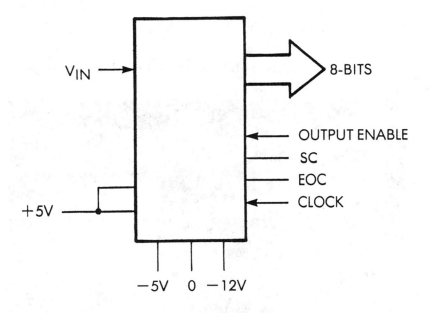

Fig. 5-41: MM4357 Pinout

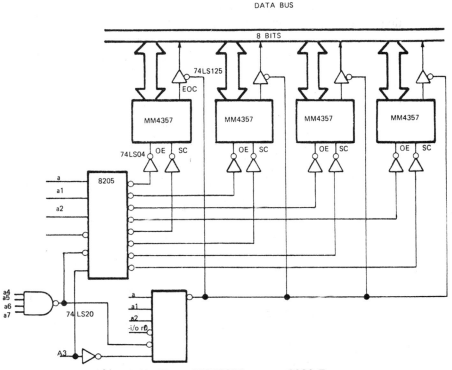

Fig. 5-42: Four MM5357 on an 8080 Bus

Most systems require more than one analog input. To provide these inputs, we can connect a number of A/D's to the bus and select them with a *decoder*. Each input would have its own A/D. Fig. 5-42 shows the schematic for four converters in an 8080 system. The 8205 decoder selects the data read from ports "F8", "F9", "FA", and "FB" hexadecimal. The ports "FC", "FD", "FE", and "FF", when read, trigger the start conversion lines on the corresponding A/D. Input port "F0" is the end-of conversion status word, with the lower four bits corresponding to the end-of- conversion outputs of the four A/D's. This port is polled by the program to control the A/D's.

Hybrids

Multilayer hybrids are frequently used to implement analog-to-digital conversion on a single package. The advantages are increased reliability, fewer interconnects, small size, and better environmental immunity (shock, vibrations). These hybrid devices may provide a combination of high resolution and high speed. As an example, the Beckman 87378 uses successive approximations to provide 12 bits with 25 us typical (± 1/2 LSB linearity). Its internal organization is shown on Fig. 5-43.

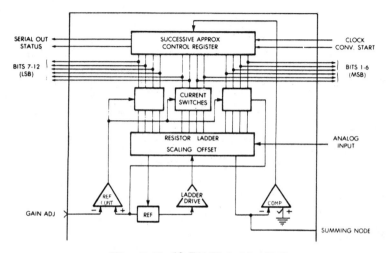

Fig. 5-43: 12-Bit Hybrid ADC

The MP21

The MP21 module contains all necessary components to provide a complete A/D system for a 6800 microprocessor. The block diagram in Fig. 5-44 illustrates the internal functions of the MP21 module. The module has a 16-channel multiplexer, that can be wired to provide eight differential inputs.

The instrumentation amplifier provides the differential-to-single-ended conversion (if required) and can be programmed by external resistors to provide different gains and offsets. If required, a sample-and-hold may be inserted in-between the multiplexer and the instrumentation amplifier. Additional multiplexers can be added at this point also to increase the number of input channels.

The heart of the unit is the 8-bit A/D converter which performs the conversion. The end-of-conversion will interrupt the 6800 through the internal-interrupt control logic on the hybrid module.

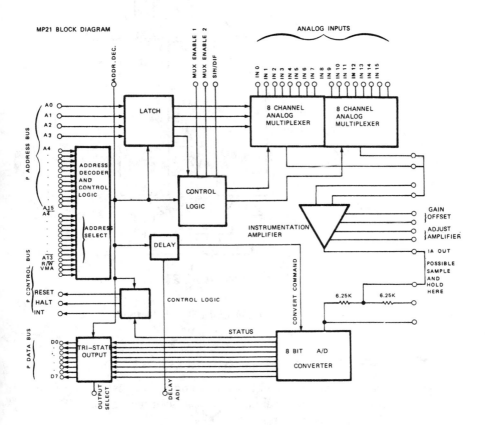

Fig. 5-44: The Internal MP21 Schematic

All necessary interfacing has been done for the user so that the module will be as simple to use as possible. Fig. 5-45 indicates the signals necessary for a typical application utilizing a 650X or 6800 processor.

ADDRESS BUS

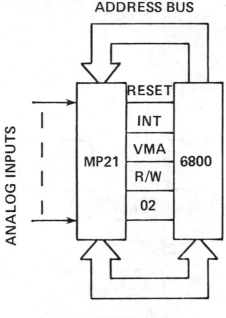

DATA BUS

Fig. 5-45: 6800 and 650X Interface

TECHNIQUES FOR INCREASING THE RESOLUTION

There are two basic techniques for extending the resolution of our A/D conversion without changing the basic accuracy of our A/D converter. These are *scaling* and *offset.*

Scaling

If the input signal is 1.0 volt and the full-scale intput of the A/D is +10.0 volts, we should increase the gain of the amplifiers before the A/D converter, so as to take advantage of the full-scale resolution of the A/D. By increasing the gain by a known amount, we can measure smaller signals more accurately. If the input were 20.0 volts, we could decrease the gain of the input amplifier in order to attenuate the input signal. This will allow us to measure larger voltages than could otherwise normally be measured. By these examples, the need for scaling becomes evident. *We scale the input to obtain maximum information upon conversion from our A/D converter.*

Offset

By connecting the output of a separate D/A to the offset input before our amplifier, we could automatically correct for offset errors, or we could offset a voltage to increase the accuracy further. If the input is 10.0 volts and we are interested in small changes around this value, we can offset the input by an equal and opposite amount. The output of the offset D/A is then -10.0 volts. Adding the two together, we get some small value which depends upon the difference between the offset D/A and our input voltage. Now, we increase the gain of the input amplifier so that any difference between the input 10.0 volts and the offset 10.0 volts can be measured with the full accuracy of the A/D converter.

Summary of Enhanced Resolution Techniques

By these methods, an 8-bit resolution A/D can be enhanced to provide many more bits of magnitude information in a coded form. The form of our information for this example is listed in Fig. 5-46.

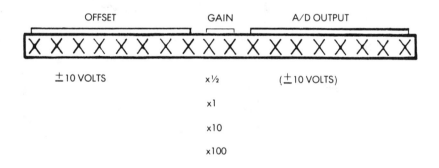

Fig. 5-46: Scaling, Offset A/D Data Format

Of course, the accuracy of the amplifier and offset D/A must be sufficient not to introduce errors of their own in the measurement process.

INTERFACING THE D/A

The D/A converter requires a parallel digital word that will remain stable as long as the analog output is needed. This is easily accomplished for eight or fewer bits, since most microcomputers have output latches eight bits wide. Fig. 5-47 shows such an interface. In the case where the D/A has more than eight bits of resolution, special techniques may be required for interfacing.

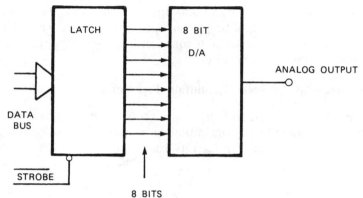

Fig. 5-47: Parallel Output D/A Interface

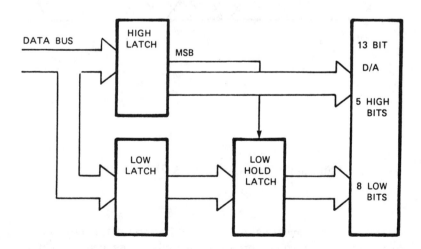

Fig. 5-48: Adding the Extra Latch

For example, take the case of interfacing a 12-bit D/A converter. If we use two separate 8-bit latches, using 8 bits from the first, and 4 bits from the second, there is a problem. When the first latch is loaded, the D/A converter immediately begins converting to the new value presented. However, some microseconds later, we change the second latch, so as to complete the needed bits for the D/A. The effect causes a *glitch* on the D/A output because of the input change. All input bits to a D/A converter must be changed at the same time in order to prevent output glitches. Fig. 5-48 indicates how an extra latch is added to the low-order latch path, in order to prevent the low bits from changing until the bits on the high latch change. The low byte is sent first, and the high byte is sent second, with the most-significant bit equal to "1". When the temporary holding low latch is strobed by the "1" from the high latch, the low-order bits will pass through to the converter, delayed by the delay of the latch. If this delay is also too severe, a fourth latch may be used in the high-bit path to equalize delays.

The new D/A converters *include an on-chip latch* for ease in interfacing.

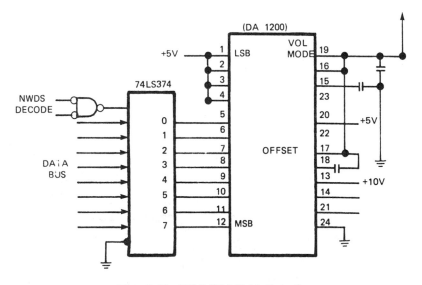

Fig. 5-49: SC/MP/ D/A Interface

Example of D/A Interfacing

Fig. 5-49 is the schematic for a D/A interface to the SC/MP microprocessor. The 74LS374 octal latch is used to hold the information while the D/A performs the conversion. Even though this converter has 12 bits of resolution, only 8 are used in this example. The *unused inputs* are tied to +5V. *Unused inputs* may be tied to either +5, or 0.0V depending on the binary coding scheme used.

DATA ACQUISITION SYSTEMS

Data acquisition refers to the collection of data from a number of analog sources simultaneously. Input transducers provide a raw signal which must then be conditioned, and finally measured in digital form. The flow-chart for a typical data acquisition loop is shown in Fig. 5-50.

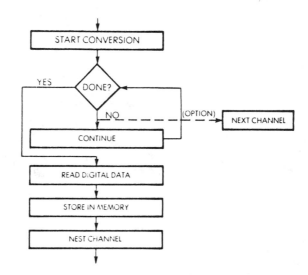

Fig. 5-50: Typical Data Acquistion Loop

- Various sensors will provide data and different formats at different speeds.
- Fast signals must be stored.
- In view of the high cost of hardware elements, and of communication lines, multiple units should share communication lines or expensive hardware, requiring multiplexing.
- Additionally, signal conditioning and processing may be necessary (filtering, etc.).

Using multiplexers

A *multiplexer* is a device which will accept n input signals and gate out only one of them in function of a selection code. A multiplexer will be used to share hardware among several input signals. The multiplexer may be placed before or after the S/H (assuming a sample-and-hold circuit is used).

The most economical case corresponds to the placement of the multiplexer before the S/H as shown on Fig. 5-51. A single S/H and a single A/D are then used for all input signals.

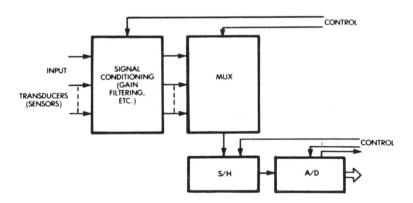

Fig. 5-51: Using a Multiplexer for Data Acquisition

Unfortunately, in high-speed system, or in systems where all data must be sampled simultaneously (this often corresponds to the case where a one-shot physical phenomenon occurs and where information must be frozen at a given time), a separate sample-and-hold must be used for every input line. The multiplexing of these lines can then be either sequential or direct access. If all lines must be converted, it will

307

be sequential. If only selected lines must be converted into digital format, a direct selection mechanism will be used. The corresponding organization is shown on Fig. 5-52. This requires a group of S/H's to avoid errors while waiting for the conversion to occur.

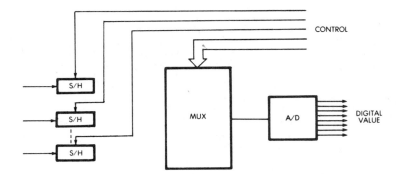

Fig. 5-52: Using Multiple S/H for Speed

An 8-to-1 Multiplexer

The internal organization of an 8-to-1 multiplexer is shown on Fig. 5-53. In response to the code "000" on the input, (on S1, S1, S2), it can be verified that the data input D0 will be selected on the output line whenever the control signal will be applied.

The use of such an 8-to-1 multiplexer in a successive-approximations converter is shown on Fig. 5-54. Similarly, assuming the use of a sample-and-hold and a monolithic ADC, the resulting organization is shown on Fig. 5-55. The microprocessor is responsible for generating a combination of signals S0, S1 and S2 which will select the appropriate input. Typically, the signals are generated on the address bus.

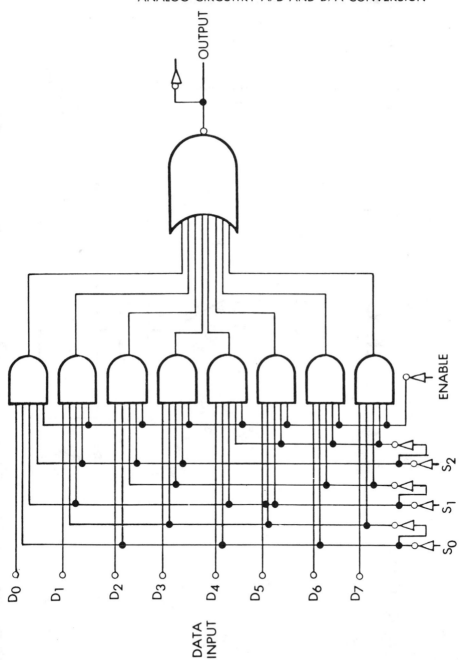

Fig. 5-53: 8 Line Multiplexer

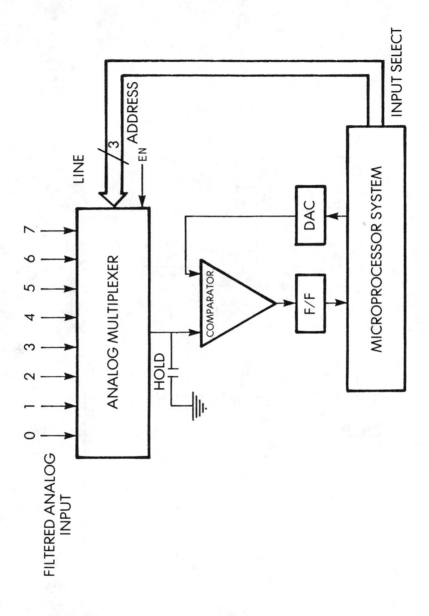

Fig. 5-54: Analog Input Multiplexing

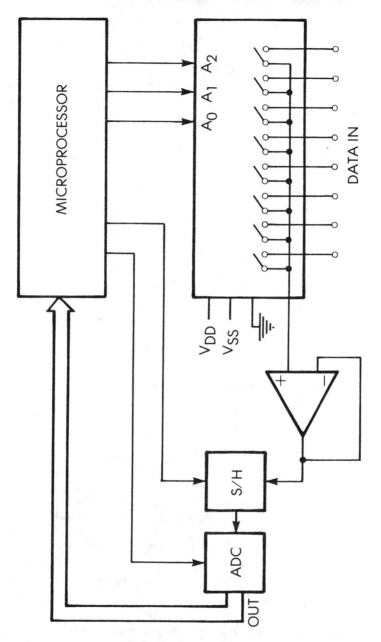

Fig. 5-55: 8 or 16 Bit Multiplexer in Data Acquisition system

A 16-channel multiplexer

Similarly, using a monolithic 16-channel multiplexer, one of 16 inputs may be selected by a combination of 4 input signals derived from A0, A1, A2, A3 on the address bus. The structure of the multiplexer is shown on Fig. 5-56.

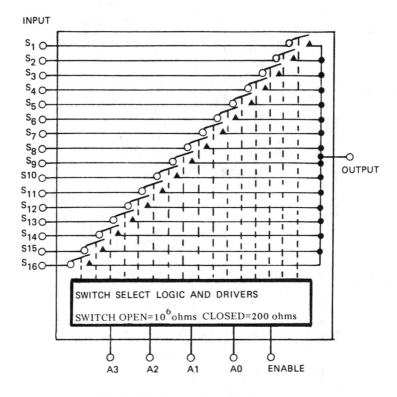

Fig. 5-56: An Analog Multiplexer

Whenever all 16 lines must be sampled sequentially, a hardware counter may be used to reduce the error overhead of the program. The resulting organization is shown on Fig. 5-57, and the resulting switching is shown on Fig. 5-58.

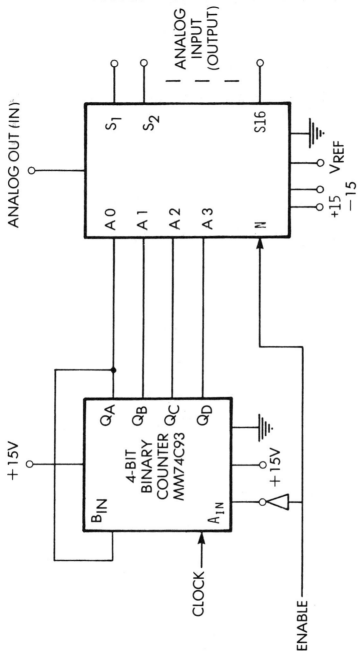

Fig. 5-57: 16 Channel Sequential Multiplexer

ENABLE	MUX SEQUENCE RATE	MUX INPUTS A0	A1	A2	A3	DG506 SWITCH STATES (– DENOTES OFF) S1	S2	S3	S4	S5	S6	S7	S8	S9	S10	S11	S12	S13	S14	S15	S16
0	0	x	x	x	x	–	–	–	–	–	–	–	–	–	–	–	–	–	–	–	–
1	0	0	0	0	0	–	–	–	–	–	–	–	–	–	–	–	–	–	–	–	–
1	1 PULSE	1	0	0	0	ON	–	–	–	–	–	–	–	–	–	–	–	–	–	–	–
1	2 PULSES	0	1	0	0	–	ON	–	–	–	–	–	–	–	–	–	–	–	–	–	–
1	3 PULSES	1	1	0	0	–	–	ON	–	–	–	–	–	–	–	–	–	–	–	–	–
1	4 PULSES	0	0	1	0	–	–	–	ON	–	–	–	–	–	–	–	–	–	–	–	–
1	5 PULSES	1	0	1	0	–	–	–	–	ON	–	–	–	–	–	–	–	–	–	–	–
1	6 PULSES	0	1	1	0	–	–	–	–	–	ON	–	–	–	–	–	–	–	–	–	–
1	7 PULSES	1	1	1	0	–	–	–	–	–	–	ON	–	–	–	–	–	–	–	–	–
1	8 PULSES	0	0	0	1	–	–	–	–	–	–	–	ON	–	–	–	–	–	–	–	–
1	9 PULSES	1	0	0	1	–	–	–	–	–	–	–	–	ON	–	–	–	–	–	–	–
1	10 PULSES	0	1	0	1	–	–	–	–	–	–	–	–	–	ON	–	–	–	–	–	–
1	11 PULSES	1	1	0	1	–	–	–	–	–	–	–	–	–	–	ON	–	–	–	–	–
1	12 PULSES	0	0	1	1	–	–	–	–	–	–	–	–	–	–	–	ON	–	–	–	–
1	13 PULSES	1	0	1	1	–	–	–	–	–	–	–	–	–	–	–	–	ON	–	–	–
1	14 PULSES	0	1	1	1	–	–	–	–	–	–	–	–	–	–	–	–	–	ON	–	–
1	15 PULSES	1	1	1	1	–	–	–	–	–	–	–	–	–	–	–	–	–	–	ON	–
1	16 PULSES	0	0	0	0	–	–	–	–	–	–	–	–	–	–	–	–	–	–	–	ON

Fig. 5-58: Sequential Mux Truth-Table

HYBRID DATA ACQUISITION SYSTEMS

A complete 8- or 16-channel data acquisition system may be implemented on a DIP using hybrid methods. Such packages are available from a variety of vendors and typically provide 8 to 12 bits of precision or more within a very small volume.

As an example, the Micronetworks 8 bit DAC uses a 32-pin DIP and is shown on Fig. 5-59.

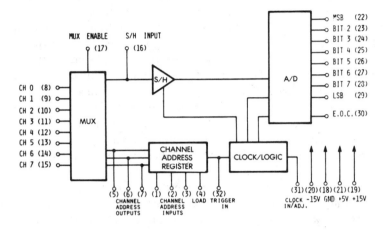

Fig. 5-59: Micronetworks 8-Bit 8-Channel DAS on a DIP

Data Translation and other companies also provide a variety of hybrid packages for most existing microprocessors and for most combinations of precision and speed required.

Programmed acquisition

It has been shown that, for any given technique, hardware may be used to implement the conversion, or else a combination of hardware and software. Additionally, hardware may be eliminated by multiplexing.

The availability of a microprocessor can be used to advantage by providing in software a number of functions such as: automatic calibration, data compression, data filtering, weighing, averaging, historical records, reasonableness testing, varying the internal precision,

315

providing fail soft through tables of values, and finally providing ease of modification and diagnostics.

THE SOFTWARE INTERFACE

In most interfacing situations, the required interfacing technique may be implemented by hardware, by software, or by a combination of both. In almost every case, part is implemented in hardware, and part is implemented in software. The usual trade-off is that a software implementation reduces the component count, but also slows down the system operation. As technology progresses, it becomes possible to implement more and more functions on a single chip at low cost. Common software algorithms can therefore be transferred onto the interface chip. This is how complex interfacing chips now incorporate not just the hardware resources required by the interface, but also the hardware version of the algorithm previously implemented by program. An example in point is the successive approximation analog-to-digital converter, or else the floppy disk controller. As technology progresses, more and more programs will become implemented in silicon.

However, it is important to stress here some of the important software techniques which should be used in virtually every control system implemented with microprocessors. These techniques are all necessary and useful. They were implemented in the past on large systems using mini-computers or large computers. They can be implemented now at minimal cost with a microprocessor, and every designer should at least be aware of them. They will be reviewed here as they form an essential part of the overall design, and should be considered part of the interface between the external world and the control program itself.

Programmed soft-fail

Soft-fail refers to the graceful degradation of a system when some of its components fail. Ideally, a system should keep operating for as long as possible, losing only an amount of performance proportional to the failure which has occurred. It should not be totally disabled whenever a limited malfunction occurs.

Four main types of failures can be distinguished: a *sensor* failure, a *control device* failure, a *power* failure, and a *system* failure. They will be reviewed now.

316

Sensor failure

Each type of failure may be either temporary or permanent. Let us examine these two cases:

Temporary

A temporary sensor failure will be detected by the *reasonableness test*.

Reasonableness testing refers to the use of a *bracket* to determine whether a given input is reasonable. For example, whenever measuring the temperature of liquid water, a temperature between 0 and 100° C would normally be deemed "reasonable". When measuring the speed of traffic in the city, a speed between 0 and 60 mph would be reasonable.

Whenever "unreasonable" data is received it is automatically rejected and will not cause an erroneous reaction from the system.

For example, assuming that a washing machine is equipped with a microprocessor control system, after telling the machine that the clothes to be washed are made of cotton, the machine will automatically reject some washing modes as they might damage the clothes. It would deem them as unreasonable.

Similarly, using a microwave oven, a 20-kilo chicken will be automatically rejected as "unreasonable".

These cases normally correspond to an operator error or else a sensor error. The essential advantage of this method is to filter out noise on the input line as well as reject any values that might otherwise throw off the operation of the system.

The operation of a reasonableness testing bracket varying with time is shown on Fig. 5-60. During the time period T0 to T1, the bracket L0 to H0 is used. During the next time period (time greater than T1), the bracket L1 to H1 is used.

The dashed line on the illustration shows the average value of the measurements during the interval and will provide a backup value in case all input data should become unavailable.

In summary, any temporary sensor failure will be detected by testing its value against the reasonableness brackets which have been predevined. Whenever the value exceeds these brackets it is rejected, and a diagnostic may be generated.

Permanent

A permanent failure of the detector is detected by the reasonableness test. It may be defined as *permanent* whenever the same sensor

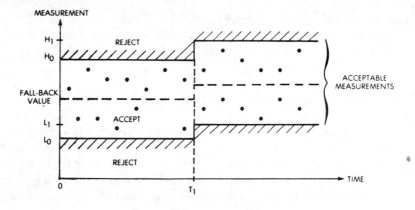

MICROPROCESSOR ACCEPTS ONLY L≤MEASURE≤H AND SIGNALS
REJECTED MEASUREMENTS

Fig. 5-60: "Reasonableness" Testing

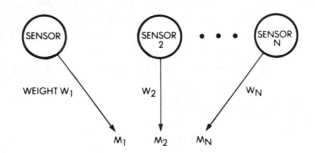

$$\text{WEIGHTED MEASUREMENT} = \frac{W_1 . M_1 + W_2 . M_2 + \ldots + W_N M_N}{W_1 + W_2 + \ldots + W_N}$$

AUTOMATIC DISCONNECT $W_1 = 0$ IF SENSOR I IS FOUND "UNREASONABLE"
OR NON-OPERATIVE

Fig. 5-61: Optimization Through Sensor Weighting

fails n/times during a given time interval. At this point, the sensor should be ignored. It can be actually *disconnected by software* by weighing it to "0", using the sensor weighting technique:

The sensor weighting technique

The sensor weighting technique is illustrated by the diagram of Fig. 5-60. A weight W_i is associated to each sensor. The weighted measurement is defined as

$$M_w = \frac{W_1M_1 + W_2M_2 + \ldots + W_iM_i + \ldots + W_nM_n}{W_1 + W_2 + \ldots + W_i + \ldots + W_n}$$

Usually, the sum of the W's is set equal to 1.

For example, if three sensors are used to measure the temperature of a room, initially all three may have the weight of .333. However, after a time, it may be found that one of the sensors is positioned at the wrong location and that its indications should not be taken in as much consideration as the indications of the other two. At this point, its weight might be reduced to .1, while the weights of the other two are boosted to .45 each.

In order to disconnect by software a sensor which has been found to be "unreasonable", its weight will simply be set to the value "0". Referring to the equation above, it can be seen that the value provided by the sensor will be ignored as long as its weight is 0. If at some time in the future it is found to become reasonable again, it can be reconnected by software by changing its weight to a non-zero value.

Additionally, back-up average values may be used for a while for one of the sensors when it becomes unavailable, if its role was crucial to the operation of the system. Naturally, a diagnostic or an alarm can also be generated.

Control Device Failure

Temporary failure

The only reasonable way to detect the failure of a control device before actual harm is done requires monitoring it. A *status-feedback* is necessary. In order to detect whether a control device has executed in order, a *tolerance bracket* is usually necessary. For example, if a relay must be closed, a time period is tolerated during which the relay may close.

If a temporary malfunction is detected, the simplest method used is the "retry". The order is simply given again, and again, up to a maximum of n times, until the control device obeys. If after n times it has not obeyed, or if such failure should occur too frequently in a given time period, it is deemed to be a *permanent* failure. This method can be somewhat compared to banging a machine after a coin has been inserted and it doesn't work. Usually this simple retry method will provide the desired result.

Permanent failure

In the case of control devices, and because of their high cost, alternate devices are not frequently available. If one is available, it should then be activated. If none is available, a back-up control strategy may be implemented which puts the system in a mode where it keeps operating at a reduced performance level. At the same time, a diagnostic or an alarm should be generated.

Power failure

A bootstrap program may be used to start the system in a *table-driven* scheduling mode. In this mode, the list of actions to be performed by the system is stored in a table. The system will revert to this mode of operation whenever a power failure will have occurred in order to provide immediate resumption of activities in a given mode. It will be able to switch to another mode of activity once enough data will have been accumulated to take reasonable action.

Naturally, backup batteries may be used to provide immunity from power failures for a limited period of time.

System failure

A system failure refers to a failure of the microprocessor system itself, or its subsystems. At this point, an alternate microprocessor or another backup device may take over.

Summary

The possible layers of software protection are illustrated on Fig. 5-62. The sensors and control devices appear on the left of the illustration. Both the measurements from the sensors and the orders to the control devices are tested for reasonableness. Additionally, the information from sensors is weighted, and may also be averaged before being passed as a parameter to the control algorithm. In the case of the control devices, status is monitored for possible malfunctions.

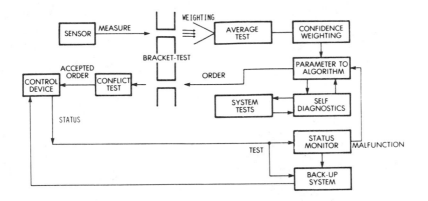

Fig. 5-62: Multi-Level Protection

The software protection discipline

The above techniques should be used in any control system to provide reliable, safe, and efficient operation. By applying them systematically to all inputs and outputs in the system, they will result in improved performance of the overall system, especially in the case where some of the hardware interfaces may malfunction. Software design should be integrated with the overall interfacing design.

SUMMARY

Our microprocessor can now be used to gather information, process it, and output that information in a new form in the analog world through the use of these conversion products. The D/A or digital-to-analog converter, providing the microcomputer with the means for generating the analog signals, and the A/D or analog-to-digital converter, providing the means for measuring the analog signals, form the basis of any conversion system. The use of sample-and-hold, multiplexers, and scaling/offset techniques, allow us to quantify any signal, process it, and pass it back in almost any form we require. A detailed case study of an analog board design is presented at the end of Chapter 6.

6

BUS STANDARDS
AND TECHNIQUES

INTRODUCTION

Connecting more than one module requires a communication path. Each module must be able to talk and listen to its neighbors. The components on a module need to communicate with one another. The problem of component interconnection has been addressed in Chapters 2 and 3. The techniques of module-to-module, and system-to-system communication will be covered in this chapter on *busing techniques*.

Two bus types will be distinguished: parallel buses and bit-serial buses. They are:

— parallel
  — microprocessor S100 bus
  — microprocessor 6800 bus
  — IEEE-488 general interface bus
  — IEEE-583 CAMAC interface system
— serial
  — EIA-RS232C asynchronous communications
  — EIA-RS422&423 asynchronous and synchronous communications
  — ASCII information standard
  — synchronous communication.

Parallel buses are useful for high-speed module-to-module communication in the case of microprocessor buses, and for system-to-system communication in the case of IEEE-488. CAMAC is the only exception—the CAMAC standard covers all communications from the component level on up.

Serial buses require fewer lines and are used to connect communications terminals to the computer system. Terminals, such as CRTs (cathode-ray-tube terminals), teleprinters, teletypewriters, and remote data collection devices, all rely on some form of bit-serial communication.

Serial standards cover the bit rates, electrical characteristics, and data format. There are basically two types of standards: asynchronous and synchronous. The asynchronous standard is used for data rates of less than 20,000 bits-per-second, and the synchronous standard is used for data rates of more than 10,000 bits-per-second. In the overlapping region, both types may be used.

An example of an S100 bus interface to an inexpensive analog-to-digital converter will be presented at the end of this chapter.

PARALLEL BUSES

Parallel buses transfer all bits of information across separate wires, at the same time. Lines must be provided for the data bus, lines for the address bus, and lines for the control bus. Each set of lines contains information on the current cycle of operation.

A typical microprocessor system will need 8 data, 16 address and 5 to 12 control lines.

— The 8 data lines are for all transfers in and out of the processor.
— The 16 address lines determine what memory location or I/O port the transfer is for.
— The 5 basic control lines will be read or write cycle line, a valid address present line, an interrupt line, a DMA request line, and a wait line.

In this basic system, the control bus will have the timing shown in Fig. 6-1.

These 29 signals are all that are needed for most simple parallel buses. Timing will vary, and separate read and write lines may be used, but all buses function in a similar fashion.

Future systems will require at least 16 data lines and perhaps as many as 24 address lines. Also, many additional control lines are desirable for flexible input-output management.

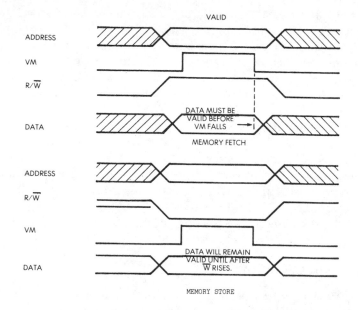

Fig. 6-1: Timing on the Control Bus

THE S100 BUS

The "hobby-computer" market was revealed at the Atlantic City conference in August 1976. The impact of one company, however, was greater than most at the time. This was MITS, the producers of the Altair microcomputers. The bus they used in their 8080-based system had 100 lines. Other manufacturers (in particular IMSAI) realized that making their memories and peripherals compatible would help them sell in this new market. Now there are over 600 different types of boards and systems available for this bus from over 100 manufacturers.

The bus signals and definitions are presented in Figure 6-2.

Some problems of this bus are: clock lines adjacent to control signals, pin layout problems, and power supply distribution.

The Φ1, Φ2, and 2MHz clock signals are near nine other control signals. All of these clock pulses have sharp rise and fall times and occur continuously. Because of this, these clock signals are most easily coupled to the other lines, unless unusual shielding measures are taken. Because of the presence of the 2MHz clock, the bus must be designed for 4MHz noise immunity when no other signal occurs at that rate.

What if a board is unplugged with the power on? The possibility of the -18 volts touching the $+8$ volts, due to misalignment, is great. If this happens...well, let us hope it doesn't. At best, only the regulators may blow out; at worst, every chip tied to $+5$ volts may be damaged.

Ideally, boards should be protected against being unplugged or reversed with power on. A symmetric arrangement of power pins that will shut down all power if boards are inserted improperly is one good idea, and the careful distribution of voltages in-between grounded pins is another good idea. Variations in supply voltage from module to module reduce noise immunity and may cause difficulties. The solution is to use high-quality regulators costing more or matching those used (an impossible job). There is no best way to solve this problem—and a central power distribution scheme has its own problems.

The interrupt lines are reserved for interrupt requests to an interrupt-controller board on the bus. No standard way of using these has been established, as Z-80s, 6500s, (and even 6800s) can also be used (and are used) in S100 systems.

PIN NUMBER	SYMBOL	NAME	FUNCTION
1	+8V	+8 Volts	Unregulated voltage on bus, supplied to PC boards and regulated to 5V.
2	+18V	+18 Volts	Positive pre-regulated voltage.
3	XRDY	EXTERNAL READY	External ready input to CPU Board's ready circuitry.
4	VI0	Vectored Interrupt Line 0	
5	VI1	Vectored Interrupt Line 1	
6	VI2	Vectored Interrupt Line 2	

Fig. 6-2: Altair Bus

PIN NUMBER	SYMBOL	NAME	FUNCTION
7	VI3	Vectored Interrupt Line 3	
8	VI4	Vectored Interrupt Line 4	
9	VI5	Vectored Interrupt Line 5	
10	VI6	Vectored Interrupt Line 6	
11	VI7	Vectored Interrupt Line 7	
12	*XRDY2 *New bus signal for 8800b.	EXTERNAL READY 2	A second external ready line similar to XRDY.
13 to 17	TO BE DEFINED		
18	STAT DSB	STATUS DISABLE	Allows the buffers for the 8 status lines to be tri-stated.
19	C/C DSB	COMMAND/CONTROL DISABLE	Allows the buffers for the 6 output command/control lines to be tri-stated.
20	UNPROT	UNPROTECT	Input to the memory protect flip-flop on a given memory board.
21	SS	SINGLE STEP	Indicates that the machine is in the process of performing a single step (i.e., that SS flip-flop on D/C is set).
22	ADD DSB	ADDRESS DISABLE	Allows the buffers for the 16 address lines to be tri-stated.
23	DO DSB	DATA OUT DISABLE	Allows the buffers for the 8 data output lines to be tri-stated.

Fig. 6-2 Continued: Altair Bus

PIN NUMBER	SYMBOL	NAME	FUNCTION
24	ϕ 2	PHASE 2 CLOCK	
25	ϕ 1	PHASE 1 CLOCK	
26	PHLDA	HOLD ACKNOWLEDGE	Processor command/control output signal that appears in response to the HOLD signal; indicates that the data and address bus will go to the high impedance state and processor will enter HOLD state after completion of the current machine cycle.
27	PWAIT	WAIT	Processor command/control signal that appears in response to the READY signal going low; indicates processor will enter a series of .5 microsecond WAIT states until READY again goes high.
28	PINTE	INTERRUPT ENABLE	Processor command/control output signal; indicates interrupts are enabled, as determined by the contents of the CPU internal interrupt flip-flop. When the flip-flop is set (Enable Interrupt instruction), interrupts are accepted by the CPU; when it is reset (Disable Interrupt instruction), interrupts are inhibited.
29	A5	Address Line 5	
30	A4	Address Line 4	

Fig. 6-2 Continued: Altair Bus

PIN NUMBER	SYMBOL	NAME	FUNCTION
31	A3	Address Line 3	
32	A15	Address Line 15	(MSB)
33	A12	Address Line 12	
34	A9	Address Line 9	
35	DO1	Data Out Line 1	
36	DO0	Data Out Line 0	(LSB)
37	A10	Address Line 10	
38	DO4	Data Out Line 4	
39	DO5	Data Out Line 5	
40	DO6	Data Out Line 6	
41	DI2	Data In LIne 2	
42	DI3	Data In Line 3	
43	D17	Data In Line 7	(MSB)
44	SM1	MACHINE CYCLE 1	Status output signal that indicates that the processor is in the fetch cycle for the first byte of an instruction.
45	SOUT	OUTPUT	Status output signal that indicates the address bus contains the address of an output device and the data bus will contain the output data when PWR is active.
46	SINP	INPUT	Status output signal that indicates the address bus contains the address of an input device and the input data should be placed on the data bus when PDBIN is active.

Fig. 6-2 Continued: Altair Bus

328

PIN NUMBER	SYMBOL	NAME	FUNCTION
47	SMEMR	MEMORY READ	Status output signal that indicates the data bus will be used to read memory data.
48	SHLTA	HALT	Status output signal that acknowledges a HALT instruction.
49	CLOCK	CLOCK	Inverted output of the 02 CLOCK′
50	GND	GROUND	
51	+8V	+8 Volts	Unregulated input to 5 volt regulators.
52	-18V	-18 Volts	Negative pre-regulated voltage.
53	SSWI	SENSE SWITCH INPUT	Indicates that an input data transfer from the sense switches is to take place. This signal is used by the Display/ Control logic to:
		b) Enable the Display/ Control Board driver's Data Input (FDI0-FDI7);	a) Enable sense switch drivers; c) Disable the CPU Board Data Input Drivers (DI0-DI7).
54	EXT CLR	EXTERNAL CLEAR	Clear signal for I/O devices (front-panel switch closure to ground).
55	*RTC	REAL-TIME CLOCK	60HZ signal is used as timing reference by the Real-Time Clock/ Vectored Interrupt Board.
56	*STSTB	STATUS STROBE	Output strobe signal supplied by the 8224

Fig. 6-2 Continued: Altair Bus

329

PIN NUMBER	SYMBOL	NAME	FUNCTION
			clock generator. Primary purpose is to strobe the 8212 status latch so that status is set up as soon in the machine cycle as possible. This signal is also used by Display/Control logic.
57	*DIGI	DATA INPUT GATE 1	Output signal from the Display/Control logic that determines which set of Data Input Drivers have control of the CPU board's bidirectional data bus. If DIGI is HIGH, the CPU drivers have control; if it is LOW, the Display/Control logic drivers have control.
58	*FRDY	FRONT PANEL READY	Output signal from D/C logic that allows the front panel to control the READY lines to the CPU.
59 to 67	TO BE DEFINED		
68	MWRITE	MEMORY WRITE	Indicates that the data present on the Data Out Bus is to be written into the memory location currently on the address bus.
69	PS	PROTECT STATUS	Indicates the status of the memory protect flip-flop on the memory board currently addressed.

Fig. 6-2 Continued: Altair Bus

PIN NUMBER	SYMBOL	NAME	FUNCTION
70	PROT	PROTECT	Input to the memory protect flip-flop on the board currently addressed.
71	RUN	RUN	Indicates that the 64 /RUN flip-flop is Reset; i.e., machine is in RUN mode.
72	PRDY	PROCESSOR READY	Memory and I/O input to the CPU Board wait circuitry.
73	PINT	INTERRUPT REQUEST	The processor recognizes an interrupt request on this line at the end of the current instruction or while halted. If the processor is in the HOLD state or the Interrupt Enable flip-flop is reset, it will not honor the request.
74	PHOLD	HOLD	Processor command/control input signal that requests the processor enter the HOLD state; allows an external device to gain control of address and data buses as soon as the processor has completed its uses of these buses for the current machine cycle.
75	PRESET	RESET	Processor command/

Fig. 6-2 Continued: Altair Bus

PIN NUMBER	SYMBOL	NAME	FUNCTION
			control input; while activated, the content of the program counter is cleared and the instruction register is set to 0.
76	PSYNC	SYNC	Processor command/ control output; provides a signal to indicate the beginning of each machine cycle.
77	PWR	WRITE	Processor command/ control output; used for memory write or I/O output control. Data on the data bus is stable while the PWR is active.
78	PDBIN	DATA BUS IN	Processor command/ control output; indicates to external circuits that the data bus is in the input mode.
79	A0	Address Line 0	(LSB)
80	A1	Address Line 1	
81	A2	Address Line 2	
82	A6	Address Line 6	
83	A7	Address Line 7	
84	A8	Address Line 8	
85	A13	Address Line 13	
86	A14	Address Line 14	
87	A11	Address Line 11	
88	DO2	Data Out Line 2	

Fig. 6-2 Continued: Altair Bus

PIN NUMBER	SYMBOL	NAME	FUNCTION
89	DO3	Data Out Line 3	
90	DO7	Data Out Line 7	
91	DI4	Data In Line 4	
92	DI5	Data In Line 5	
93	DI6	Data In Line 6	
94	DI1	Data In Line 1	
95	DI0	Data In Line 0	(LSB)
96	SINTA	INTERRUPT ACKNOWLEDGE	Status output signal; acknowledges signal for INTERRUPT request.
97	SWO	WRITE OUT	Status output signal; indicates that the operation in the current machine cycle will be a WRITE memory or output function.
98	SSTACK	STACK	Status output signal; indicates that the address bus holds the pushdown stack address from the Stack Pointer.
99	POC	POWER-ON CLEAR	
100	GND	GROUND	

Fig. 6-2 Continued: Altair Bus

The other host of signals are control signals. The S100 bus has far more than anyone will ever need of these, and suffers from being designed before a system-controller chip was made available for the 8080. Because of this, many of the signals are due to the original Intel problem with pin limitations, as discussed in Chapter 2. Obviously, a new S100 bus would be needed, with these control signals reduced to a manageable number. This will probably never happen. *A standard can always be improved; but it won't be—this is why it is a standard!*

333

The S100 bus is a practical bus and will perform well in most applications. The problems mentioned here should be avoided when new bussing schemes are being considered in the next few years for future systems.

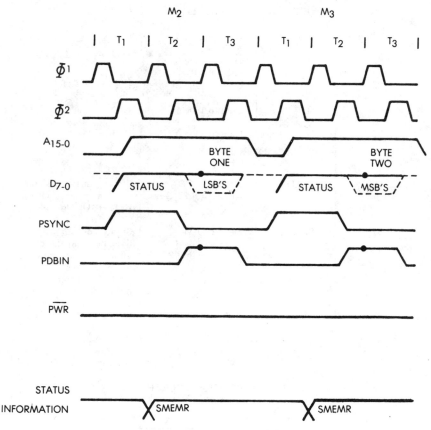

Fig. 6-3: Memory Read Cycle on S100 Bus

The bus provides: 8 data in, 8 data out, 16 address, 3 power-supply, 8 interrupt and 39 control lines. Other pins are unused or reserved for future use.

The *data bus* has been changed from the normal bidirectional 8080 bus to two unidirectional data buses. One is for data input to the processor and one for data output from the processor. In this system, there is no real advantage to this, as many peripherals actually hardwire the two buses together. There is also no real disadvantage, except

334

the need for eight more pins.

The *address bus* is the typical buffered 16 address lines, which are found in every standard microprocessor system.

The *power supplies* are most interesting. There are two philosophies for power distribution: regulate at a control location and distribute power, or regulate locally on each module. Altair chose the latter. It is a good choice because power distribution to the modules is simplified, and noise cross-coupling between the modules is reduced. It is a more expensive choice in that the regulators cost much more than a single good regulator would cost, and it is a marginal choice due to the variations in regulated voltages between modules.

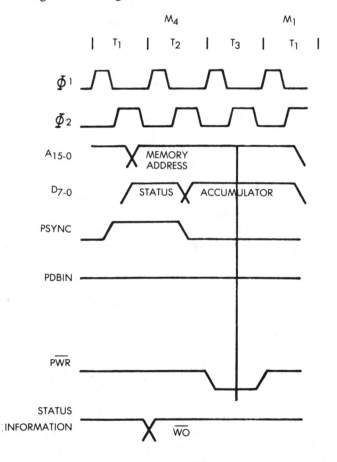

Fig. 6-4: Memory Write Cycle on S100 Bus

The design of an S100-bus-compatible peripheral is discussed in the example at the end of this chapter. Timing diagrams for memory-fetch and store cycles are presented in Fig. 6-3 and 6-4. They illustrate the basic timing of the 8080 system, and the basic *signals* used for these transfers. Note how the most important signals are $\overline{\text{PWR}}$ and PDBIN. These two signals control the direction of the data on the buses: fetching or storing. In conjunction with the status information, all memory transfers can be identified by these few lines.

A 6800 SYSTEM BUS

Described here is the Altair-680B 6800-system bus. This bus was well thought-out, in comparison with the problems of the S100 bus.

The system has eight bidirectional lines for data, sixteen unidirectional lines for address, and nine control lines.

The data and address buses are quite the same as any other system's buses. The control lines contain the minimum number of useful lines needed. They are: clock Φ2, reset, halt, R/$\overline{\text{W}}$, VMA, DBE, R/$\overline{\text{W}}$-P, BA, and TSC. These are summarized in Fig. 6-5. Not described in the Table are the IRQ and NMI interrupt-request lines. They appear also on the control bus.

This bus provides clean, concise signals for fetching and storing information. It is an example of a well thought out design. Unfortunately, the Φ1, and Φ2-drive clock signals are present on this bus for no reason, except presumably to decrease noise-immunity. One well isolated high speed clock is all that most buses can have, without resorting to unusual and expensive shielded backplanes.

IEEE-488-1975

This bus is intended for connecting systems, rather than modules. Such devices as computers, voltmeters, power supplies, and frequency generators and can be equipped with a 488 bus. The 488 bus was a result of three years of discussion in the IEC (International Electrotechnical Commission). In 1974, the IEEE approved the IEC draft, resulting in IEEE-488-1975. Hewlett-Packard was one of the prime influences in the development of this bus, and the handshake technique used is patented by Hewlett-Packard. All producers of a 488-compatible interface must purchase the license to use the bus handshake circuitry. (The bus is sometimes called HPIB or Hewlett-Packard Interface Bus.)

The System Control Bus consists of the following signals:

CLOCK: The system clock is a 500 KHz asymmetrical, two-phase, non-overlapping clock that runs at the Vcc voltage level. Phase one(ϕ1) is used for internal chip operations. All data transfers take place during Phase Two(ϕ2). Therefore,ϕ2 is used throughout the system to enable memory and interfaces such as the Asynchronous Communication Interface Adapter (ACIA).

RESET: This input is used to initialize the system after a power-down condition due to either an initial start-up or power failure. It is also used to reinitialize the MPU at any time after start-up. When a positive edge is detected on the RESET input which is caused by a manual front panel reset, the MPU will begin the restart sequence. Within the restart sequence, the Program Counter is loaded with the contents of the reset vector location (FFFE, FFFF), which contains the starting address of the System Monitor.

HALT: The Halt line is used for external control of program execution. When in the high state (RUN), the MPU will fetch the instruction addressed by the program counter and begin program execution. When the Halt line is low, all of the activity within the MPU will be halted. The Bus Available (BA) signal will then go high and the Read-Write (R/W), Address and Data lines will all be in the high-impedance state. With BA high, the front panel addressing and data deposit functions will be enabled.

R/W: Read/Write controls and indicates the direction of data transfer. When in the high state (READ), data is read into the MPU from memory and peripherals. When in the low state (WRITE), data is written into memory or peripherals. When the processor is halted, R/W will turn to the off (high impedance) state.

VMA: The VMA output indicates to the memory or the peripherals, such as an ACIA, that a stable, valid memory address is on the bus.

Fig. 6-5: System Control Bus

DBE: The DBE input is the three-state control signal for the MPU data bus and will enable the bus drivers of the 6800 when in the high state. Phase 2 is used to drive this input directly. During an MPU read cycle, the data bus drivers are disabled internally, i.e., within the MPU.

R/W-P: Read/Write-Prime is developed by NANDing the Read/Write signal and $\phi2$. The Read/Write-Prime signal assures that data will always be read or written while the data bus in enabled and not during a period of invalid data.

Fig. 6-5 Continued: System Control Bus

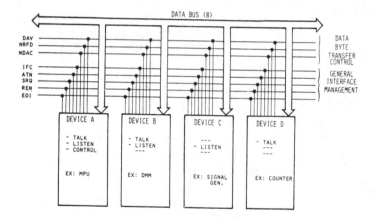

Fig. 6-6: 488 Bus Signals

The basic bus connects to devices that can do one or more of the following:

1. control other units — *controller*
2. take information from the controlling unit — *listener*
3. give information to the controlling unit — *talker*.

The bus consists of eight bidirectional data lines, three byte-transfer control lines, and five general control lines.

The eight data lines will carry: device commands (only 7 bits used), address and data (8 bits).

Since this system *has no address or complete-control buses,* the data bus is used to perform all these functions. The rest of the lines control the function of the data bus and how it is used.

The transfer-control lines are used to implement the "handshaking" required between the device outputting and the device inputting.

The last five lines control the general conditions of the system. These are: Attention, Interface Clear, Service Request, Remote Enable, and End-or-Identify.

Attention, when false, indicates that the data lines contain data from one to eight bits. When true, the data bus contains a seven-bit command or seven-bit address.

Interface Clear puts the system in a known state. It is similar to a system-reset.

Service Request, when set true, flags the controlling unit to indicate a device needs attention.

Remote Enable sets the mode of each device, in conjunction with other codes, to operate remotely or locally.

End-or-Identify is used to flag the controlling unit, as to the end of a data transfer.

The "handshaking" function is used when devices must wait for information to become available. One line says, "How do you do?" The other replies, "Fine, thank you, I have something for you." In return, the reply is: "Please give it to me, I am ready." The dialogue continues with ,"OK, here it is," and ends with, "Thank you, nice meeting you."

In our case, we have three lines: DAV (data valid on data lines), NRFD (not-ready-for-data; true indicates information accepted by listening device), and NDAC (not-data-accepted; true indicates system module ready to accept data). The timing of the handshake appears in **Fig. 6-7.**

Note how all listening devices must accept the transfer of data before the next transfer is initiated. If it appears complex—it is! Use of this standard requires complete knowledge of all the states allowed by the protocol.

Some simple examples are presented in Figs. 6-7 and 6-8.

In the "talk" example, the controller sends the address and command-to-talk to the talker, by using ATN and the data bus. Upon recognizing its address, and the command, the talker will then send information to a listener, via the data bus, using the handshake

339

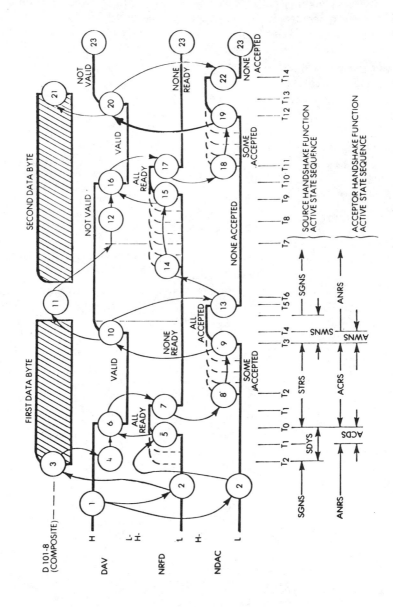

Fig. 6-7: 488 Handshake Timing

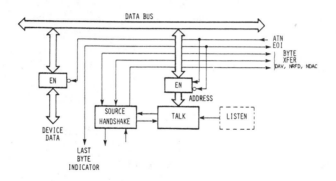

Fig. 6-8: Talker

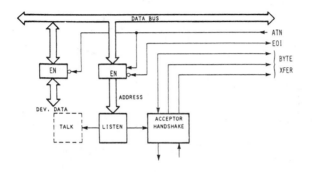

Fig. 6-9: Listener

signals. When the transfer is finished, the EOI line may be used to indicate the end of the block.

The "listen" example works similarly. The controller sends the address via the data bus, using the ATN line as before. In this case, the command sent next is for the device to listen to a talker. The transfer of data, byte by byte, is then begun using the data bus, and handshake signals. The EOI then indicates that the transfer is complete.

In summary, the IEEE-488 bus represents quite an advancement in intelligent data acquisition systems. As more manufacturers produce compatible equipment, the standard will become even more widespread. In fact, the Commodore Business Machines' home microcomputer system is equipped with an IEEE-488 bus interface. This may indicate a new trend in home computing as well as in industry.

The example presented here illustrates how a 6800 system can be interfaced to the 488 bus. The schematic appears in Fig. 6-10, and contains the 6800 CPU, the new 68488 bus interface chip from Motorola, and the bus transceivers required for the IEEE bus.

The chip allows the 6800 to be interfaced easily to the IEEE bus. The unit may be either a talker or listener. Illustrated in Fig. 6-11 is a small 6800 system with GPIB interface. The program in ROM will take data from the RS232C serial channel and put it on the 488 bus when requested. When data appears on the 488 bus, it is output through the ACIA onto the serial channel.

Fig. 6-12 is a subroutine for the listener function to ACIA output. This routine assumes that the talker does not talk faster than the ACIA can output. Further refinements can be added to buffer the data, convert it to ASCII, if it isn't already, add EOI messages, and so on.

By using some more logic, the full controller function may be added to this system.

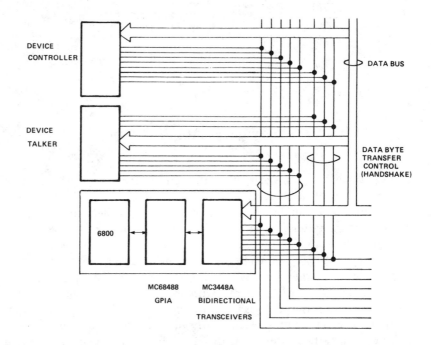

Fig. 6-10: IEEE-488 Bus Block Diagram

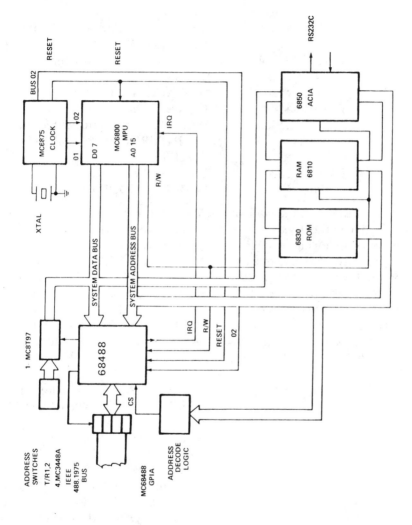

Fig. 6-11: Small GPIB 6800 System

LDAA	#$XX	Load ACIA control to ACC A.
STAA	$5008	Store baud rate, parity and number of characters to ACIA control.
LDAA	$5004	Read the device's address on the ADDRESS SWITCHES.
STAA	$5004	Write the address into the ADDRESS REGISTER.
LDAA	#$00	Load ACC A with zeros.
STAA	$5003	This clears the reset bit.
STAA	$5000	Mask all interrupts (if desired) in the INTERRUPT MASK REGISTER.
STAA	$5002	Select no special features in the ADDRESS MODE REGISTER.

NOTE: At this time the controller will address the device to LISTEN in the following manner: ENABLE ATN and send mla (my listen address) on the D101-8 lines which would be X0100100 ($26). Now DISABLE ATN. A READ of $5002 ADDRESS STATUS REGISTER will show $86 ma (Bit 7), LACS (Bit 2), and

LPAS (Bit 1) will be set HIGH. At this time the device is ready to LISTEN. B1 (Bit 0) of the INTERRUPT STATUS REGISTER will be LOW. B1 will go HIGH to indicate that a data byte is available in the DATA-IN REGISTER at $5007. Reading the DATA-IN REGISTER will reset B1 (Bit 0).

LOOP 1 LDAA	$5000	Load ACC A with contents of INTERRUPT STATUS REGISTER.
TAP		Transfers ACC A contents to CONDITION CODE REGISTER.
BCC	LOOP 1	Loop until carry bit is set. This indicates B1 is set in R0R.
BVS	LOOP 2	Branch to LOOP 1 if overflow is set, indicating END, bit 1, of R0R has set (i.e., controller has sent EOI).

Fig. 6-12: Software Listener Program

```
         LDAA    $5007    Load DATA-IN REGISTER into
                          ACC A. This resets bit B1.
         STAA    $5009    Store the data byte in the ACIA.
         INX              Increment pointer.
         BRA     LOOP 1   Branch back to LOOP 1 and
                          check to see if B1 is set.
LOOP 2   INX              Increment pointer.
         LDAA    $5007    Get the last byte of data from
                          the DATA-IN REGISTER.
         STAA    $5009    Put last byte in the ACIA.
         RTS              End of subroutine; block has
                          been transferred.
```

ADDRESS MAP

Hexadecimal Address	MC68488 Registers (R/$\overline{\text{W}}$)
$5000	Interrupt Status/Interrupt Mask
$5001	Command Status/ −
$5002	Address Status/Address Mode
$5003	Auxiliary Command/Auxiliary Command
$5004	Address Switch/Address
$5005	Serial Poll/Serial Poll
$5006	Command Pass-thru/Parallel Poll
$5007	Data In/Data Out
$5008	ACIA Control
$5009	ACIA Data

Fig. 6-12 Continued: Software Listener Program

CAMAC

The IEEE-583 standard describes what is known as the "Computer-Automated-Measurement-and-Control-Standard" or CAMAC. These also cover CAMAC-related standards.

The CAMAC concept covers all areas of instrument interfacing. There are the rack and card-cage standards for physical dimensions, there are the power-supply standards, and there is the "Dataway" bus standard. In addition, there are standards for the inter-rack bus: the "parallel highway," and serial inter-rack communications: the "serial highway."

345

It was developed for the nuclear industry, and all domains of the CAMAC standard contain rigorous specifications. CAMAC systems are required to be built to quite exacting standards.

Physical Dimensions

Fig. 6-14 illustrates a CAMAC "crate." The crate is the basic system sub-unit. It contains a controller and up to 24 peripheral interfaces. The size of each card, and the connector types, are all specified.

Power Supply

The power supply is a four-voltage type, supplying regulated ± 6 and ± 24 volts. Stability, regulation, and transient suppression are all covered in the standard. Remember that the power supply, while often ignored, is the basic most important unit in any system. Any flaws in the power supply will show up everywhere else in the system. Thus, CAMAC does something no other standard does: it guarantees the user that the power supply will be the least of all problems in the system. Fig. 6-15 illustrates the crate and power supply. (Pictures are courtesy of Lawrence Berkeley Laboratory.)

Dataway

The CAMAC Dataway bus consists of the following lines: three control, five command, five address, twenty-four read, twenty-four write, two timing, and four status. The lines are described in Fig. 6-16.

The three controls are: initialize, inhibit and clear. These signals are used to put all devices on the dataway into a known state.

The five command lines determine the function to be performed. The 32 possible functions are all defined in the standard. Some functions are for read, write, and status transfers. Others are either reserved for future use, or not defined.

The 24 read and write lines form the data bus. If extra address information is required, the data buses may be used to load further address information. 24 bits allow for simultaneous transfer of three 8-bit bytes for efficient operation. Since some CAMAC systems contain microprocessors, these 24 lines could carry the address and data from the microprocessor. Since data transfers may occur as fast as 10^6 per second, this bus has a greater bandwidth than the other buses so far described.

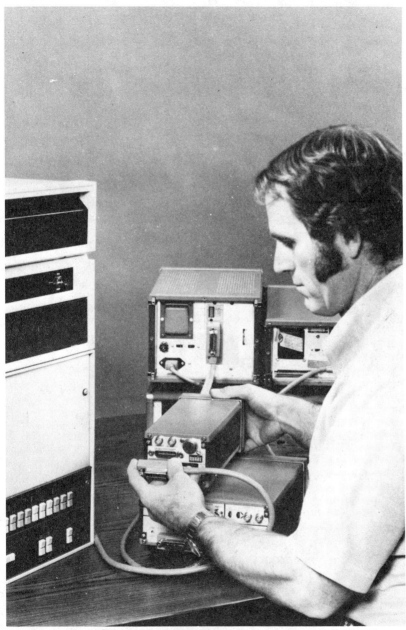

Fig. 6-19: IEEE-488 Instruments (Hewlett-Packard)

Fig. 6-14: CAMAC Crate with Modules

Fig. 6-15: Crate and Power Supply

CAMAC can transfer 24 bits $\times$ 10^6 transfers/second, or 24 million bits/second. This is important in nuclear applications, where large amounts of data must be transferred quickly during each experiment.

The two timing signals provide the information necessary to indicate when data are valid.

The status lines are used to monitor the requests for service to the controller from the peripheral Dataway interfaces. There can be 24 separate requests in a single crate.

In summary, the CAMAC standard truly implements a *concept.* It covers all aspects of the communication problem. It includes standards for data formatting and crate-to-crate communications, as well as software conventions.

A list of Dataway Signals Available at Each of the Normal Stations 1 through 24 of a 25-Station CMAC Crate		
Title	Designation	Use in Module
Common Control Signals		
Initialize	Z	Sets registers or control functions in a module to an initial state, particularly when power turned on.
Inhibit	I	Disables features for duration of signal.
Clear	C	Clears registers, or resets flip-flops.
Commands, addressed Function codes	F1,2,4,8,16	Carried on Dataway in binary code. Defines the function to be performed in a module during command operations.
Addressing Station number	N	Selects the module. There is an individual line from crate controller to each station.
Subaddress	A1,2,4,8	Also binary coded. Selects a location, within the module, to which the command is directed. There are 16 possible subaddresses.
Data Read bus	R1-R24	Transmits digital information from module to Crate Controller. Format is bit-parallel words, 24 bits maximum.
Write bus	W1-W24	Transmits digital information from Crate Controller to module. Format is same as for Read bus.
Timing Strobe 1 and Strobe 2	S1,S2	These strobes are generated by CC during every Dataway operation. Used by modules for timing acceptance of data or execution of features of an operation.
Status Look-at-Me	L	A signal from module to Crate Controller indicating request for service or attention. There is an individual line from each module to control station.
Q-Response	Q	A one-bit reply by module to certain commands issued by Crate Controller.
Command Accepted	X	Indicates the ability of a module to execute the current command operation.
Busy	B	Indicates a Dataway operation is in progress.

Fig. 6-16: Dataway Signals

SERIAL STANDARDS

Serial transmission requires only one or two wires to carry all necessary signals between modules or systems. In order to transmit address, data, and control, they must be sent bit by bit.

Described here are the RS232C, RS422 and 423, asynchronous and synchronous communication standards. In addition, data standards such as ASCII and SDLC will be covered.

EIA-RS232C

The Electronics Industry Association (EIA) standard RS232C covers the electrical specifications for bit-serial transmission, as well as the physical specifications. It defines the handshaking signals used to control standard telephone connection equipment, and standard modulator-demodulators (modems).

Electrically, the standard uses nominal plus and minus 12-volt pulses to effect information transfer. The RS232C standard specifies a 25-pin connector with the signals shown in Fig. 6-17. All 25 lines are specified, but only the first fifteen in the Table will be described.

- GROUND	
- XMIT DATA	(TO COM EQUIPMENT)
- REC DATA	(FROM COM)
- REQUEST TO SENT	(TO COM)
- CLEAR TO SEND	(FROM COM)
- DATA SET READY	(FROM COM)
- DATA SET READY	(FROM COM)
- DATA TERMINAL READY	(TO COM)
- RING INDICATOR	(FROM COM)
- RECEIVED LINE SIGNAL DETECTOR	(FROM COM)
- SIGNAL QUALITY DETECTOR	(FROM COM)
- DATA RATE SELECTOR	(TO COM)
- DATA RATE SELECTOR	(FROM COM)
- TRANSMITTER TIMING	(TO COM)
- TRANSMITTER TIMING	(FROM COM)
- RECEIVER TIMING	(FROM COM)
· ⁵ SECONDARY DATA AND REQUESTS	

Fig. 6-17: EIA RS232C Signals

The secondary lines provide the data and control paths for a second serial channel running at a much lower speed than the primary channel. The second channel is then identical to the first, except for speed. The second channel is hardly ever used, but when it is it contains control information for the modems connected at each end of the communications line.

The main signal lines are transmit data and receive data. These lines are used to send serial information between the two systems. The bit rate may be any one of the following standard rates:

19,200	1,200	110
9,600	600	75
4,800	300	50
2,400	150	

Other rates are also occasionally used. The teletypewriter terminals run at 110, 150, or 300 bits/second. CRT terminals typically use any of the speeds above 1,200.

Quite often, serial data are transmitted over telephone voice-grade lines. The data must first be modulated, so that they may be transmitted. For bit rates of less than 300, the method of modulation is known as FSK: frequency-shift-keying. The "marking" or logic "1" condition is represented by a tone of given frequency, and the "spacing" or logic "0" condition is represented by a second, different, frequency. Bit rates above 300 must use phase-modulation techniques, due to the lack of available bandwidth. Quite often, voice-grade lines are too noisy for high-rate communications. More expensive data-grade lines must be used.

The other signals are used to indicate the status of the modulator-demodulator (modem) communications link. Signals such as: "request-to-send," "clear-to-send," "data-set-ready," "data-terminal-ready," are used to control the modem link.

The timing in Fig. 6-18 is meant to show a typical communications transaction. Note how the signals between the modem (communications equipment) and the computer (or terminal) implement a similar kind of handshake to that used in most buses—especially the IEEE-488. The difference, in this case, is that the handshake is used only at the beginning, and end, of a block of serial data.

RS232C is popular, as almost all dial-up time-share systems use this standard in their communication subsystems. A similar standard is *current loop*. This is used in the mechanical teletypewriters. A good thing to do is to convert all loop devices to EIA-RS232C via a loop-to-EIA converter. In this way, all communications become standardized. A loop-to-EIA converter for a teletype is shown in Fig. 6-19. Also useful is what is known as *auto loop back,* shown in Fig. 6-20. This is where the computer, terminal, or modem, does not have the full standard implemented. The jumpers specified will usually allow the devices to believe that all conditions are "OK" for data to pass.

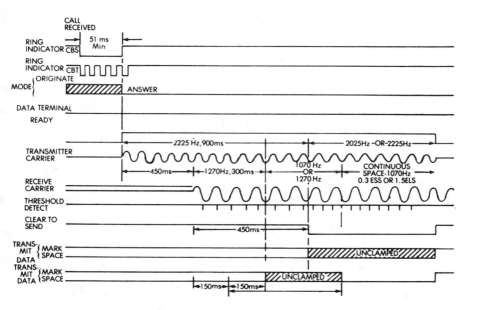

Fig. 6-18: EIA RS232C Modem Handshake

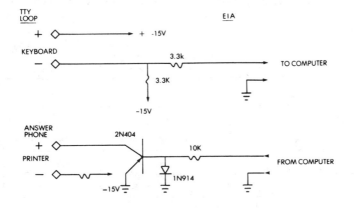

Fig. 6-19: Loop-To-EIA Converter

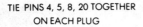

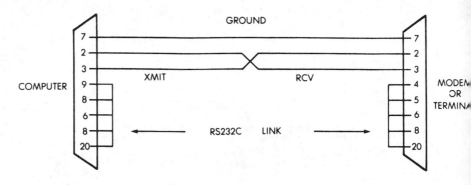

Fig. 6-20: Auto Loop Back Connection

RS422 and 423

RS232C transmits signals as single-ended voltages. The "mark" or "space" condition is represented by the voltage between two wires. Thus, the transmit path has two wires, and the receive path has two wires. The advantage is that the path may be physically longer between devices, due to the noise immunity of a differential channel. In the same way, the data rate may be higher, due to reduced noise effects.

CHARACTERISTIC	RS232	RS422	RS423
MAXIMUM LINELENGTH	100 ft.	5000 ft.	5000 ft.
MAXIMUM BITS/SEC.	2×10^4	10^6	10^5
DATA "1' = MARKING DATA " 0' = SPACING	-1.5V →-.36V +1.5V→+36V	VA>VB VA<VB	VA = - VB = +
SHORT CIRCUIT	100	100	100
POWER OFF LEAKAGE MAXIMUM VOLT APPLIED TO UNPOWERED	300	100 A	100 A
RECEIVER INPUT, MINUMUM	1.5V (SINGLE-ENDED)	100 mV (DIFFERENTIAL)	100 mV (DIFFERENTIAL)

Fig. 6-21: Comparison of RS232C, RS422, and RS423

Table 6-21 illustrates the difference between the three standards. Fig. 6-22 shows the types of drivers and receivers used for the lines. RS422 and 423 are not used often due to the already widespread use of RS232C and the infrequent need for such high data rates and line lengths.

Of course, the data sent back and forth may be formatted in many ways. The topics of asynchronous and synchronous data transmission and standards for information exchange will be covered next.

ASYNCHRONOUS COMMUNICATION

When data are sent in bursts of equal duration, without clock information, they are being sent *asynchronously,* without a clock. When data are sent with synchronizing character codes imbedded within the blocks, they are being sent *synchronously:* with a clock.

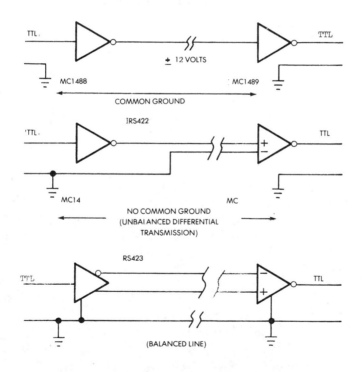

Fig. 6-22: Drivers for RS422 and RS423

The most common asynchronous data structure, shown in Fig. 6-23, is used by most CRT's and teletypewriters. It consists of the 10 (or 11) bits described in Chapter 4. The start bit, eight data, and one or two stop bits, comprise a *character*. The most popular standards for character codes are ASCII and EBCDIC.

ASCII stands for "American Standard Code for Information Exchange." It uses seven bits to encode 128 possible characters. An eighth bit may be used for parity. Note that many codes are used for controlling the functions of a data link. Codes such as: "Begin Text," "End of Text," etc., are used to format and transfer blocks of characters.

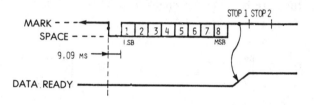

Fig. 6-23: Asynchronous Serial Data Format

EBCDIC is similar except that the 128 codes are encoded differently. Simple code-conversion ROMs can convert ASCII to EBCDIC, and EBCDIC to ASCII. Such an ROM has 8 inputs: seven address lines for the data input, and one address line to specify the conversion (either ASCII to EBCDIC or EBCDIC to ASCII). It has seven outputs for the converted character. The size of this ROM would be 256 bytes by 7 bits/byte. This is a small ROM by today's standards, and it is relatively inexpensive to program or purchase.

Who uses EBCDIC? IBM. Who uses ASCII? Practically everyone else. Other codes exist, such as the five-bit Baudot code (obsolete today), which can also be converted by a look-up ROM.

Naturally, a program may also be used to convert from one code to another.

BIT NUMBERS									0	0	0	0	1	1	1	1
									0	0	1	1	0	0	1	1
									0	1	0	1	0	1	0	1
b_7	b_6	b_5	b_4	b_3	b_2	b_1	HEX 1 / HEX 0		0	1	2	3	4	5	6	7
			0	0	0	0	0		NUL	DLE	SP	0	@	P	`	p
			0	0	0	1	1		SOH	DC1	!	1	A	Q	a	q
			0	0	1	0	2		STX	DC2	"	2	B	R	b	r
			0	0	1	1	3		ETX	DC3	#	3	C	S	c	s
			0	1	0	0	4		EOT	DC4	$	4	D	T	d	t
			0	1	0	1	5		ENQ	NAK	%	5	E	U	e	u
			0	1	1	0	6		ACK	SYN	&	6	F	V	f	v
			0	1	1	1	7		BEL	ETB	'	7	G	W	g	w
			1	0	0	0	8		BS	CAN	(	8	H	X	h	x
			1	0	0	1	9		HT	EM	)	9	I	Y	i	y
			1	0	1	0	10		LF	SUB	*	:	J	Z	j	z
			1	0	1	1	11		VT	ESC	+	;	K	[	k	{
			1	1	0	0	12		FF	FS	,	<	L	\	l	¦
			1	1	0	1	13		CR	GS	-	=	M	]	m	}
			1	1	1	0	14		SO	RS	.	>	N	^	n	~
			1	1	1	1	15		SI	US	/	?	O	_	o	DEL

(Abbreviations are explained in Fig. 6-25.)

Fig. 6-24: ASCII Code Table

SYNCHRONOUS COMMUNICATION

An asynchronous transmission format contains at least two extra bits per character: start and stop. When data are sent as a continuous stream of bits, with no start or stop, the receiver might loose its timing, and scramble the incoming data. To prevent this, *synchronizing characters* are sent every hundred or so bytes. There exists the necessary logic, at the receiving end, to resynchronize the decoding circuitry, often enough to remain locked in. Using this method, known as *synchronous communication,* there will only be eight extra bits for every 800 bits. This is 1% extra data versus 20% extra data in the case of asynchronous communication.

ACK	Acknowledge
BEL	Bell
BS	Backspace
CAN	Cancel
CR	Carriage return
DC1	Direct control 1
DC2	Direct control 2
DC3	Direct control 3
DC4	Direct control 4
DEL	Delete
DLE	Data link escape
EM	End of medium
ENQ	Enquiry
EOT	End of transmission
ESC	Escape
ETB	End transmission block
ETX	End text
FF	Form feed
FS	Form separator
GS	Group separator
HT	Horizontal tab
LF	Line feed
NAK	Negative acknowledge
NUL	Null
RS	Record separator
SI	Shift in
SO	Shift out
SOH	Start of heading
SP	Space
STX	Start text
SUB	Substitute
SYN	Synchronous idle
US	Unit separator
VT	Vertical tab

Fig. 6-25: Abbreviations of ASCII Code Table

HEXA-DECIMAL	EBCDIC 8-BIT	HEXA-DECIMAL	EBCDIC 3-BIT	HEXA-DECIMAL	EBCDIC 8-BIT	HEXA-DECIMAL	EBCDIC 8-BIT	HEXA-DECIMAL	EBCDIC 8-BIT	HEXA-DECIMAL	EBCDIC 8-BIT
0		2D		5A	$	88	h	B6		E3	T
1		2E		5B	*	89	i	B7		E4	U
2		2F		5C	)	8A		B8		E5	V
3		30		5D	;	8B		B9		E6	W
4		31		5E		8C		BA		E7	X
5		32		5F		8D		BB		E8	Y
6		33		60		8E		BC		E9	Z
7		34		61		8F		BD		EA	
8		35		62		90		BE		EB	
9		36		63		91	j	BF		EC	
A		37		64		92	k	C0		ED	
B		38		65		93	l	C1	A	EF	
C		39		66		94	m	C2	B	F0	0
D		3A		67		95	n	C3	C	F1	1
E		3B		68		96	o	C4	D	F2	2
F		3C		69		97	p	C5	E	F3	3
10		3D		6A		98		C6	F	F4	4
11		3E		6B		99		C7	G	F5	5
12		3F		6C	%	9A		C8	H	F6	6
13		40	BLANK	6D	—	9B		C9	I	F7	7
14		41		6E		9C		CA		F8	8
15		42		6F	?	9D		CB		F9	9
16		43		70		9E		CC		FA	
17		44		71		9F		CD		FB	
18		45		72		A0		CE		FC	
19		46		73		A1		CF		FD	
1A		47		74		A2	s	D0		FE	
1B		48		75		A3	t	D1	J	FF	
1C		49		76		A4	u	D2	K		
1D		4A		77		A5	v	D3	L		
1E		4B		78		A6	w	D4	M		
1F		4C		79		A7	x	D5	N		
20		4D	(	7A	:	A8	y	D6	O		
21		4E	+	7B	#	A9	z	D7	P		
22		4F		7C	@	AA		D8	Q		
23		50	&	7D	'	AB		D9	R		
24		51		7E	=	AC		DA			
25		52		7F	"	AD		DB			
26		53		80		AE		DC			
27		54		81	a	AF		DD			
28		55		82	b	B0		DE			
29		56		83	c	B1		DF			
2A		57		84	d	B2		E0			
2B		58		85	e	B3		E1			
2C		59		86	f	B4		E2	S		
				87	g	B5					

Fig. 6-26: EBCDIC Code Table

Various kinds of SDLC or *synchronous data-link control* schemes have been proposed. Many are presently being used by IBM, Burroughs and others. All of these schemes have the same basic formats.

Data are transmitted in blocks of many characters at a time, called *frames*. Each frame has a number of *fields*. Each field is one or more bytes of data. In this example, the frame has seven fields. The frame is shown in Fig. 6-27. All transmitters and receivers share the same wire. Only one unit may transmit at a time, but more than one unit can receive. Any unit that wants to transmit must wait until the line is not busy.

The start character will indicate to the receivers that a frame has begun. All SDLC interfaces will begin listening to the frame. If it is not their address, they will go back to waiting. If their address is recognized, the whole frame will be received, and checked for errors. A return frame will be sent back to the transmitting unit to indicate if data were received intact or how many errors were present and if retransmission is necessary.

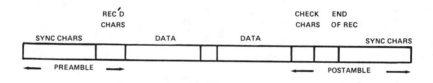

Fig. 6-27: Synchronous Data Format

There are two or more types of frames that can be transmitted. They differ in that their control bytes will have different information. An *information* frame will contain data for a listener. A *protocol* frame will contain data concerning supervision and management of the network's transmissions.

The data part of the frame will contain some multiple-of-8-bit bytes of data. This data may be in ASCII, binary, or some other format.

The check characters, the CRCC and LRCC, are used to detect and correct single-bit errors, and detect double-bit errors. These 32 bits contain enough redundant check information to do this. The stop character is the same as the start character and will indicate that the frame has ended.

In the process of transmission, resynchronization characters or bits may be inserted automatically to maintain system timing. As in the case of the floppy disk address marks, the start and stop characters may be special bytes of 1's and 0's that are easily detected by a hardware unit.

The new synchronous serial adapter integrated circuits, such as Intel's SDLC controller, Motorola's XSDA, or Zilog's Synchronous Serial Interface, will all handle the various protocols by some combination of software in the processor and hardware in the controller chip. A typical controller will recognize start characters, insert and delete sync bits automatically, and do some block checking. The software must assemble the frame from the fields and decode the frames from the fields. The program must also set up the initial network protocols.

ERROR DETECTION AND CORRECTION

Many devices such as cassettes, disks, dynamic memories, and modems make errors in reading or writing data. There are three basic schemes for detecting these errors: *parity, checksums,* and *cyclic redundancy check characters.* In order to not only detect but also correct errors, other information is needed. Two ways of correcting errors will be described here: *hamming code* and *cross parity.*

Parity

In a byte of data, there are either an even number of 1's occurring or an odd number of 1's occurring. The eighth or sometimes ninth bit added to every byte to make the number of one bits even or odd is the parity bit.

By recording or storing a parity bit with every byte, errors can be detected. After the byte is read, a new parity is generated from the eight bits of the byte. If the regenerated parity bit does not match the recorded parity bit, there is an error of at least one bit. *Note that two bits changing from 1 to 0 and 0 to 1 will not be detected.*

Checksums

To verify that an entire block of data is correct, a one-byte check character is generated and added at the end of the block. To check, the block is read, and a new check character generated. The check character stored is compared with the one generated; if it is different, there is an error in the block.

361

A checksum can be generated by adding all the bytes in the block together using add-with-carry instructions. One eight-bit number is then "related" to information in the block. Another way is to exclusive OR every byte together. The resulting byte is actually the parity across the block rather than the parity of the byte. The more checksum information, the more accurate the error detection.

Cyclic Redundancy

This is explained in the floppy disk section, and the reader is referred to Chapter 4. Besides the algorithm presented for the floppy disk data format, other cyclic redundancy check algorithms are also used.

Hamming Code

By adding redundancy to our stored byte, one can not only detect but also correct single-bit errors.

Using eight bits for our byte, one must add ($\log_2 8$) + 1 bits to the byte for hamming bits. That implies using a twelve-bit word for eight bits of data. The four extra bits will be parity bits for different subgroups of the eight original bits.

```
b0      b3      b6  ──►  h2      parity for row
b1      b4      b7  ──►  h3
b2      b5
 │       │
 ▼       ▼
h0      h1
parity for column
b0 b1 b2 b3 b4 b5 b6 b7 = byte
h0 h1 h2 h3 = hamming bits
```

If the correction circuitry finds the generated bit h1 is different from the read-back h1, and all the rest are correct, bit b5 is reversed. If h2 and h1 are wrong, bit b3 is reversed. All single-bit errors can be corrected, and two-bit errors detected.

Cross Parity

Expanding the hamming concept to blocks, one can apply parity across a block of bytes and apply parity to each byte to vector any single bits in error.

9 bits	b0	.	b0	l0	parity across
	b1	.	b1	l1	the block
	.	.	. . . .	.	
	.	.	.	.	
	b7	.	b7	.	
	p0	pl	pn	l8	

BLOCK
parity down
the block

If bits l0 and p0 are wrong, bit b0 of the first byte is reversed.

These error detection and correction schemes have been simplified for discussion here. There are obvious problems which arise that require extra study. Such situations as: what if l8 and p0 are wrong in the hamming example—which bit is wrong? Many mathematical discussions have been written on error correction techniques in binary data and the reader is referred to these for a more thorough discussion.

A CASE-STUDY:
INEXPENSIVE ANALOG BOARD FOR S100 BUS

The circuit in Fig. 6-28 shows a digital-to-analog converter with analog-to-digital conversion capability. The circuit has 6 integrated circuits: one triple three-input NAND gate, one 74LS138 decoder, one 74LS125 tri-state bus driver, one 8212 octal latch, one MC1408 D/A converter, and one LM324 quad operational amplifier. With these components, an S100 bus analog measurement assembly has been designed.

Features of this module are:

— S100 bus compatible, only 1 LSTTL load per bus line
— 8-bit resolution for both D/A and A/D
— D/A conversion in 20us
— A/D conversion in 1ms
— 0-10 volt input and output with extra 1 to 1000 gain stage for low-level inputs.

The circuit will be described part by part, to explain the function of each component.

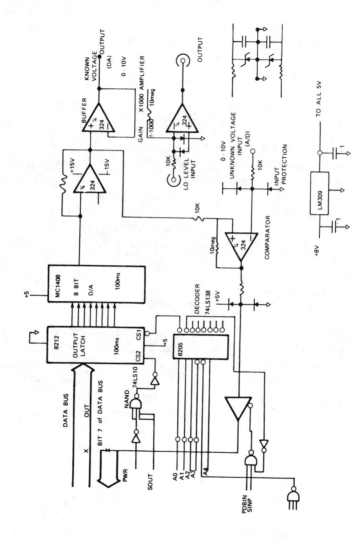

Fig. 6-28: S100 A/D, D/A Board

The Hardware

The output data bus, which performs all data transfers to memory or output ports, is connected to an 8212 latch. Each bit is loaded by an input of the latch. Each input represents ⅔ of a low-power-Schottky input load.

The 74LS138 decoder, along with the 74LS10 and 74LS04, decodes the output to port "F8" (hexadecimal). The address is partially decoded by ⅓ of the 74LS10, so that bits A7, A6, A5 must all be 1's to enable the 74LS138 decoder. Then the bits A0, A1, A2, A3, and A4 are decoded by the 74LS138. The first output represents "F0" on the low eight address bits. This enables one of the chip selects on the 8212 latch.

The other chip select is driven by the condition $\overline{PWR}$ false and SOUT true. This is done by inverting $\overline{PWR}$ and "NANDing" it with SOUT. The output of the NAND is passed through an inverter to the second chip select of the 8212.

This way, the output data bus is latched into the 8212 latch when the address is "F0", and the control signals indicate an output instruction is being executed. The timing is shown in Fig. 6-29.

The latched data is sent to a MC1408 digital-to-analog converter. At the output of the converter, a current proportional to the binary input is present. In order to convert it to a voltage, a current-to-voltage converter circuit is used. It is implemented with ¼ of the LM324 quad op-amp.

The output is now a voltage between 0 and 10 volts for inputs between "00" and "FF" (hexadecimal). The next op-amp, in the LM324, is used to buffer the output so that an output may be driven without affecting the comparator section.

The third op-amp is used as a comparator for the analog-to-digital conversion. The op-amp compares the unknown input with the output of the D/A. If the unknown signal is too small, a variable-gain amplifier, implemented with the fourth op-amp, is used to boost the signal. Note the protection diodes, that are used so that no damage will be caused to the inputs, as long as voltage transients there are kept below 100 volts.

The output of the comparator is clamped to TTL levels by the resistor-diode combination, so the 74LS125 tri-state driver can be driven. The driver is enabled by an input command and the address "F9" (hexadecimal). The decoding is done similarly to that of the output port, except that the second output of the 74LS138 is used to decode

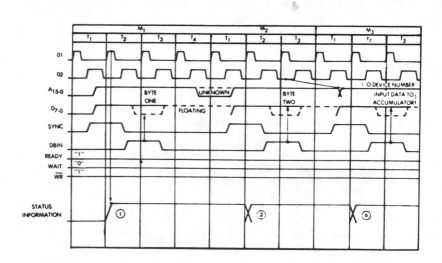

Fig. 6-29: S100 Output Write-Cycle Timing

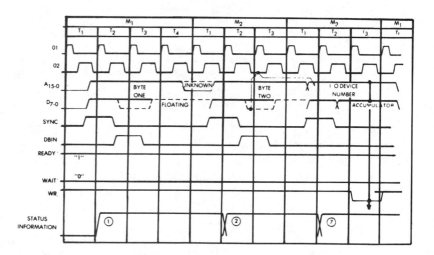

Fig. 6-30: S100 Input Read-Cycle Timing

the address "F1." In addition, the control lines PDBIN and SINP are "ANDed" with the address, to enable the driver to bit 7 of the data bus.

By driving bit 7, we can input from port "F1", rotate bit 7 into the carry bit, and test the carry to see if we are above, or below, the unknown input voltage. Outputting a new value to port "F0" and checking bit 7 again will form the basis of our analog-to-digital converter. Timing for an input operation appears in Fig. 6-30

Power is supplied by the +5-volt voltage regulator for all Vcc pins and the Zener diode regulators for the + and −15-volt voltages, required for the op-amp package.

Note that three of the bus drivers were used as inverters. Fig. 6-31 shows how this is done.

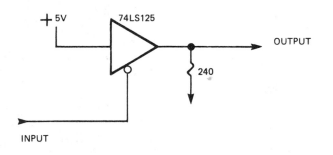

Fig. 6-31: Use of 74LS125 as an Inverter

When the input is low, the driver is enabled, and the output will be pulled up to a logic "1". When the input is high, the driver is disabled, and the 240-ohm resistor pulls the output to a logic "0". We could have used a hex inverter for these functions, but it would have increased the part count.

The Software

For digital-to-analog conversion, the binary value to be converted is output to port "F0". Each step represents 10.0 volts/256 = 39.0625 millivolts. This means that if you want 2.5 volts out, the binary number is:

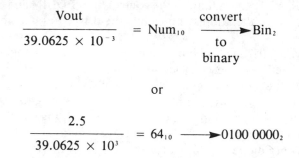

$$\frac{Vout}{39.0625 \times 10^{-3}} = Num_{10} \xrightarrow[\text{to binary}]{\text{convert}} Bin_2$$

or

$$\frac{2.5}{39.0625 \times 10^3} = 64_{10} \longrightarrow 0100\ 0000_2$$

or 40 hexidecimal. 80 hex will be 5 volts, because the converter is linear. In software we need:

> MOV A, M : get value from memory to output
> OUT F0H : output

QUESTION: What is the highest frequency we could generate with this converter?

ANSWER: Since the sampling theorem states we need to sample, or, alternatively, to output a value at least at twice the rate of the highest frequency, we would have:

$$\frac{1}{\text{conversion}} \cdot \frac{1}{2} = f\ max$$

or

$$\frac{1}{20 \times 10^{-6}} \cdot \frac{1}{2} = 250\ KHz$$

In practice, our program will not be able to fetch information fast enough to use this bandwidth, but we will be able to generate music or voice range sounds.

Analog-to-Digital Conversion

To perform the A/D conversion, we need to implement the successive approximation algorithm in software. Another technique which can be used is the counter-conversion technique. Both will be discussed.

368

Successive approximation was presented in Chapter 5. In order to code this into an 8080 assembly-language subroutine, we need to examine the flowchart of Fig. 6-32.

A program that will perform this conversion appears in Fig. 6-33. Note how this program uses the "NOP" and "CMP E,M" instructions to balance the timing of the "JC" instruction. This is done so that the conversion will take the same amount of time to execute through either path of the flowchart.

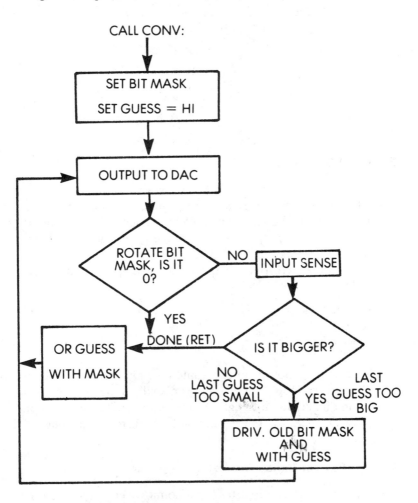

Fig. 6-32: Successive Approximation Flowchart

The conversion time is 373.5 uS according to the instruction execution times, without a wait state. We can only sample approximately every 380 uS.

QUESTION: What is the highest frequency we can sample?

ANSWER: Again, according to the sampling theorem it is:

$$\frac{1}{\text{conversion time}} \cdot \tfrac{1}{2} = f \text{ max}$$

$$\frac{1}{380 \times 10^{-6}} \cdot \tfrac{1}{2} = 1316 \text{ HZ}$$

This means our converter can just barely go fast enough to digitize speech.

POWER SUPPLIES

Now that the circuitry is connected, where are the $+5.0$ volts ($\pm 5\%$) at 10 amperes? *Power supplies,* which are at the heart of any system, are often the most overlooked element of a system. If the power supply is not properly specified, the system does not have even a chance of working reliably.

Power-supply performance is measured simply by the following parameters:

— voltage current ratings
— regulation
— efficiency.

The design of a power supply would take another book this size to describe. Power-supply engineering is actually a much harder skill to learn than digital-circuit design or programming. There are a number of good references for power-supply design listed at the end of this chapter.

Voltage, Current Rating

Power supplies are rated by the amount of energy or power that they can deliver to the load by the voltage and current specifications. For example, a five-volts-at-five-amperes power supply will deliver

370

```
                MVI      D, 80H :  temp mask in D
                MVI      B, 80H :  mask in B
                MVI      C, 80H :  guess in C
GUESSOUT:       MOV      A,C
                OUT      DAC    :  OUTPUT GUESS
                MOV      A,B
                RRC
                RC              :  done if carry
                                   bit set
                MOV      B,A
                IN       SENSE
                RLC
                JC       bigger
                MOV      A,D
                RRC
                MOV      D,A
                MOV      A,C
                ORA      B
                MOV      C,A
                CMP      E,M
                JMP      GUESSOUT
BIGGER:         MOV      A,D
                CMP
                AND      C
                MOV      A,D
                RRC
                MOV      D,A
                NOP
                JMP      GUESSOUT
```

Fig. 6-33: Program For A/D Conversion

25 watts to the load, maximum.

To know the voltages the circuits will require involves looking them up in the data sheets. But how much current will the whole system draw? Again, the current requirement for each part is in the specification sheets. Listed as minimum, typical, and maximum current drain, or alternatively as power dissipation, all the typical figures are simply added together to get a rough estimate of the operating current. For specification of the power supply the current rating of the supply should be twice the average or typical system-load current requirement. Maximum values should also be tabulated, as well as minimum values for power-supply regulation specification.

Regulation

Power supplies are not perfect. They cannot deliver exactly 5.000 volts under all load conditions. This is why they are also rated as to the ability to *regulate,* or hold the output voltage current.

Specifications are divided into *load-regulation tolerance,* and *load-no-load regulation* tolerance. Also important is the *turn-on overshoot,* and *stability* under varying load conditions.

If the load is constant, and our input line voltage from the wall socket is whatever range of values the utility company will allow, the variation in output voltage over temperature and time is the *load-regulation tolerance.*

For example, if our system is an 8048 single-chip microcomputer, one requires a load regulation of ±5%: 4.75 to 5.25 volts in the range of guaranteed operation. The power supply should typically be two times better than this if one wishes to be safe. By not choosing carefully, one may operate the system right at the limit of the guaranteed operating range, and this situation combined with other marginal circuit factors, such as loading of the buses, temperature, and clock frequency, may cause the system to never work!

If the load varies, one would like to know how much the voltage will change. This is known as the *no-load, load regulation* measurement, or the *step-load* measurement. As an example, if one takes a 5-volts-at-5-amperes supply and attaches a 1-ohm load, the supply should deliver 5 volts at 5 amperes. If one measures the voltage under this condition, and then disconnects the load and measures again, one should see optimally *no change.* In reality, step-load tolerance of less than ½% is usual.

In addition to the tolerance, the overshoot and stability measurements are extremely important. *Overshoot* is the supply, when turned on or off, goes above the rated output voltage—and by how much. *Stability* is a measure of whether the supply can oscillate under varying load conditions.

If we are driving standard TTL, the circuits will not tolerate an overshoot of greater than 8 volts, or the circuits will be destroyed. Most commercial power supplies have little or no overshoot.

In contrast, most home-built power supplies tend to be unstable. This is due to layout and construction techniques. Remember, even though one may think the highest frequency in a power supply is the line frequency, regulators have a feedback loop capable of operating in the megahertz range. Why so fast? The regulator must respond quickly to a load change to meet the requirements stated earlier. The tighter the regulation and step response, the faster the regulator must operate. The faster it operates, the greater the chance of instability through a design error.

Efficiency

If a supply delivers 25 watts to a load, how many watts is the supply taking from the wall socket to do this? This ratio, of output power divided by input power, is the efficiency. Typical power supplies are 40% efficient. That is, for the 25-watt model, it will draw 62.5 watts from the power line. There are high-efficiency regulators of the *switching* type which will deliver efficiencies of about 90%, but they are more expensive than the typical linear regulator.

Choosing Your Supply

The question always asked is: "Should I build or buy?" First buying will be examined. The best units are those known as OEM or *Original Equipment Manufacturers* supplies. These are commercial units that are used by most companies in their products. They are expensive, typically $50.00 for a 35-watt supply, or 5 volts at 7 amperes. The advantage of an OEM supply is that the user is receiving the result of hundreds of thousands of dollars in power-supply engineering. The heart of a system will be a healthy one. The general rule for costs is about $1.50 for every watt required.

If one builds the supply, there are many design choices to be made. The transformer, diodes, and capacitors must all be chosen by certain design rules and formulas. The regulator itself must then be matched to the transformer, diode, capacitor combination so that stability and efficiency problems do not occur.

For anything less than 3 amperes at five volts, there are simple monolithic voltage regulators available, such as the popular LM309 or 78XX series. These regulators' specification sheets contain typical circuits for their application. Above 15 watts, it is suggested the user look to the references listed, and good luck. Remember, if a supply does work, do not be too proud—in quantities of hundreds with component variations half may never work due to a marginal design.

Fig. 6-34 lists the typical specifications of an OEM supply from the Power One Corporation. Fig. 6-35 illustrates the supply itself.

AC Input:	105–125 VAC, 47–440 HZ (Derate output current 10% for 50 HZ operation).
DC Output:	See Voltage—Current Rating Chart. Adjustment range, ±5% minimum.
Line Regulation:	±.01% for a 10% line change.
Load Regulation:	±.02% for a 50% load change.
Output Ripple:	1.5 mv PK-PK, 0.4 mv RMS max.
Transient Response:	30 seconds for 50% load change.
Short Circuit & Overload Protection:	Automatic current limit/foldback.
Reverse Voltage Protection:	Provided on output and pass element.
Remote Sensing:	Provided, open sense lead protection built-in.
Stability:	±.05% for 24 hours after warm-up.
Temperature Rating:	0°C to 50°C full rated, derated linearly to 40% at 70°C.
Temp. Coefficient:	±.01%/°C maximum, .002% typical.
Efficiency:	5V units: 45%, 12 & 15V units: 55%, 20 & 24V units: 60%.
Vibration:	Per Mil-Std-810B, Method 514, procedure 1, curve AV (to 50 HZ).
Shock:	Per Mil-Std-810B, Method 516, procedure V.

Fig. 6-34: Power One Supply Specifications

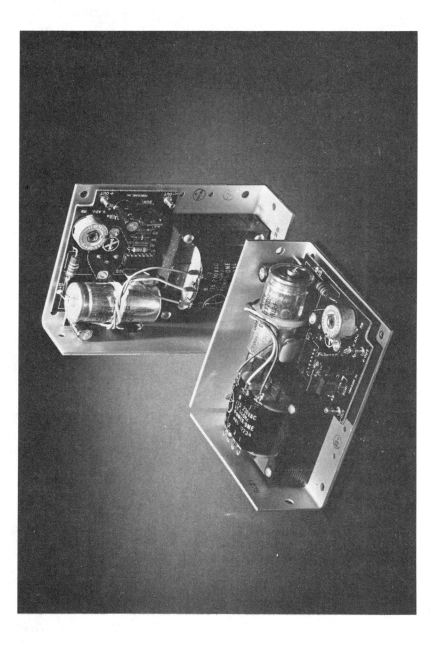

Fig. 6-35: Power One OEM Supply

SUMMARY

We have designed an analog data collection and control board. It was designed to be connected to the S100 bus. Software was written to use the features of this D/A and A/D converter.

The buses and standards described are intended to make the job of interfacing easier. To plug the device into a system with no extra work is every interface designer's dream. We have seen how the many users of the S100, CAMAC, IEEE-488 and EIA-RS232C standards create a large need for standard-compatible devices, modules, and systems. If at all possible, *stay within a standard*. The design will be easier and your time may be spent on the harder problems.

Parallel and serial bus standards, methods of communication between modules, and an actual bus interface example were presented. The S100 bus is the most popular parallel bus used now, with over 600 different types of compatible boards being produced. The serial RS232C standard is the most popular standard for data communications, and versions of data formatting are used, with modems, to store and retrieve data from cassettes and cartridges, as described in Chapter 4.

Power supplies are the heart of a system. Regulation, stability, and some design parameters have been discussed. The OEM solution is obviously one of the best, as the power supply manufacturer is a specialist in regular and custom supply requirements.

7

THE MULTIPLEXER —
A CASE STUDY

INTRODUCTION

This system is intended to concentrate 32 EIA RS232C-compatible terminals onto a single two-way high-speed transmission line. Each terminal has buffered output and character-by-character input. Thus, the host computer can spend less time executing the multiplexing task.

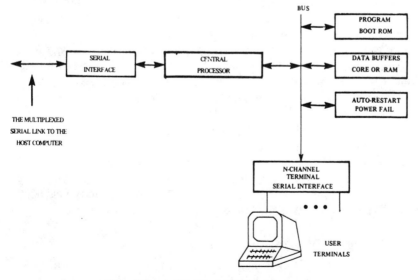

Fig. 7-0: A 32-Channel Multiplexer

Designed for a PDP 11/70, the system is also applicable, with only code changes in the host machine, to almost any host computer. The cost of providing this function is $50 per channel, as compared to usually around $250 per channel. The system is also cost-effective in clusters of fewer than 32 terminals.

The system uses the 8080 microprocessor, 8251 USRT, 8259 interrupt controller, and other components in the 8080 family. The system has no modem-control features, as it was intended to be at the site of the terminals, saving even more money in man-hours of time and cost of wire for connection. This does not even include the cost benefit of fewer telephone lines and modems.

THE SPECIFICATIONS

The task of connecting a large number of terminals to a time-sharing facility always presents the engineer with a number of problems. Most have to do with the interconnection headaches of modems, telephone wiring, patchboards for testing, and internal machine interfacing.

Remotely-located concentrators would eliminate many problems. The new problem: cost. The design goal here is to service 32 terminals at an input rate never exceeding 30 characters-per-second, and an output rate as fast as possible. Given that the 8080A could execute roughly 300 instructions in the time between characters at 9600 baud, if it were to service 32 terminals on input, it would have to have fewer than 300 instructions in the polling loop for the terminals. Any time left over would be used for output. The code would have to be thought out byte-by-byte, with all coding being carefully optimized. A prototype was built, under the assumption that it could service at least 16 terminals in a degraded mode.

The typical statistics of our input was a maximum of 150 baud for any second, and a rate of 50 baud for all 32 terminals combined. Thus, when completed, the multiplexer could handle a maximum of 150 baud on all 32 at once, or a maximum of 300 baud on one. The output was a minimum of 300 baud for all 32 at once, and typical 6000 baud when there was a specific demand from a single user.

ARCHITECTURE

The architectural block diagram is presented in Fig. 7-1. Each terminal has its own USART, because each needs a dedicated serial interface. The USARTs are grouped into fours and then placed onto cards, which are on the 8080A system bus. There are 8,192 bytes of RAM for data storage, and 1,024 bytes of EAROM for program, in the system. Lastly, there is an interrupt controller and high-speed-channel card, which is on the bus.

Each terminal, through its USART, has a 128-character buffer associated with it, for buffering output to the terminal. This takes 4,096 bytes of the available RAM. The terminals-to-host queue is 256 characters long. These lengths were chosen to optimize the communication-channel transfers. The method will not be discussed here.

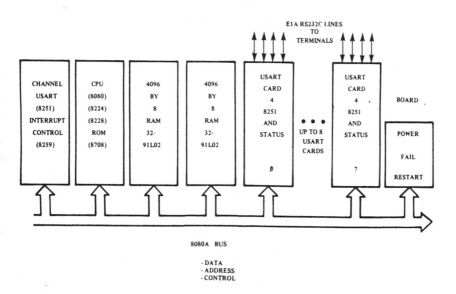

Fig. 7-1: Multiplexer Block Diagram

There are three processes, running one at a time: input-output service polling routine, host-to-terminal buffer interrupt process, and terminal-holding-queue to host interrupt process. They will be described in the following section.

SOFTWARE

A flowchart of the software appears in Figs. 7-2, 7-3, 7-4 and 7-5. The software can be divided into four parts: the initialization routine, the polling routine, the interrupt routine to fill terminal buffers from the host, and the interrupt routine to empty the terminal-to-host waiting queue.

The initialization runs only when reset, then the latter processes may run, one at a time. They communicate only through the output data buffers and share no other common memory space, other than pointer tables.

The initialization routine clears all memory, sets up tables, finds which boards are plugged in, resets all USARTs, and will print out errors, if a debug board is installed. This is roughly all the system housekeeping. It sets the stack pointer, resets and sets the mode, speed, and number of bits-per-word on the USARTs. This section of the program is 60% of the code used for the whole application.

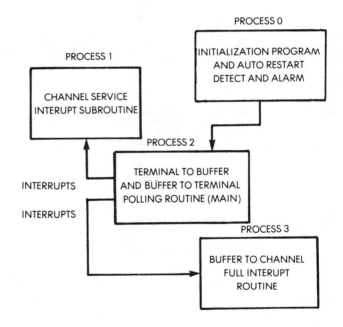

TOTAL 8080A BYTES FOR PROGRAM: 526 BYTES! LESS THAN ¾ OF THE 2708 USED

Fig. 7-2: Multiplexer Software: Overall Program Flow

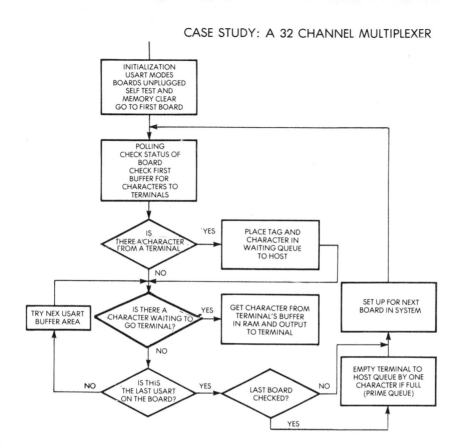

Fig. 7-3: Multiplexer Software: Polling Loop

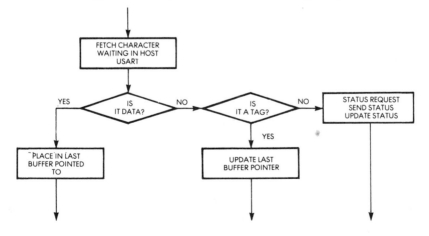

Fig. 7-4: Multiplexer Software: Host to Mux Interrupt

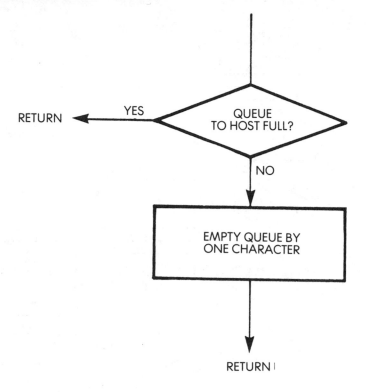

Fig. 7-5: Multiplexer Software: Mux to Host Queue Interrupt

The polling routine goes through the list set up by the initialization program, testing to see if there has been a character typed by a terminal, or if there is data in a buffer, to be output to a terminal. Thus, each of the 32 terminals is serviced once during each pass. If the channel-to-host is busy (it takes 1 millisecond to transmit a character at 9600 baud), the characters are put into a waiting queue that will be serviced when the "channel-not-busy" interrupt comes in. If the channel is not busy, the waiting queue is emptied by one character, and the character currently waiting is placed at the end of the line, in the queue. In this way, the queue-service routine is primed and will continue to interrupt, when not busy, to empty all the characters waiting for the channel. The format used for data transmission is the following: the tag for that terminal is sent first, and then the character is sent to the host, via the queue routine. Each board has its own priority table, so that only one input is processed, per pass, per board. After a character is transmitted, or, if a board has no characters, the buffer area for each terminal is then checked to find if there is an output character pending (these are placed in the buffer by the host-interrupt routine). If so, the buffer gives its character to the USART to be transmitted, and all the pointers are updated. When there are no incoming characters, and no buffer is full, the system still polls each board for input, and each USART buffer for output.

The channel-queue-interrupt routine looks at the queue, and transmits a character, if there is one waiting; otherwise it returns. This routine will not be called again by interrupt, until the polling routine primes it by sending a character.

The host-interrupt routine waits for information to come from the 11/70, or host machine, before it executes. When a character is received, and ready, an interrupt is generated that then starts this interrupt process. This process checks the incoming character and, if it is data, places it in the appropriate output buffer area. After this, polling resumes. Other characters from the host perform status requests, data-tag-switch, and soft-restart commands.

The host-interrupt routine may interrupt at any time during polling. It first saves the status vector of the machine, then picks up the character that caused the interrupt. If the most-significant-bit (MSB) is a "1", the character is a tag, or a command. If it is a tag, it is stored, so that the following data characters are loaded into the buffer pointed to by the last tag.

The most-significant-bit could also mean that it is a command. The commands allowed are: "status-request," "status-change," and "soft-restart." "Status-request" will send back a status tag followed by the status of that USART. "Status-change" will take the next character, and transfer it to the USART control register. This can be used to turn ports on or off, and change baud rate by a factor of four. "Soft-restart" will reinitialize the entire system. Caution is advised in the use of these controls: do not expect the data buffers to be unaffected by their use! This is because these commands require more time than is allowed to poll all the terminals. Thus, interrupts are locked out and characters may be lost. These commands are usually used to re-intitialize the system from the host, after the host crashes.

The most-significant-bit being "0" means that the character represents data. This character is then loaded into the last place in the buffer pointed to by the last tag. All following characters will load into the same buffer, until a new tag is sent.

The CPU and PROM Module

In Fig. 7-6, we see the 8080 CPU board schematic. This board contains all of the necessary CPU interface circuitry along with one 2708 programmable ROM and the necessary bus buffers.

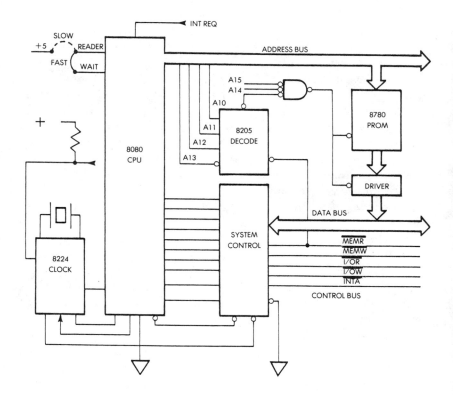

Fig. 7-6: CPU Board Schematic

The 8080 needs a clock and a system controller. These functions are provided by the 8224 and the 8228 chips, respectively. The 8224 provides the necessary timing from the 18-megahertz crystal to drive the two-phase clock of the 8080. It also provides the reset signal synchronization necessary.

The 8228 system controller provides the system with the control bus and also buffers the data bus, so that all of the modules in the system can be driven with no load limitation.

Also on this board are 1,024 bytes of EPROM provided by the 2708. Notice that the selection of this device is fully decoded. The EPROM will only respond to addresses from "0000" hexadecimal to "03FF" hexadecimal. This is where the multiplexer program resides.

The selection is done as follows: all address bits A10 through A15 must be low, to enable the EPROM, as well as the $\overline{\text{MEMR}}$ signal. The first four of those signals, along with this $\overline{\text{MEMR}}$, go to a 1-of-8 decoder, an 8205. If all of these are zero, then the first output is selected. Then this output is checked with the last two address lines. If all are zero, then the $\overline{\text{CS}}$ is held low, selecting the EPROM. The EPROM bus driver, an 8212, is also enabled at this time to drive the appropriate cells' data onto the data bus, to be read by the processor.

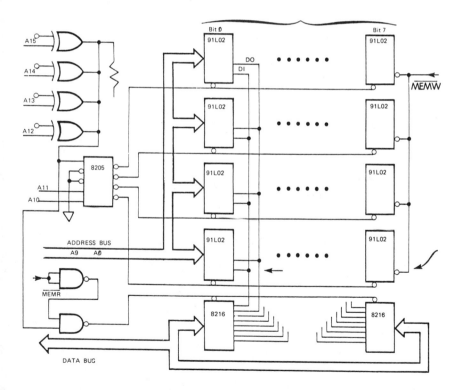

Fig. 7-7: RAM Board

RAM Modules

There are two memory cards in this system. They are both identical, except one is for addresses "1000" hexadecimal through "1FFF" hexadecimal, and the other is for addresses "2000" hexadecimal through "2FFF" hexadecimal. These two cards provide 8,192 bytes of RAM storage.

Each card contains 32 static 1,024 × 1-bit RAM chips, bus drivers and receivers, and address-selection logic.

A single RAM chip can store 1,024 bits of information. In order to store 4,096 × 8 bits, we need to organize these chips into a *memory array*. Note that we need one chip for each bit, and that we need four sets for 4,096 bytes.

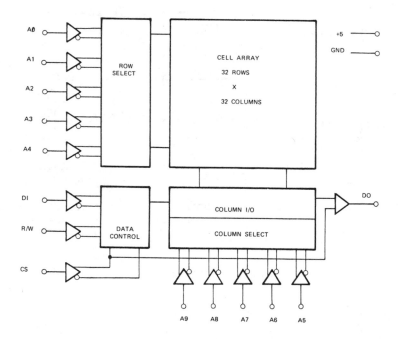

Fig. 7-8: Detail of 91L02C

Since, for any group of 1,024 bytes, eight 91L02s will need to be enabled, the chip-selects for each of the groups of eight are tied together. From there, these four group-selects go to a 1-of-8 decoder.

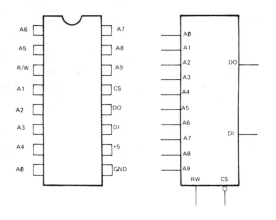

Fig. 7-9: Pinout of 91L02C

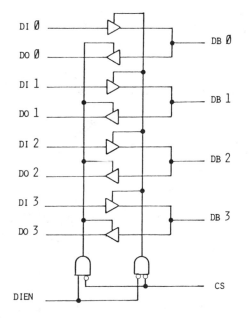

Fig. 7-10: 8216 Bidirectional Bus Drivers

The data bits are bussed from each group in the direction perpendicular to the chip select. All bit 0s should be tied together, as well as bit 1s, bit 2s, bit 3s, etc. Since 91L02's cannot drive the bus directly, all input data lines come from an 8216 bidirectional bus driver and receiver. In a similar fashion, all data outputs from the 91L02s go to the 8216 bidirectional bus drivers. An illustration of the 8216 appears in Fig. 7-10.

Two of these devices will provide a standard method of listening to, and driving, the data bus. The DIEN signal controls whether the bus is driven by the 8216, or whether the bus is listened to. The CS enables the outputs to drive both the bus and the D0 outputs. If CA is high, all of the DB and D0 pins are in the high-impedance state.

The direction of data-flow is determined by the MEMR signal. When it is low, the RAM will put data out onto the DI lines of the 8216s. The bus-drivers will be enabled, to drive the 8080 data bus with this data. At all other times, the memory array listens to the bus. The only time it will write data into the memory is when the MEMW signal goes low and the chips are selected.

The address selection is performed in a way so that the address of the board may be selected by jumper wires. The low ten address bits go directly to the 91L02s. The next two bits go to a 1-of-8 decoder (8205) to select one of the four sets of eight memory chips. The enable line of the 8205 comes from a wire-ANDed combination of exclusive-or (XOR) gates.

Only when all of the outputs from these four gates are high will the memory board be enabled. Each XOR gate compares an address bit with a jumper wired to "1" or "0". If both are identical, the output will be "0". If they are different, the output will be "1". To set these jumpers for the right address, we set the jumper to the opposite of what the high four address bits should be. If we want "0010", for A15-A12, the jumpers should be tied to "1", "1", "0", "1", respectively. In this way, the board will respond only when an address lies in the area of $0010XXXXXXXXXXXX_2$. This is pages "20" through "2F" hexadecimal, or "2000" through "2FFF" hexadecimal. *Exercise for the alert reader: What should the jumpers be for "1000" through "1FFF"?*

The USART Board

In Fig. 7-11, the basic card for all the terminals' interface is shown. This card contains four 8251 USARTs, a baud-rate clock generator, and a priority-encoded status-generation PROM.

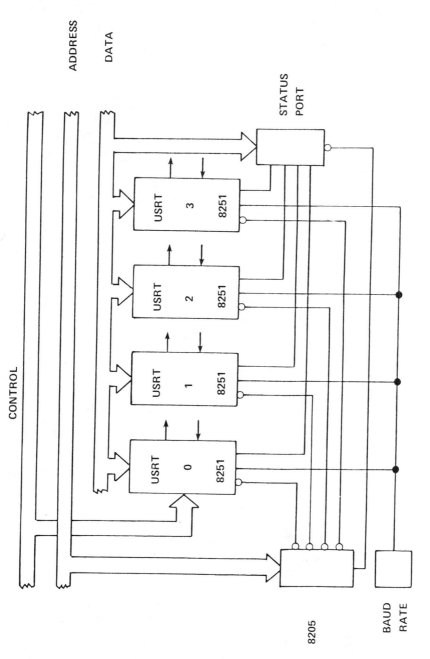

Fig. 7-11: USART Board

The 8251 is the basic serial interface element. Grouped four to a card, they are connected on their data buses to form an on-card data bus. Similar to the memory card, this on-card bus is buffered by 8216s onto the system bus. This is because the 8251 cannot drive more than eight other LSTTL loads. The 8251 is selected by implementing an address-decoding technique, using an 8205. Note how these devices are memory-mapped input-output. That is, since the same signals that control memory (MEMW, MEMR) control the USARTs, they appear as memory locations. According to our memory map, when bit A15 is high, we are addressing input-output. This corresponds to locations from "8000" to "8FFF" hexadecimal. Note that since the lower eight address lines are not decoded, these are "don't cares" in our memory-mapped I/O map.

The first card starts at "80XX" (where "XX" means that these bits do not matter) and, since each USART has two registers (input-output and control), the address ends at "87XX" hexadecimal. The next card goes from "88XX" to "8FXX", and so on, with the last card addressed by "B8XX" to "BFXX". The even page-addresses are the status registers, and the odd ones are the data-in and data-out registers.

Note also that there is a special PROM on the card, which is decoded by a separate decoder. Its address is "70XX" for the first card and "77XX" for the last card. The function of this PROM is to place on the data bus the actual address of the USART which has received a character from its terminal. How is this done? Each of the "RxRdy" lines on the USARTs indicate whether a character has been received. These four lines, one from each USART, are tied to the *address lines* of the PROM.

One of 16 possible bytes may be selected by the decoding. The fifth address bit is jumpered to a one or a zero. In this way, the same PROM can be used for board 0 or board 1, by placing in the other 16 locations the addresses for board 1, and setting the jumper on the fifth address bit to a 1 (jumper to zero for even, one for odd). What are these 16 locations? They are simply a table of the addresses "81", "83", "85" and "87" hexadecimal for board zero, and "89", "8B", "8D", "8F" for board one. Similar PROMs are made for the other six boards.

The values are placed in such a way that the first location in the PROM is a byte of zeroes. That way, when no USART has a character and all RxRdy lines are low, the byte of status is all zeroes, indicating that there is "nothing" to do for this board. If it is not zero, then a character is waiting. To make sure that it is easy to tell which USART is waiting, the next location contains the value "81": if the first USART is waiting, and all the others are not, the program will receive an "81" from the status PROM. The program can then use this value to directly address the actual character waiting. What is more, the value "81" can be masked, to form the tag for the data fetched.

The next two locations contain "83", the next four "85", and the next eight, "87". In this way, a priority table is formed so that, as each USART is serviced, the next one waiting will be serviced in turn.

This method of addressing the status PROM allows the program to use only a few instructions to identify which USART, out of 32 possible ones, is ready with a character, fetch the character, and generate the proper tag from that status information.

There are two interface chips to take the TTL serial inputs and outputs from the USARTs and convert them to EIA-RS232C + 12 and − 12 volt-serial pulses. These are simple level-translator integrated circuits.

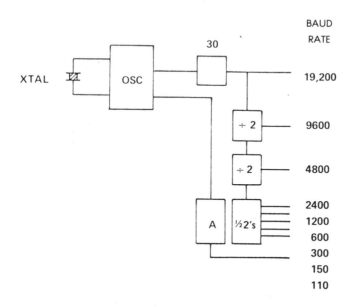

Fig. 7-12: Baud-Rate Generator

The last section consists of an astable multivibrator, synchronized by a crystal, to provide the timing for the serial-bit clocks. Two simple dividers are on each board to provide the USARTs with all of the common serial rates. This is shown in Fig. 7-12.

The Host Interface Board

This module contains: the host USART, the interrupt controller, and a baud-rate generator for the host-to-multiplexer communication rates. It appears in Fig. 7-13.

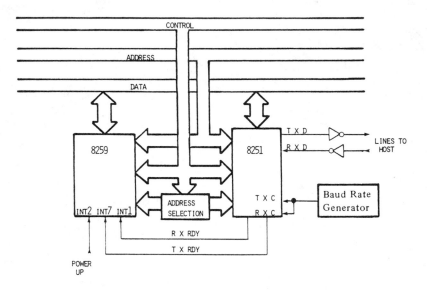

Fig. 7-13: Host Interface Board

The units on this board are addressed as input-output ports, instead of memory locations. The USART is addressed as ports "F9" and

PORTS F7 AND F8 ARE PIC

CONTROL	ADDRESS	DATA	OPERATION	
WRITE I/O				
WRITE I/O	F8	32	SETS LOW ADDRESS FOR CALL ⎤	FOR INT 1
WRITE I/O	F7	00	SETS HIGH ADDRESS FOR CALL ⎦	
WRITE I/O	F8	F2	SETS LOW ADDRESS FOR CALL ⎤	FOR INT 7
WRITE I/O	F7	00	SETS HIGH ADDRESS FOR CALL ⎦	
WRITE I/O	F7	70	ENABLES ONLY INT 1 AND INT 7	
WRITE I/O	F8	A0	SETS ROTATING PRIORITY RESET MODE	

Fig. 7-14: PIC Software Load Format

```
0000                        ORG OH          ;INITIALIZATION STARTS
0000 00        RST0:        NOP
0001 31FF2F                 LXI SP,2FFFH    ;SET THE STACK POINTER
0004 F3                     DI              ;DISABLE THE INTRRUPTS
0005 C3D700                 JMP INIT        ;SYSTEM RESTART UPON RESET
0008 C5        RST1:        PUSH B          ;HOST TO MUX RST VECTOR
0009 D5                     PUSH D          ;PUSH STATUS VECTOR
000A E5                     PUSH H
000B F5                     PUSH PSW
000C CD4900                 CALL INT70      ;INT70 GETS THE CHARACTER FROM
000F 3E08                   MVI A,0008H     ;HOST--DECODES IT AND RETURNS.
0011 D3F8                   OUT 00F8H       ;INTERRUPT CONTROLLER RESET INT 1
0013 F1                     POP PSW
0014 E1                     POP H
0015 D1                     POP D           ;FLAG
0016 C1                     POP B           ;POP STATUS VECTOR
0017 EF                     RST 5           ;PRIME QUEUE
0018 FB                     EI

0019 C9                     RET
0020                        ORG 0020H
0020 CDC700     RST4:       CALL SND50      ;SOFTWARE RESET
0023 C7                     RST 0

0028                        ORG 0028H
0028 F5         RST5:       PUSH PSW        ;SAVE A AND FLAGS
0029 DBFA                   IN 00FAH        ;READ THE USRT STATUS
002B E601                   ANI 0001H       ;CHK FOR TXRDY
002D CA3100                 JZ POPAF        ;IF USRT IS BUSY RETURN
0030 FF                     RST 7           ;ELCE CALL RST7 FOR FIFO SERVICE
                                            ;TO CHK IF ANYTHING IS IN THE
                                            ;FIFO TO SEND TO 11/70
0031 F1         POPAF:      POP PSW
0032 C9                     RET
0038                        ORG 0038H
0038 C5         RST7:       PUSH B          ;MUX TO HOST RST VECTOR
0039 D5                     PUSH D
003A E5                     PUSH H          ;CHANNEL NOT BUST
003B F5                     PUSH PSW
003C CD1802                 CALL OINT       ;OINT IS OUTPUT A CHARACTER
003F 3E08                   MVI A,0008H
0041 D3F8                   OUT 00F8H       ;FROM QUEUE
0043 F1                     POP PSW
0044 E1                     POP H
0045 D1                     POP D
```

Fig. 7-15: Example of Interrupt Control

RST0;   Hardware Initialize.

RST1;   Character from Host has arrived.

RST4;   Soft-reset on program fail ROM
             detect.

RST5;   Channel to Host is not-busy check.
             Mux to Host buffer queue should be
             emptied.

RST7;   Channel to Host is not-busy. Check
             buffer queue for characters, if any
             transmit, if not, return.

Fig. 7-16: Vectors in Software

"FA" hexadecimal, for control and data, respectively. There is a duplicate of the baud-rate circuit here to generate the "TxC" and "RxC" signals for the host-to-multiplexer USART, as these rates may differ from any of the others in a typical system.

The interrupt controller takes the "RxRdy" and TxRdy" signals from the USART and generates two interrupt vectors, number 1 and number 7. Number 1 is to signal that a character has been received from the host and should be processed, and number 7 indicates that the USART can be reloaded to transmit another character to the host.

The 8259 interrupt controller is set up by the initialization routine, to call the service routines at the proper locations and service the interrupts on a rotating basis. After an interrupt has been serviced, the software will reset the corresponding bit flag in the 8259, and proceed with polling, until a new interrupt arrives.

Fig. 7-14 illustrates the initialization procedure of the PIC and Fig. 7-16 presents the interrupt-handling code at the beginning of memory.

PICTURES OF MULTIPLEXER PROTOTYPE P.C. BOARDS:

Fig. 7-17: CPU

395

Fig. 7-17: RAM

Fig. 7-19: Terminals' USARTs

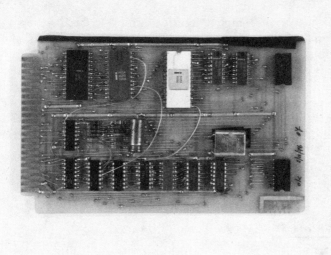

Fig. 7-20: Host and Interrupt Control

The channel-to-host was set to 9600 baud in both directions. The characters from each terminal must be echoed, as this is a full-duplex system. For every character generated, the host must process and return the echo. There are 24 Lear-Siegler ADM-3s terminals, set to 9600-baud input and output. There are also four 300-baud terminals and four 300-baud dial-up lines on the multiplexer.

Typical averaged input rate is ten characters-per-second. Average output rate is 200 characters-per-second. Buffers in the host, for characters waiting for output channel, are 95% of the time empty, indicating the host can get rid of data as fast as the channel can handle it, rather than as fast as the terminals can print. Maximum rates measured are 15 characters-per-second on input, and 620 characters-per-second on output. The maximum and typical figures were obtained over a 17-hour period, when 90% of the terminals on the multiplexer were in use.

Error rates were entirely due to the channel, or at least indistinguishable from other errors, such as operator errors and host errors.

Photographs of the printed-circuit boards appear in Figs. 7-17, 7-18, 7-19, 7-20.

397

CONCLUSION

In this chapter, a complete interface was described. A step-by-step discussion of how each component was integrated into a module, how the modules created a subsystem and then the overall system, should enable the reader to follow through almost any other microprocessor interface application. This particular application utilizes most of the techniques discussed in previous chapters: interrupts, memory and I/O management, integrating special techniques for software reduction in hardware, and external device interface were used here.

THE SYSTEM OVERVIEW

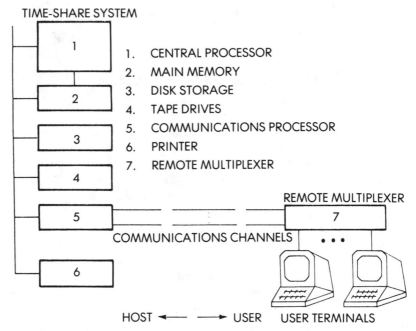
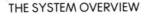

1. CENTRAL PROCESSOR
2. MAIN MEMORY
3. DISK STORAGE
4. TAPE DRIVES
5. COMMUNICATIONS PROCESSOR
6. PRINTER
7. REMOTE MULTIPLEXER

Fig. 7-21: Overall System

8

TESTING

INTRODUCTION

What do you do when it doesn't work? What went wrong and why? The debugging process, also known as testing or trouble-shooting, is an integral part of any system design. Murphy's Law usually holds: if anything can go wrong, it will.

When faced with a misbehaving system, there are a number of techniques available to the designer for identifying and correcting problems. In this chapter, the causes of common problems, and their solutions, will be presented. Problems such as component failure, software failure, and noise-induced failure will be analyzed, and methods for identifying them will be presented.

The tools necessary in order to identify and locate these problems will also be described: voltmeter, logic probe, signature analyzer, oscilloscope, digital analyzer, in-circuit emulator, emulator, and simulator.

Finally, a case history of the "One Bit in 16,384" will be presented. The example illustrates the debugging phase in the actual design of the multiplexer presented in Chapter 7.

WHAT GOES WRONG?

Four essential problems may arise in a system: wiring fault—a short or open circuit; component failure—including wrong value components; software bugs; and noise or interference—either internal or external.

Wiring faults are detected by a resistance check from point to point in the system. Check each wire: *make sure it goes to the right pin and no other* on the integrated circuit. Make sure you look up circuit pinouts twice. *Do not be confident that the schematic is without fault until the system works.*

Wiring faults are the most common and troublesome problems. They are easily solved—although they take time. Most circuit boards are "buzz-tested" with a simple continuity-checker that emits a tone for a short, and no noise for an open. Such a tester leaves both hands and eyes free to keep track of the wiring.

Component Failure

Components such as resistors, capacitors, inductors, transformers, transistors, diodes, integrated circuits, and connectors may all experience failures. Resistors crack open; capacitors leak out their electrolyte. In short, *no component is perfect. Everything fails sooner or later.* Each component is given a figure of merit, known as its *mean-time-between-failures* or *MTBF*. This is a statistical prediction, in hours, of *how long the part will last in a given environment.* A table of percent/1000 hours failure rate is shown in Fig. 8-1 for applications in military avionics.

Component	(%/1,000 hr) Failure Rate
1. Capacitor	0.02
2. Connector contact	0.005
3. Diode	0.013
4. Integrated circuits, SSI, MSI, and LSI	0.015
5. Quartz crystal	0.05
6. Resistor	0.002
7. Soldered joint	0.0002
8. Transformer	0.5
9. Transistor	0.04
10. Variable resistor	0.01
11. Wire-wrapped joint	0.00002

Fig. 8-1: Failure Rates for Military Applications

Some parts last longer, on the average, than others. Of course, *this table assumes that all parts are being used properly.* These figures are based on accelerated-life tests on a large sample for each part.

Failure rate is defined as 1/MTBF. Knowing the failure rate of each component in a system will yield the failure rate for the entire system. The rule is to add the failure rates of all of the components in the system. This gives the system failure rate—the inverse of which is the system meantime-between-failures.

For example, suppose we have three LSI chips, one crystal, ten resistors, ten capacitors, a printed circuit board with connectors, a transformer, four diodes, and an IC voltage regulator. This system is to be used in the same environment as the components that were tested. What is the system failure rate? Using Fig. 8-1, we find:

four ICs	.06
crystal	.05
ten resistors	.02
ten capacitors	.50
P.C. board	∼.60 (10 connectors, 500 soldered points)
transformer	.50
diodes	.052
TOTAL	1.82%/1,000 hours

This yields a MTBF for the system of:

$$1/1.82\%/1,000 \text{ hours or} \approx 60,000 \text{ hours}$$

Suppose we made 1000 of these systems, and used them in the specified environment? After 1000 hours, it would be most probable that 18 would have failed. After 10,000 hours, 180 would have failed.

How often do parts fail? This simple question, which we have answered on an average basis, tells us nothing about the *distribution of failures*. It gives the *mean*. Most components exhibit the following lifetime characteristics shown in Fig. 8-2.

Most failures occur when new, or when old, and fewer failures occur in the "middle-age" of the components.

"New" and "old" differ for each component. In-depth analysis of the entire system involves simple but time-consuming calculations concerning each component's lifetime failure history.

A "burn-in" test tries to weed out the *"infant-mortality"* part of the curve before parts are shipped to the buyer.

The table is accurate only for the environment specified. Commercial, industrial, and military applications all lead to different ways of measuring the MTBF. A unit designed for a child's toy may last five

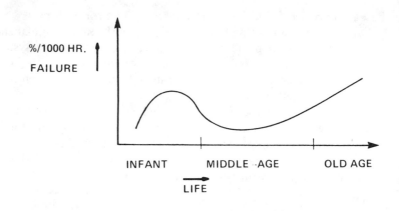

Fig. 8-2: %/1000 Hr. Failure versus Age

years, if used as a toy; if shot into space, it would not last five minutes. The application's environment determines the basic reliability statistics to be used.

So far, we have only addressed the topic of *reliability.* A separate problem is *quality.* Contrary to intuition, high quality doesn't always mean high reliability. Quality refers to how well a component will last, doing its job. The part may be noisy, dissipate lots of heat—but it may also work longer than a part that is quiet and dissipates less heat. Only thorough statistical analysis can determine reliability. Quality is easily measured on a part-by-part basis.

Software

Software can be at fault. For example, suppose there is a special routine in the program for handling a power failure. The problem is that, when coding, a mistake was made in the part of the program which restores the machine when power returns. *If you never tested this routine, it may not be used until the power fails. Only then will you know that your machine does not meet specifications.*

A second example is when an arithmetic calculation causes an overflow-and-halt condition only when some measured input value is "0". The system may work well for months, and then stop mysteriously every two days after that. Software problems, or *bugs,* are often the hardest to identify.

Tools for finding who is at fault, engineer vs. programmer, will be after the noise discussion. However, software problems are the most common in a microcomputer system. No program is ever perfect. A program is limited in precision, speed, and flexibility. The smart programmer is a complete pessimist about his software until it has been running for a number of years.

Noise

Noise is everywhere. Whenever there is a current in a wire, there is an electromagnetic field. Thus, fields from power transformers, motors, and electrical wiring are everywhere. In addition, with all the radio, television, citizens' band, and amateur radio transmitters—any length of wire becomes an antenna. *Not only can noise come from the outside, but it can be generated inside your system.*

Four examples are:

1. When integrated circuits switch, they generate small current changes in their power requirements because of internal circuit characteristics. If too many circuits switch at once, the power-supply voltage may change enough to affect other parts of the circuit. There are usually bypass capacitors near each integrated circuit to prevent this type of noise.
2. If two wires are close together, a pulse traveling along one induces a pulse in the other, because of the transformer action between the two. The induced pulse may reflect, and toggle a flip-flop, or cause the data to be incorrect. To prevent this, twisted and shielded pair transmission lines are used.
3. The power-supply may not be properly designed. There is a small amount of 60-cycle ripple on the 5-volt supply. This may affect the contents of memory and cause an improper read or write. Proper power-supply design accounts for the droop in voltage under heavy load before the regulation circuits.

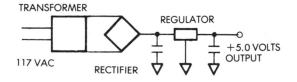

Fig. 8-3: Noise Spike on Power Line

4. In Fig. 8-3, there is a typical noise spike from turning on a teletype on the power line. Notice what happens to that noise spike in a plain power supply in Fig.8-4, without noise filters. If that glitch happens at a crucial moment, data are lost and the machine fails.

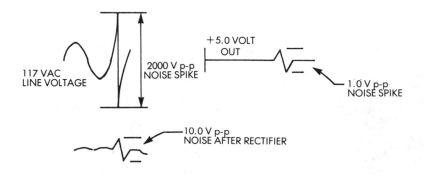

Fig. 8-4: Power Supply without Line Filter

The solution here is to use a line filter and a shielded transformer, that prevent high-frequency noise pulses from getting through, as in Fig. 8-5.

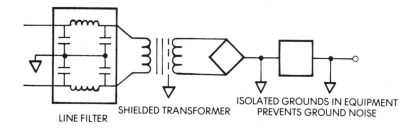

Fig. 8-5: Power Supply with Line Filter

Summary of Common Failures

Components fail at predictable rates, software may not be reliable and correct, and noise may be happening all around and inside the system. How do we go about finding the fault in a rational fashion?

The next section will deal with the tools used to find the faults and identify them. In this discussion of tools, the tell-tale signs of each problem will be discussed.

The Trouble-Shooting Tools

We will present here the tools available and the kinds of problems which can be identified with them. Tools will be examined closely as to their own limitations.

Fig. 8-6 presents a short summary of problems and tools. The discussion will follow this table and expand on each problem—what a tool can do to find it, and how long it would take.

Simple Problems

Short and open conductors, wrong voltages—these are the most common problems. Luckily, they are the easiest to detect. Any ohm meter can check for gross conditions, such as open, or short, and a digital voltmeter (DVM) or volt-ohm-milliampmeter (VOM) will suffice to check voltage and currents. If you know your components and design, it is an easy matter (although time-consuming) to make sure everything goes where it belongs and draws the right currents from the proper voltages.

The VOM

To measure a voltage, the meter is placed in parallel with the circuit element. Fig. 8-7 shows the measurement of the power-supply voltage at the output of a regulator. The VOM will easily measure all such voltages, but be warned that it will not detect excessive ripple or noise on the power supplies.

To measure a current, the meter must be placed in series with the component. This means the circuit must be broken. If possible, connections should be made, so that in-circuit current measurements need not cut wires or traces. Any dynamic behavior of the circuit may not be measurable, yet could cause problems.

THE DEBUG MATRIX: PROBLEMS & TOOLS

You can solve problems like:	You have Equipment						
	VOM	PROBES	SGN.ANA.	OSC.	D.D.A.	I.C.E.	EMU.
· shorts, opens, wrong voltages	yes	maybe	no	yes	maybe	maybe	no
· bad resistors, caparitors	yes	no	no	yes	no	no	no
· unknown logic signals bad-fault tree already generated	yes	yes	yes	yes	yes	no	no
· unknown logic signals bad-fault tree available	yes	yes time consuming	no	yes time consuming	yes	yes	no
· software problem	no	no	no	maybe	yes	yes	yes

To fix a typical Problem:	You need at least						
Eventually	yes	yes		yes			
In an average time	yes			yes	yes		
Fastest way possible	yes			yes	yes	yes	

TABLE OF ABBREVIATIONS

VOM	VOLT-OHM-MILLIAMPMETER
PROBES	LOGIC PROBES
SGN.ANA.	SIGNATURE ANALYSER
OSC.	OSCILLOSCOPE
D.D.A.	DIGITAL DOMAIN ANALYSER
I.C.E.	IN CIRCUIT EMULATOR
EMU.	SOFTWARE EMULATOR OR SIMULATOR

Fig. 8-6: Problems and Tools

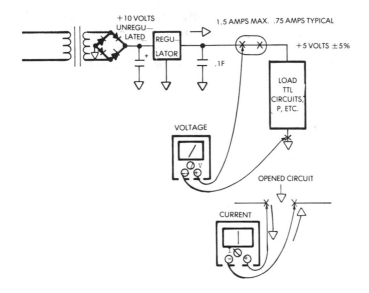

Fig. 8-7: Measuring Voltage and Current with a VOM

In the power-supply example, the meter measured the voltage across the load, and then by disconnecting the load and reconnecting it through the meter, the current was measured. Be sure to check that these measurements are within the required tolerances. Improper values may indicate later trouble.

Bad Components

Resistors, capacitors, diodes, and transistors can all be checked against known good devices. They can be measured with the DVM or VOM to determine whether they are basically functional. Other special test equipment is needed for diodes and transistors to establish device characteristics.

Integrated circuits are difficult to test without expensive equipment. When debugging, several of each device used should be kept in stock, in order to replace a device with an inherent malfunction. Once the entire circuit is working, all devices in stock should be tested in the prototype system, to make sure that no marginal problems occur in production due to component tolerance changes.

Simple problems usually prevent the system from working at all. Intermittent failures are most often due to connector or bad solder-joint problems. These should be checked first, before assuming something else is at fault. All intermittent problems will require an oscilloscope (preferably with storage) or a logic-analyzer for quick, effective debugging.

All static problems can be solved. This is the first step; be completely confident about this stage before continuing.

Design Problems

You thought you knew what you wanted—but you didn't. Yes, we all make mistakes, so we might as well admit it. Design errors are divided into two general categories: *improper specification* and *improper use*. Examples of each follow.

Improper Use

Passing too much current through a resistor will cause it to burn up. Applying too much voltage to a capacitor will cause it to short. Every device has its limits. The "too much" problem is the most common. For example, too many loads on a single output line may cause the system to read or write improper data values intermittently, depending on temperature variation.

Improper Specification

If we believe a part to be able to drive 30 bus loads when it can only drive 20—this is improper specification. It simply was not noticed in the data sheet upon specification.

More subtly, the timing of a particular part may be misunderstood. For example, if the address gated to a memory part must be stable 20 nanoseconds before the data and write pulses, this may have been overlooked and the system timing design may violate this condition.

Design problems require a full range of equipment for proper troubleshooting, but a VOM-oscilloscope combination will suffice if time is of little concern. These problems manifest themselves primarily in an intermittent fashion in the case of overloading bus lines, and in burning and smoking parts in the case of overvoltage/current.

The burning parts problems are simple—get a bigger part or improve the design so it will work with the parts you have.

408

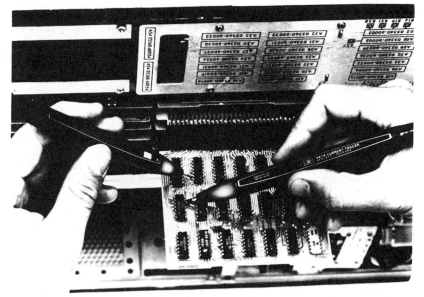

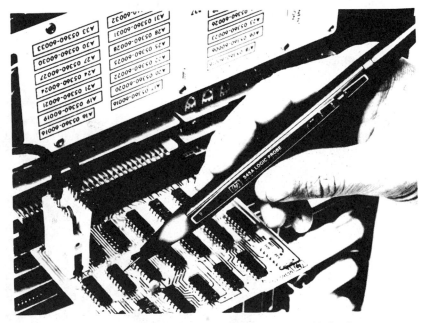

New Hewlett-Packard Model 545A Logic Probe for fast troubleshooting

Fig. 8-8: Logic Probes

The intermittent problems require that all input-output loading be checked, all device specifications be checked, and the system operated at different temperatures to localize the sensitive component(s).

A can of freeze spray and a heat lamp can locate temperature sensitive problems quickly and easily, by selectively heating and cooling the suspected parts.

Logic Probes

Logic probes can verify logic levels quickly, so as to isolate any static conditions efficiently. The probes will indicate whether a signal is a 0, 1, or undetermined by using an LED indicator or light bulb. Watch out for undetermined states; unless it is a tri-state bus floating, and it is supposed to be floating, something may be wrong. Fig. 8-8 illustrates a logic probe in use.

DYNAMIC PROBLEMS

In operation, the system doesn't work. *The VOM, logic probe, etc., will not indicate time. Thus, they are of little use in the dynamic case.* We need devices which will indicate that the logic-level timing is correct.

The Oscilloscope

To obtain timing information, the *oscilloscope* is most commonly used. With one or more traces, events may be measured accurately in amplitude and duration, in function of time. In microprocessor systems, events as short as 10 nanoseconds should be observable with an oscilloscope. A 10-nanosecond square wave will appear as a sine wave on a 10-megahertz oscilloscope. Thus, to see these events clearly, a 50 or 100-megahertz scope is desirable. Fig. 8-9 illustrates the trace on a typical oscilloscope of a TTL logic-control signal.

The logic zone definitions here are for standard TTL. The logic "0" signal is for any voltage between -0.6 and $+0.8$ volts. The logic "1" signal is from $+2.0$ volts to $+5.5$ volts. Anything in the zone from $+8.0$ to $+2.0$ is considered undefined. Transitions from one level to the other should occur in much less than one microsecond to avoid noise problems. The oscilloscope will indicate if a bad logic level is present. For example, if two TTL outputs are connected, we have violated a design rule. If the condition occurs, in which the two outputs wish to go in opposite directions, one of the gates may be destroyed. If the condition occurs for only a few microseconds at a time, no harm will be done; however, the fault will cause problems. Fig. 8-10 shows a trace for such a condition. Note how the logic "0" level is not correct.

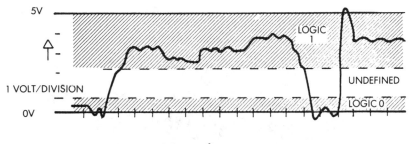

Fig. 8-9: TTL Logic Signal

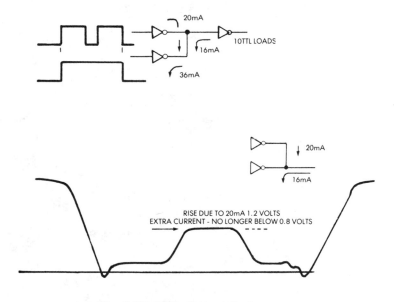

Fig. 8-10: TTL Output Fault

Such a measurement, along with the knowledge of the logic family drive specifications, will indicate to the trouble-shooter where the fault lies.

Observing chip-select, control and bus lines with the oscilloscope will clue you to load problems, timing problems, and noise problems. Make sure that the logic levels are well-defined. TTL "0" should be from -0.6 to $+0.8$ volts. TTL "1" should be from 2.0 to 5.5 volts. Anything else means trouble.

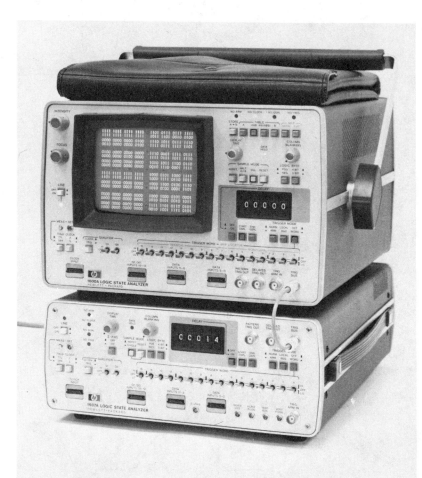

Fig. 8-11: HP 1600S Analyzer

STATE MEASUREMENT

All system timing and system logic levels are correct when observing any single bit or line—but we need to observe all the lines at once in time. We could gather 16 oscilloscopes together (and early analyzers were simply multi-channel oscilloscopes), but it is not specially convenient to observe 32 tiny traces on the face of an oscilloscope tube. For this reason, we developed *logic analyzers,* or more accurately, *digital-domain analyzers.*

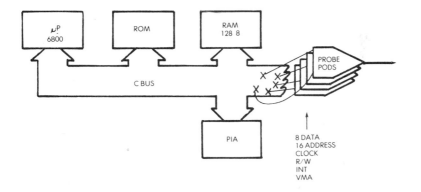

Fig. 8-12: Connecting the Analyzer

Logic Analyzer

What does a digital-domain analyzer do? It allows us to observe up to 32 nodes in the system *simultaneously.* It will display these bits in binary, octal, hexadecimal, or in the form of conventional oscilloscope traces. It will begin displaying the information when a given combination of bits, or *trigger,* occurs. It will store every clock cycle, or more often a new set of signals, and be able to display a few sets of signals *before* and *after* the trigger set. Each set of signals in time is known as a *state.*

Available analyzers fall into two categories: those that emphasize *timing* information, and those that emphasize *state* information.

Timing-oriented analyzers are merely multi-channel oscillocopes. These devices are useful where logic glitches, noise, or logic-level problems are suspected.

State-oriented analyzers attempt to present the flow of the system's program by monitoring all important circuit points. State analyzers are effective in debugging software and complex software-hardware faults.

Example of a State Analyzer

The Hewlett-Packard 1600S Analyzer has 32 channels, two clocks, four trigger qualifiers, and many other features. The instrument will take a "snapshot" of the state of the system on every clock cycle. We will use the HP1600S to observe the interrupt cycle in a 6800-based processing system.

Fig. 8-13 lists the format of the data displayed on the 1600S. The probes were attached to the lines indicated. The clock was connected to Φ2.

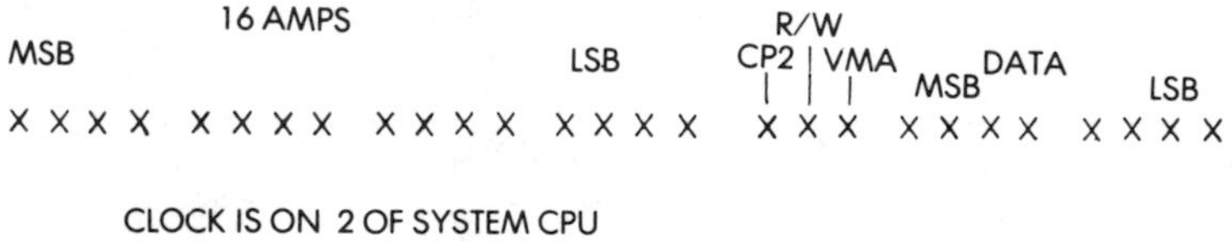

```
          16 AMPS                          R/W
 MSB                              LSB    CP2 | VMA    DATA
                                          |  |  | MSB       LSB
 X X X X   X X X X   X X X X   X X X X    X X X   X X X X   X X X X

        CLOCK IS ON  2 OF SYSTEM CPU
```

Fig. 8-13: HP 1600S Display Format for 6800 Interrupt

The 1600S was triggered by the interrupt signal. In Fig. 8-14, the state flow is displayed. The data displayed are:

1. The current instruction cycle is finished. Instruction is an "F2" hex at location "1385" hex.
2. The status is now pushed onto the stack, before going to the service-routine vector location. Note the stack is at locations "3FF" hex downward. The program counter, index register, accumulators, and flags are stored in successive locations in the stack.
3. The microprocessor now fetches the contents of addresses "FFF8" and "FFF9" hex. The contents are transferred to the program counter.
4. Interrupt-service routine begins at "1351" hex. Execution continues from this point.

With such a device we have a roadmap of where the system was, where it is, and where it is going.

Some analyzers store a proper sequence of states, continuously

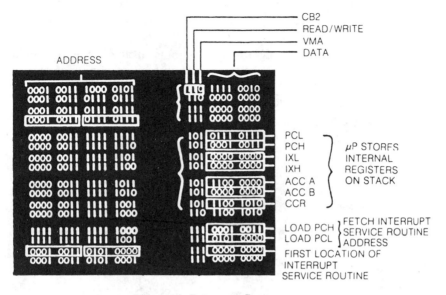

Fig. 8-14: Interrupt Sequence

compare those with the current states, and stop upon a mismatch. Others display a "1", "X", or "0" for each bit in a page of memory, and indicate if that bit has been read or written. Some store more states than others. However, all of these analyzers have similar basic characteristics of being able to observe a number of states in a system, in a time sequence.

The digital-domain analyzer allows the designer to monitor software execution so that wrong data, wrong addresses, or wrong instructions may be found. If a digital-domain analyzer is used to trigger an oscilloscope, noise problems and subtle timing problems may also be identified.

In-Circuit Emulation

In-circuit emulation allows us to "get inside" the microprocessor itself, dynamically watch where it is going, what it is reading and writing. It makes it possible to monitor the processor itself. It includes breakpoints and test routines to allow you to "catch" a specific section of code as it goes by and display the contents of the internal registers. By checking these against what you expected, the fault may be located.

Shown in Figures 8-15 and 8-16 are Biomation's Timing Analyzer and Hewlett-Packard's In-Circuit Emulator State Analyzer.

415

Signature Analysis

There is a whole range of special tools; usable after the initial
system has been built and tested. These systems rely on the known behavior of the original system in order to predict what went wrong in
the system, in the field.

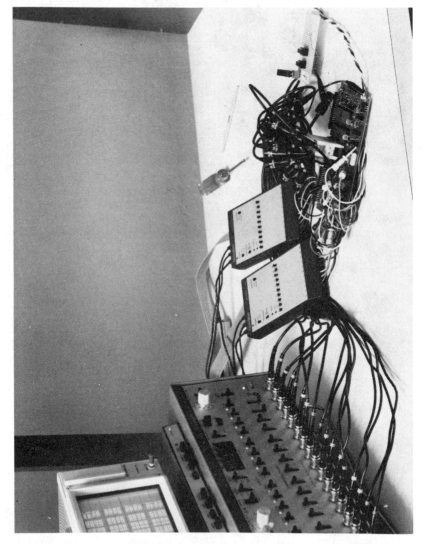

Fig. 8-15: Biomation Logic Analyzer

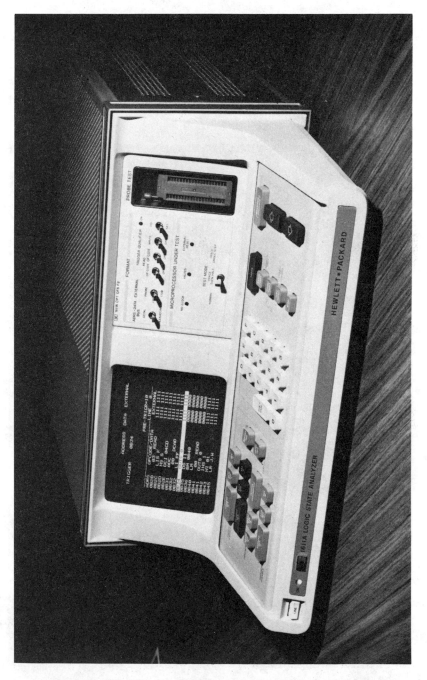

Fig. 8-16: HP ICE for 8080 System Mnemonic Analyzer

These techniques rely on a *fault-tree*. That is: everything that could go wrong has been made to go wrong, and, in each case, nodes in the circuit were measured to discover just how such a failure would manifest itself. Some fault-trees are short: if the fuse blows, replace it; if the fuse blows again, call the service department. Some trees walk the service person through the entire system, depending on measured values.

Fig. 8-17: HP 5004A Signature Analyzer

A Signature Analyzer

This device relies on the fact that any repetitive sequence of signal values may be stored in a recirculating shift register, whose value, clocked into a display each time around, will have a certain value. A device can be designed so that the probability of two bit streams having the same value or "signature" is extremely small.

Thus, each node in a system will have its own signature when it is working correctly. It will also have a special signature for each possible problem. By using a fault-tree method, developed by using the analyzer, all faulty equipment can be debugged quickly, down to a faulty component.

It will not find initial software problems, or the cause of intermittent failures in a system.

In Fig. 8-18 we see the trouble-shooting flowchart, using a HP 5004A Signature Analyzer. These signatures were generated on a good instrument and the chart developed to speed repair.

SOFTWARE TESTING TECHNIQUES

The underlying principle of all testing techniques is to compare an existing board, component, or system, to "what it should be." The problem naturally may be to know what it should be, or else to implement a reasonable procedure for performing this comparison in a systematic manner. In addition, two supplementary problems arise: making the measurements themselves, and recording the history of the last n signals. For this purpose, a number of new hardware and software tools have been developed. The test instruments and techniques used in performing such comparisons have been described in the preceding section. As usual in the computer world, either hardware or software methods can be used. The purpose of this section is to explain the software testing techniques.

Comparison Testing

In this method, a device, or a board, is compared to a known "good" device, or "good" board. They share the same common input, and outputs are compared. This is a hardware method, and the required tools have been presented. The next three techniques are essentially software techniques.

419

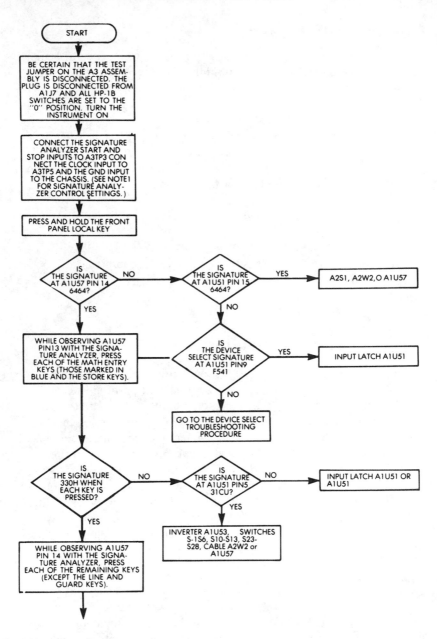

Fig. 8-18: Fault Tree

Self-Diagnostic

In the self-diagnostic method, the microprocessor system itself determines whether it is operational, and if not, which part of the system is defective. The basic principle of self-diagnostic is to execute a "worst-case" sequence and to observe the results. In the case of the MPU itself, a worst-case sequence of instructions is usually available from the manufacturer. Typically, such a sequence will exercise all the machine's instructions, in a pre-determined order. In addition, it may include some critical sequence of instructions which has been found to fail in some cases. Clearly, this information is usually available only from the manufacturer. Most of them are cooperative in supplying such a program. Naturally, the following question arises: *what if the MPU itself is indeed defective?* If it is defective, it is likely that the program will not terminate successfully, and that the system will "crash," with no external warning. When performing a self-diagnostic, an automatic warning mechanism must be used. For example, the system will print a message on the printer saying "undergoing diagnostic testing at time X." At time X plus one minute, the system should have completed diagnostic testing, and should print the message "diagnostic testing completed successfully." If such a message is not printed, the system will be assumed to have failed. Optionally, external devices may be set. For example, an external alarm, with its own timing mechanism, may be actuated at the beginning of the test. Unless the timer is reset within a specified amount of time, the alarm will go off, automatically signaling an MPU failure.

Such self-diagnostic programs are used extensively on systems enjoying idle time. It is a simple matter to write the basic test program using most of the machine instructions and residing in some unused portion of the ROM. Whenever the microprocessor is idle, such a program may be run thus verifying the machine integrity. In addition, if it is run continuously for a period of time, it will help isolate intermittent failures of the system. Naturally, it need not reside in ROM, and may be loaded in RAM from an external device.

Self-diagnostic is also used to test memory or input/output facilities. The topic of memory testing will be addressed in detail in a paragraph below on algorithmic pattern generation. In the case of an ROM memory, the simplest form of self-diagnostic is called *checksum validation*. In this technique, each block of data, such as 16, 32, or 256 words, is followed by a one-byte or two-byte checksum. Typically, such a checksum is computed by summing the n half-bytes of the

421

block of n words, using hexadecimal arithmetic. This sum is then truncated to the last four binary digits, and the checksum character is the ASCII encoding of the resulting hexadecimal digit. A simple program executing in a secure area of the ROM (a portion of the ROM which is assumed to be good) can read the contents of the rest of the ROM, recompute the checksum, and then compare it to the value which has been stored. If a mismatch is detected, an ROM failure has been identified.

Testing input-output interfaces and I/O devices is usually complex, in view of the delicate timing relationships involved. However, a rough checking is possible as to the correct overall operation of the devices themselves. Provided that feedback information is available from the device, an order will be issued by the program such as: "close relay A." If the feedback path is available, relay closure can be verified within n milliseconds. In this way, the system can exercise all of the external control devices, and verify their proper overall operation. In addition, during systems operation, "reasonableness tests" are usually run on all input devices (see book C201 for a complete discussion). Such tests will compare the value of input parameters to values in a table, stored in the memory, and determine whether this input data is "reasonable." For example, when measuring the temperature of water, temperatures below 0 °C and over 100 °C will be deemed "unreasonable." Similarly, for a microprocessor controlling a traffic light at an intersection, detecting vehicle speeds over 200 mph will be deemed unreasonable. Naturally, tests can be much finer than the simplified examples, in a specific environment. Such reasonableness testing will detect intermittent and permanent failures of input devices and will set off an external alarm.

Stored-Response

In the stored-response method, a large-scale computer system is used to emulate, or simulate, the device or the board under test. First, a program is used to measure the characteristics of the device, or system, under test, preferably under dynamic circumstances. This data is then recorded, and will be used by the comparison program. The comparison program is then applied to the device. It will generate input signals. The outputs are measured and compared to the previous response of the system, as stored in the tables. In such a system, two phases are necessary. The first phase is a characterization phase, where the computer system is used to record essential responses of the system that will later be used as references. Once these responses are obtained, in phase two, the system will only run in comparison mode by executing a specific test program and measuring the response.

This method is used essentially in production, and for incoming testers. The cost of the system required to provide efficient stored-response testing, plus the programs, can range from $50,000 to $500,000.

Algorithmic Pattern Generation

Algorithmic pattern generation is essentially used for testing RAM memory. The principle is to write a pattern in the memory, and then verify that:

1. It was written correctly.
2. Nothing was written anywhere else because of an RAM malfunction.

The two basic pattern-generation techniques used in RAM testing are fixed-pattern tests, and galloping-pattern tests.

Fixed-Pattern Testing

In a *fixed-pattern* test, identical, alternating, cyclical patterns are successively written, then read, at each memory location. This will detect gross RAM failures. However, this will not detect *pattern-sensitivity* problems. Pattern sensitivity is a typical source of failure in high-density chips. Because of the geometrical layout of the chip, some combination of bits written at some instant of time in memory cells might cause some other bit position elsewhere in the device to turn on or off. This problem can happen in RAM memories or in microprocessors themselves. Whenever this problem occurs in a microprocessor, it is a basic design failure, and there is not much the user can do about it. The best that can be done by the user is to run a worst-case program, supplied by the manufacturer, which has been shown to make similar units fail because of the specific sequence of instructions involved. This problem will not be considered here, as it is deemed highly infrequent once a chip has been in the field for more than a year. In the case of memory, however, especially in the case of high-density memory, pattern sensitivity is a frequent problem, which can be diagnosed relatively easily using an algorithmic pattern-generation test. This will be described in the following section.

Galloping-Pattern Testing

The galloping pattern test is usually abbreviated "galpat." The principle of this technique is to write successive binary values into memory cells, then compare them to all of the rest of the memory, before moving on to the next memory location. In this way, if writing into memory cell zero affected the contents of memory cell 102, this will be detected by the test. In a typical galpat, the memory will be initialized with a known content, such as all ones or all zeros. The basic test algorithm is the following:

1. The contents of a location L-1 are tested against the contents of all other memory locations. They should match.
2. The address L-1 is then incremented by one, and step one is carried out until all memory locations are tested.
3. The initial data pattern is then complemented, and one goes back to step one.

Many variations are possible on this basic galpat. They have been nicknamed "marching ones and zeros," "walking ones and zeros," and "galloping patterns" (galpat one and galpat two).

Ideally, one should write all possible patterns in each memory location, and, after writing a pattern in every word, check every other word of the memory to verify whether it might have been changed. In addition, after checking each of the other memory words, one should immediately come back to the original memory location under test in order to verify that its pattern has not been changed by the tests performed on another memory location. It could happen that the fact of checking every other memory location would modify the original contents of the memory cell, then modify them again so that eventually they would have the correct initial contents. A possible failure would then not be detected if one did not come back every time to verify the contents of the initial cell. It is easy to see that such exhaustive testing will require a very high number of operations. A simple memory exerciser, checking a 32 K memory, will typically run for several minutes. It will, for example, write all zeros, or all ones, or write its own address in each memory location, and then rotate these addresses through the available memory. If the test uses galpat techniques, it could easily run for half an hour, or even for several hours. For this reason, these tests are usually run only during the initial debugging phase of the system, or when a malfunction is suspected. It is not practical to consider their use once the microprocessor system is operational, unless a simplified version is used.

SIMULATION AND EMULATION

Let us first introduce the basic definitions. *Simulation* refers to the functional replacement of a hardware device by a program. It is said that the device is simulated by software. The program will generate the same outputs as the hardware device, in response to the same inputs. Unfortunately, it will perform such a simulation much more slowly than the original device.

Emulation refers essentially to a simulation performed in *real time*. In fact, many emulators will simulate the operation of a complete system even faster than the model. For example, many bit-slice systems emulate the instruction set of another computer. They will execute all the instructions of the processor being emulated at the same speed, or sometimes even faster.

Simulation is used for two essential devices: the microprocessor itself and the ROM memory. ROM simulation, or emulation, is performed by executing programs out of RAM, as if they were in ROM. This is normally done during the development phase of all programs. Clearly, an initial program will contain a number of bugs and should not be placed directly in a final ROM or PROM. In a typical development system, such a program will be installed in RAM memory and will be tested and debugged there. The two main problems are to convert the addresses of the final program into those required by the ROM and to maintain speed compatibility. Typically the RAM board resides at a specific physical address which will not correspond to the actual address of the ROM chip in the final system. The second problem is a synchronization problem whenever a slow RAM is used initially, and a program is then installed on a faster ROM. Such ROM-emulation or ROM-simulation facilities are a normal part of any microcomputer development system and will not be addressed in greater detail here.

Simulating and emulating the microprocessor itself is much more complex. Simulating the microprocessor is used in two cases:

1. when the MPU itself is not available
2. for convenience in debugging.

These two cases will not be detailed. When programs are developed on a large-scale system, *cross programs* are used. A cross assembler will create, for example, 8080 code on an IBM 370. It is necessary to test the correct execution of the resulting 8080 code. This will be performed with a simulator. An 8080 simulator will be used, which executes all the 8080 instructions in simulated time. In this way, the complete logic of the program will be tested. The essential limitation of such a simulator is the fact that no input-output can be tested unless the user deposits known data at the right time into selected memory locations. Input-output registers are then simulated by memory locations. Unfortunately, the timing of input-output is often random and almost always complex. For this reason, a simulator is only used to test the overall logic of a program. This is fine for testing numerical algorithms, such as a floating-point package. It is inadequate for debugging a complex input-output interface.

In any system where the user must test real input-output in real time, one of the most significant aids in testing is the emulation of the microprocessor itself. This is called "in-circuit emulation."

In-Circuit Emulation

In-circuit emulation was originally introduced by INTEL on its MDS system, and is now available on every leading microprocessor development system, as well as on independent systems. The picture of an actual "in-circuit emulator" (ICE) appears in (Fig. 8-19). A special board, which provides the in-circuit emulation facility, has been inserted on the INTEL MDS system. The system under development will be connected to the cable. The 8080 itself has been removed from its socket, and a special cable, called the "umbilical cord," has been plugged into the socket. This is the cable appearing in the illustration. This 40-line cable is terminated by a 40-pin connector identical to an actual 8080. The difference is that all the signals carried by this cable are generated by, or under the control of, the in-circuit emulator, rather than the real 8080. What is the purpose of replacing an actual 8080 by a software emulator? The facility provided by the emulator is to completely control and test the system under development (on the right) from the console. It is possible to stop the operation of the 8030. It is possible to examine the registers or change them. Doing this on an actual 8080 would require opening up the package, removing the lid, and placing microprobes under a microscope, to obtain the contents of the registers, if indeed this were possible. The contents of the registers are not available in an actual 8080. Only the values on the buses are. Using an emulator, it is possible to stop the operation of the 8080 automatically, using breakpoints in the program. This facility will be clarified below. It is possible to examine, or change, registers, as well as the contents of the memory. It is possible to sit at the keyboard and execute actual input-output instructions,

Fig. 8-19: Software Development

such as closing a relay, by hitting a key on the keyboard. It is then possible to stop the processor again and examine the buses, the registers, or the memory. In addition, all the operations may be performed in conjunction with the powerful software aids available in a development system. Examining, or changing, memory can be performed in symbolic form, rather than in binary or hexadecimal. This is called symbolic debugging.

Breakpoints are a facility for specifying and addressing where the program will automatically stop. Addresses are selected, and a list of breakpoints is given to the emulator. When the specified location is reached during execution, the emulated microprocessor will automatically stop and allow the user to verify contents of registers, buses or memory. In addition, an in-circuit emulator provides a capability called trace-back. It provides a snapshot of the history of the signals on the buses during a specified length of time. In the case of the INTEL ICE, it provides a 44-machine-cycle trace-back. Whenever a breakpoint is encountered, the in-circuit emulator stops the execution and provides the user with a symbolic debugging facility. Typically, when an error is detected at the breakpoint, it was not caused by the instruction at the breakpoint, but was the result of a previous instruction in the program. The problem is to locate the previous instruction which caused the problem. This is a tracing problem. With the traceback capability, it is possible to examine the previous signals, and to determine which were the instructions executed before the detection of the error. If this historical record is not long enough, an earlier breakpoint can be set-up and an additional segment of the history of the system will become available. This process can be repeated until the error is finally identified.

An in-circuit emulator does not require an important configuration for software or hardware to execute. It is a debugging capability. As it provides for the first time a tool for checking the operation of the complete system including the actual input-output boards, or interfaces, the availability of an in-circuit emulator is essential.

DEBUGGING A CONCEPTUAL PROCESSOR

After all logic levels are verified to be reasonable, the system is ready for some *simple* test programs. Do not get too ahead of yourself here! Try simple things such as: address sequentially every possible memory location, jump to "0000" hexadecimal continually, input from a port, and output the data input to an output port. Put these tests in separate PROMs so that they can be executed individually.

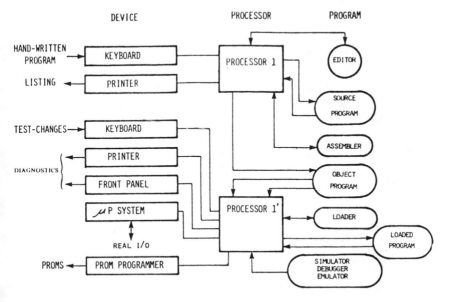

Fig. 8-20: Debug Flowchart

The address test should result in each of the address bit lines toggling at increasing long time with square waves.

The jump test is so short, that it is usually possible to observe all lines with an oscilloscope to check all dynamic conditions. Also, all of the address bits—from bit A2 to bit A15—should be all zeroes in the suggested test.

The input-output will allow each input bit to be tested. If the bit is held high, the corresponding bit on the output should also go high. If it does not, there is a fault with the input-output scheme in the system, or the microprocessor.

Now it can get interesting. Try larger programs, working your way up to the final applications program. *At this point, all problems should be software ones. If you are sure it is hardware—why? Go back and write different simple test programs to establish whether you are right or wrong. Remember: if a few instructions work OK, usually they all work OK.*

A helpful point here is that small debugging systems' software ROMs are available for most prototyping situations. They are usually called Hex (or Octal) Debug and Test Programs, or System Monitors. Fig. 8-20 illustrates the debug flow for a typical situation.

Typical Problems Unique to Micros

The following is a list of some interesting problems the authors have found:

— A bad address bit on the microprocessor, causing any program beyond "1FFF" hex to not execute properly.

— Excessively leaky EPROM lost its data before you could plug it back into the system from the PROM programmer.

— PMOS and NMOS circuits cannot always be connected without buffering. This is true of all logic families. "TTL-compatible" means it will connect to TTL—*not that it connects to something else labelled TTL-compatible!* This may cause serious problems. As an example: a PMOS address line to an NMOS RAM may cause one bit in the RAM to go bad *at random!* These problems are usually heat and power-supply sensitive. Your system should work over a wide range of temperatures and over a specified power-supply range. Check all specifications closely.

— Dynamic RAMs can and do go bad at one single bit location at random. This is the reason for error detection, parity, and error-correction in large memory systems.

— Know your buses. As a rule, connect no more than one input and one output to any bus line. Overlooking this may cause noise-sensitivity problems due to overloading. The most common line that violates this rule is the RESET line.

— *Don't plug it in upside down or skewed down by one pin. Know which way is up, down, right and left.* If in doubt, measure your circuit at the socket and call the manufacturer to find where pin one is.

A trouble-shooting flowchart is presented in Fig. 8-21.

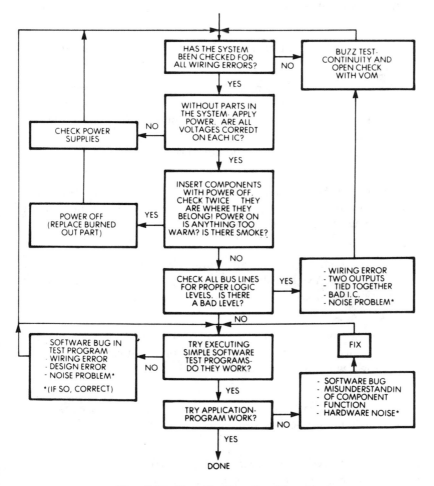

Fig. 8-21: Trouble-Shooting Flowchart

THE ONE BIT IN 16,384

The multiplexer design described in Chapter 8 took six man-months to debug completely, with two full-time engineers assigned to this task, with all of the tools mentioned in this chapter available to them. Thus, the real cost of debugging this system was:

— 6 months' salary: $10,000
— 6 months' equipment: $15,000 (if rented)
$ 8,000 (five-year use).

This section will focus on actual problems, as they were found.

Week 1:
Wire-wrapped version of design finished. Buzz-testing begun.

Week 2:
Buzz-test finished. Each module has about 20 errors out of 1000 connections. Power applied and one board has a short between power and ground. Power supply blew up. Wire found by applying large current to board with no part in it, and "burning out" the short. It was a shorted bypass capacitor on a memory board.

Week 3:
Each board being checked for logic signals, etc., separately. Average of one more error per board found in wiring. Printed-circuit boards being made for wire-wrap modules.

Week 4:
Prototype system executes all simple test routines. Bad memory chip found in RAM boards on a memory test program that wrote alternate ones and zeroes into every cell.

Week 5:
Bus-loading problem with system program. EPROM on CPU card, a buffer added to this card. Applications program can do input and output for a while without crashing.

Week 6:
Looks like only software problems now. P.C. layouts are ready for wiring check before boards are made.

Week 7:
P.C. board layout approved, about 5 errors per board found. System has a baffling problem: will run for a few hours then give garbage to host system.

Week 8:

P.C. boards back and debugged. Replaced wire-wrap boards with P.C. boards, one at a time, to check for errors.

Week 9:

Still fixing wiring errors on P.C. boards. System still acting funny. Logic analyzer is being used extensively to find the problem.

Week 10:

Bad bus driver on host USART card found. Now only crashes every day or so. P.C. boards finished. System will sometimes pick up improper data from terminal. In-circuit emulator being used to check the data pick-up routine on a trace-back basis. Problem only happens every 8 hours or so—thus, truly difficult to catch.

Week 11:

Argument between programmers and designers—unhealthy finger-pointing session. Friday the fault is found. Two problems.

Week 12:

There was a bad bit in the EPROM used for the program, and the carry bit was not cleared upon entering the interrupt routines, where an add-with-carry instruction was used, instead of an add-with-no-carry instruction. The instruction determined the location of the data to be transmitted, hence it would occasionally get the wrong data upon encountering a carry set after an interrupt. The problem of the bad bit came by checking the PROM against the listing four times (it escaped detection that long!). The problem of the wrong instruction was traced back using the logic analyzer, when it triggered on a read from the wrong place.

Epilog:

Except for statistical failures, three identical systems have been in use since the end of Week 12. There have been fewer failures in the multiplexers, with ten times less downtime, than in the main computers to which they are connected.

SUMMARY

Components, software, and noise are the only "things to blame" if a problem occurs. The flowcharts presented have described a simple method of approaching typical microprocessor-related problems. The equipment needed for a good microprocessor debugging station was presented, and examples of each have been given. For reference, all of the equipment required in a prototyping situation is illustrated in Fig. 8-22. Note the cost: typically $45,000. Use anything less, and the time required to fix things or find out what is wrong will increase.

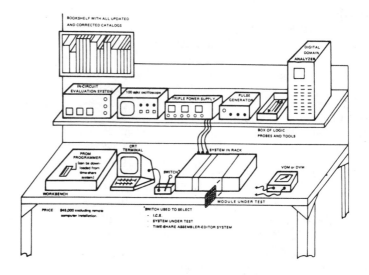

Fig.8-22: Prototyping Equipment

Future hardware debugging tools will be oriented towards the state-type of analyzer discussed. A large number of state, trace, and trigger-capabilities, as well as the ability to format the display of the states in any machine's mnemonics, will be features of the new machines. Also their use on minicomputers and large computers will become wide-spread, with some systems including an analyzer in the unit for self-diagnosis.

REMEMBER!
DON'T

Don't handle an IC unless you are properly grounded, or the ambient humidity is high. A static charge, such as the one generated by walking on carpeting on a dry day, will destroy most MOS chips with a several-thousand-volt discharge.

Don't install a board in your computer unless:

1. Power is off
2. You have waited 15 seconds (all charges should have dissipated by then).

Don't turn your computer ON or OFF with the diskette inserted: transients may wipe it out. Always turn the computer ON first, insert diskette, remove diskette, then turn the computer OFF.

Don't select several devices for input simultaneously by generating incorrect addresses, or else have spare MPU chips available.

Don't trust voltage levels. Check them.

Dont't give up.

Fig. 8-23: 8080 Family I.C.s

9

EVOLUTION

TECHNOLOGICAL EVOLUTION

Beginning with the fundamentals of system interconnection, we have traveled through the interfacing techniques. Throughout, the direction of the evolution has been towards the use of completely integrated interfaces. The original racks, full of circuitry, previously required, have now been reduced to a small number of LSI chips. The future will bring more intelligent peripheral chips which will result in increased performance and flexibility.

The central processor at the heart of every system is now a single LSI chip. The interconnection of the memories and processor will be eliminated in the future by *one-chip microcomputers*. These one-chip devices will contain ROM, RAM, and input-output facilities adequate to perform most interface tasks. Such devices are already being introduced: the Texas Instrument 9940, the Intel 8048, Fairchild Mostek 3870, and others. They are characterized by a 1K to 2K ROM, plus 64 to 128 words of RAM, plus clock and timer on the MPU chip. The 16 pins freed by the unnecessary address bus become available as two 8-bit input-output ports.

The Texas Instrument 9940 is a 16-bit microcomputer with 1K ROM, RAM, and input-output in a single chip. The power of a 16-bit instruction allows the implementation of a complete instruction set, including hardware multiply and divide. Unfortunately, the small ROM is a major limitation.

The Intel 8048 integrates a 1K by 8 PROM and a 32-byte register file on a single chip, and provides 27 lines of input-output. An EPROM version, the 8748, allows the program to be erased and reprogrammed during development. The versatility gained by using an eraseable ROM, on the same chip as the processor and input-output, makes 8748 easily adaptable to changing interface requirements.

In fact, the first interface of this type is now available from INTEL. Called the UPI or 8041, it is a complete microcomputer on a chip dedicated to controlling a single peripheral. Since it may be programmed, it is a general-purpose programmable interface that will connect your 8080, 8085, or 8048 system to almost any peripheral requiring control rates of fewer than 20,000 bytes per second.

The Mostek Fairchild 3870 integrates a 2K ROM, plus RAM, and is software-compatible with the F8.

PROGRAMMABLE INTERFACES

Because of the low-cost of one-chip processors, device interface chips are becoming "intelligent," i.e. processor-equipped. They receive instructions from the MPU, and implement all required control and sequencing. The decoding and sequencing are usually accomplished by a microprogram internal to the chip.

It is interesting to note that the complexity of a standard MPU is about 6000 transistors.

One-chip interfaces are special-purpose processors for device control. As integration progresses, the complete controller will eventually be shrunk into a single chip.

COST

The cost of interfaces will probably remain higher than the cost of a processor, because of higher complexity and lower volume. However, it has become almost negligible compared to the cost of peripherals.

"PLASTIC SOFTWARE"

As soon as a software algorithm becomes well-defined, it can be solidified into LSI at low cost. This is "plastic-software": programs can be purchased as a plastic LSI chip.

In the next step of evolution, it is likely that many of the algorithms or programs which have been presented throughout this book will be implemented as part of complex LSI chips. They will have become plastic software.

Interfacing will then have been essentially reduced to the simple interconnect of the required chips. When this time comes, it is hoped that the techniques presented here will contribute to understanding it.

In conclusion, many techniques have been presented in a step-by-step fashion, ranging from interfacing the CPU to the RAM, ROM and I/O device, to complete floppy-disk intelligent interfacing. Along with the discussion of interfacing, such diverse topics as power supplies and analog to digital conversion have been covered. These topics are needed to complete the digital microprocessor designer's talents. The interface begins at the wall socket, and ends only at the front panel of the most remote peripheral. As the technology improves, the interface designer will evolve into more of a programming person. In order for his profession to remain useful, the incorporation of other skills, such as power supply design and analog design might be necessary. At that point, one can interface anything to anything else—and have it work.

APPENDIX A
MICROPROCESSOR MANUFACTURERS

AMD (Advanced Micro Devices)
901 Thompson Place
Sunnyvale, CA 94608
(408) 732-2400
Telex: 346306

AMI (American Microsystems)
3800 Homestead Road
Santa Clara, CA 95051
(408) 246-0330

Data General
4400 Computer Drive
Westboro, Mass. 01581
(617) 366 8911

Digital Equipment Corp.
146 Main St.
Maynard, MA 01754

Electronic Arrays
550 East Middlefield Road
Mountain View, CA 94043
(415) 964-4321

EMM Semiconductor
3216 West El Segundo Blvd.
Hawthorne, CA 90250
(213) 675-9241

Fairchild Semiconductor
1725 Technology Drive
San Jose, CA 95110
(408) 998-0123

GI (General Instruments)
600 West John Street
Hicksville, NY 16002
(516) 733-3107
TWX: (510) 221-1666

Harris Semiconductor
Box 883
Melbourne, FL 32901
TWX: (510) 959-6259

Hitachi
2700 River Road
Des Plaines, IL 60018
(312) 298-0840

Hughes Microelectronics
500 Superior Avenue
Newport Beach, CA 92663
(714) 548-0671

Intel
3065 Bowers Avenue
Santa Clara, CA 95051
(408) 246-7501
Telex: 346372

Intersil
10090 North Tantau Avenue
Cupertino, CA 95014
(408) 996-5000
TWX: (916) 338-0228

ITT Semiconductors
74 Commerce Way
Woburn, MA 01801
(617) 935-7910

Zilog
10460 Bubb Road
Cupertino, CA 95014
(408) 446-4666
TWX: 910-338-7621

Western Digital Corp.
3128 Redhill Avenue
Newport Beach, CA 92663
(714) 557-3550
TWX: (910) 595-1139

MMI (Monolithic Memories)
1165 East Arques Avenue
Sunnyvale, CA 04086
(408) 739-3535

MOS Technology
950 Rittenhouse Road
Norristown, PA 19401
(215) 666-7950
TWX: (510) 660-4033

Mostek
1215 West Crosby Road
Carollton, TX 75006
(214) 242-0444
Telex: 30423

Motorola
5005 E. McDowell Road
Phoenix, Arizona 85008
(602) 244-6900

RCA
Box 3200, Rte. 202
Sommerville, N.J. 08876
(201) 685-6000

Rockwell International
3310 Miraloma
P.O. Box 3669
Anaheim, CA 92803
(714) 632-3698

SGS-ATES
79 Massosoit Street
Waltham, MA 02154
(617) 891-3710
Telex: 923495WHA

Sharp
10 Keystone Place
Paramus, NJ 07652
(201) 265-5600
Telex: 134327

Siemens
3700 East Thomas
Box 1390
Scottsdale, AZ 85252
(602) 947-2231

Signetics
811 East Arques Avenue
Sunnyvale, CA 94086
(408) 739-7700

Solid State Scientific
Montgomeryvale, PA 18936
(215) 855-8400
Telex: (510) 661-7267

Synertek
3050 Coronado Drive
Santa Clara, CA 95051
(408) 984-9800
TWX: (910) 338-0135

TI (Texas Instruments)
Digital Systems Division
P.O. Box 1444
Houston, TX 77001
(713) 494-5115

Thompson-CSF, Sescosem
50 Rue JP Timbaud
Courbevoie 92, France
788-50-01
Telex: 610-560

APPENDIX B

S 100 MANUFACTURERS

Advanced Microcomputer Products
P.O. Box 17329
Irvine, CA 92713
(714) 558-8813

Affordable Computer Products
Byte Shop No. 2
3400 El Camino Real
Santa Clara, CA 95051
(408) 249-4221

Ai Cybernetic Systems
P.O. Box 4691
University Park, NM 88003

ALF Products, Inc.
128 S. Taft
Lakewood, CO 80228

Alpha Micro Systems
17875 N. SkyPark North
Irvine, CA 92714
(714) 957-1404

Altair (see MITS)

Artec Electronics, Inc.
605 Old Country Road
San Carlos, CA 94070
(415) 592-2740

Associated Electronics
12444 Lambert Circle
Garden Grove, CA 92641
(714) 539-0735

Base-2, Inc.
P.O. Box 9941
Marina del Rey, CA 90291

Byte Shop
1450 Koll Circle, No. 105
San Jose, CA 95112

CHP, Inc.
P.O. Box 18113
San Jose, CA 95158

Comptek
P.O. Box 516
La Canada, CA 91011
(213) 790-7957

Computalker Consultants
P.O. Box 1951
Santa Monica, CA 90406

Computer Data Systems
English Village, Atram 3
Newark, DE 19711

Crestline Micro Systems
P.O. Box 3313
Riverside, CA 92519

Cromemco
2432 Charleston Road
Mountain View, CA 94043
(415) 964-7400

Cybercom
2102A Walsh Avenue
Santa Clara, CA 95050
(408) 246-2707

Computer Kits Inc.
1044 University Avenue
Berkeley, CA 94710
(415) 845-5300

Computer Graphics Associates
56 Sicker Road
Latham, NY 12110

Computer Hobbyist Products, Inc.
P.O. Box 18113
San Jose, CA 95158
(408) 629-9108

COMPU/TIME
P.O. Box 417
Huntington Beach, CA 92648
(714) 638-2094

Computer Power & Light
12321 Ventura Blvd.
Studio City, CA 91604
(213) 760-0405

Crea Comp System, Inc.
Suite 305
4175 Veterans Highways
Ronkonkoma, NY 11779
(516) 585-1606

DAJEN
David C. Jenkins
7214 Springleaf Court
Citrus Heights, CA 95610
(916) 723-1050

Data Sync
201 W. Mill
Santa Maria, CA 93454
(805) 963-8678

DigiComm
6205 Rose Court
Roseville, CA 95678

Digital Systems
1154 Dunsmuir Place
Livermore, CA
(415) 413-4078

Digiteck
P.O. Box 6838
Grosse Point, Michigan 48236

Duston, Forrest
885 Aster Avenue
Palatine, Il 60067

Dutronics
P.O. Box 9160
Stockton, CA 94608

E & L Instruments, Inc.
61 First Street
Derby, Conn. 06418
(203) 735-8774

E.E. & P.S.
Electronic Eng. & Production Ser
Route No. 2
Louisville, Tennessee
(615) 984-9640

Electronic Control Technology
P.O. Box 6
Union City, NJ 07083

El Paso Computer Group
9716 Saigon Drive
El Pase, TX 79925

Environmental Interfaces
3207 Meadowbrook Blvd.
Cleveland, Ohio 44118
(216) 371-8482

Equinox Division
Parasitic Engineering
P.O. Box 6314
Albany, CA 94706
(800) 648-5311

Extensys Corp.
592 Weddell Drive, S-3
Sunnyvale, CA 94086
(408) 734-1525

Forethought Products
P.O. Box 386-A
Coburg, Oregon 97401

Franklin Electric Co.
733 Lakefield Road
Westlake Village, CA 91361
(805) 497-7755

Galaxy Systems
P.O. Box 2475
Woodland Hills, CA 91364
(213) 888-7233

GNAT Computers
8869 Balboa, Unit C
San Diego, CA 12123

Godbout Electronics
Box 2355
Oakland Airport, CA 94614

Hayes
P.O. Box 9884
Atlanta, GA 30319
(404) 231-0574

Heuristic, Inc.
900 N. San Antonio Road
Suite C-1
Los Altos, CA 94022

Hornestead Technologies Corp.
891 Briarcliff Road N.E.
Suite B-11
Atlanta, GA 30306

iCOM Division
6741 Variel Avenue
Conoga Park, CA 91303
(213) 348-1391

IBEX
1010 Morse Avenue, No. 5
Sunnyvale, CA 94086
739-3770

INFO 2000
P.O. Box 316
Culver City, CA 90230

Integrand Research Corp.
8474 Avenue 296
Visalia, CA 93277
(209) 733-9288

International Data Systems
400 North Washington Street,
Suite 200
Falls Church, VA 22046
(703) 536-7373

Kent-Moore Instrument Co.
P.O. Box 507
Industrial Avenue
Pioneer, Ohio 43554
(419) 737-2352

Lewis and Associates
68 Post Street, Suite 506
San Francisco, CA 94104
(415) 391-1498

Lincoln Semiconductor
P.O. Box 68
Milpitas, CA 95035
(408) 734-8020

Logistics
Box 9970
Marina Del Rey, CA 90291

North Star Computers
2465 Fourth Street
Berkeley, CA 94710

443

MECA
7344 Warnego Trail
Yucca Valley, CA 92284
(714) 365-7686

Micro Data
3199 Trinity Place
San Jose, CA 95124

Microdesign
8187 Havasu Circle
Buena Park, CA 90621
(415) 465-1861

Micro Designs, Inc.
499 Embarcadero
Oakland, CA 94606
(415) 465-1861

MicroGRAPHICS
P.O. Box 2189, Station A
Champaign, IL 61820

MicroLogic
P.O. Box 55484
Indianapolis, IN 46220

Micromation
524 Union Street
San Francisco, CA 94133
(415) 398-0289

Micronics, Inc.
P.O. Box 3514
Greenville, NC 27834

Micropolis Corp.
9017 Reseda Blvd.
Northridge, CA 91324

Midwest Scientific Instruments
220 West Cedar
Olathe, Kansas 66061

MIKRA-D, Inc.
P.O. Box 403
Hollister, Mass. 01746

Mini Micro Mart
1618 James Street
Syrecuse, NY 13203

MiniTerm Associates
Box 268
Bedford, Mass. 01730

MITS (Altair)
2450 Alamo S. E.
Albuquerque, NM 87106

Morrow's Micro-Stuff
Box 6194
Albany, CA 94706

MRS
P.O. Box 1220
Hawthorne, CA 90250

Mullen Computer Boards
Box 6214
Hayward, CA 94545

Mountain Hardware
Box 1133
Ben Lamand, CA 95005

National Multiplex Corp.
3474 Rand Avenue, Box 288
South Plainfield, NJ 07080

Objective Design, Inc.
P.O. Box 7536 Univ. Station
Provo, Utah 84602

PerCom Data Company
4021 Windsor
Garland, TX 75042

Peripheral Vision
P.O. Box 6267
Denver, Colorado 80206

Phonics, Inc.
P.O. Box 62275
Sunnyvale, CA 94086

Prime Rodix Inc.
P.O. Box 11245
Denver, Colorado 80211

Processor Applications, Ltd.
2801 East Valley Veiw Avenue
West Covina, CA 91792

Quay Corporation
P.O. Box 386
Freehold, NJ 07728

Realistic Controls Corporation
3530 Warrensville Center Road
Cleveland, Ohio 44122

R.H.S. Marketing
2233 El Camino Real
Palo Alto, CA 94306

RO-CHE Systems
7101 Mammoth Avenue
Van Nuys, CA 91405

S. D. Sales
P.O. Box 28810
Dallas, Texas 75228

Sargent's Dist. Co.
4209 Knoxville
Lakewood, CA 90713

Scientific Research Instruments
P.O. Drawer C
Marcy, NJ 13403

Seals Electronics
Box 11651
Knoxville, TN 37919

Smoke Signal Boardcasting
P.O. Box 2017
Hollywood, CA 90028

Solid State Music
MIKOS
419 Portofino Drive
San Carlos, CA 94070

Stillman Research Systems (SRS)
P.O. Box 14036
Phoenix, AZ 85063

Suntronics Company
360 Merrimack Street
Lawrence, MA 01843

Synetic Designs Company
P.O. Box 2627
Pomona, CA 91766

Szerlip Enterprises
1414 W. 259th Street
Harbor City, CA 90710

TEI Inc.
7231 Fondren Road
Houston, Texas 77036

T&H Engineering
P.O. Box 352
Cardiff, CA 92007

Tarbell Electronics
20620 South Leapwood Avenue
Suite P
Carson, CA 90746

Technical Design Labs Inc.
342 Columbus Avenue
Trenton, NJ 08629

Vandenberg Data Products
P.O. Box 2507
Santa Maria, CA 93454

Vector Electronics Company, Inc.
12460 Gladstone Avenue
Sylmar, CA 91342

Vector Graphic Inc.
717 Lakefield Road, Suite F
Westlake Village, CA 91361

Western Data Systems
3650 Charles Street, No. Z
Santa Clara, CA 95050

WIZARD Engineering
8205 Ronson Road, Suite C
San Diego, CA 92111

Xybek
P.O. Box 4925
Stanford, CA 94305

APPENDIX C

CONVERSION TABLE

DECIMAL	BINARY	HEX	OCTAL
0	0000	0	0
1	0001	1	1
2	0010	2	2
3	0011	3	3
4	0100	4	4
5	0101	5	5
6	0110	6	6
7	0111	7	7
8	1000	8	10
9	1001	9	11
10	1010	A	12
11	1011	B	13
12	1100	C	14
13	1101	D	15
14	1110	E	16
15	1111	F	17

APPENDIX D

RS232C SIGNALS

PIN	FUNCTION	
1	Protective chassis ground	
2	Transmit data to communication equipment	(TxD)
3	Receive data from communication equipment	(RxD)
4	Request to send to communication equipment	(RTS)
5	Clear to send from communication equipment	(CTS)
6	Data set ready from communication equipment	(DSR)
7	Signal ground	
8	Data carrier detect from communication equipment	(DCD)
20	Data terminal ready to communication equipment	(DTR)

APPENDIX E

IEEE-488 SIGNALS

D I01-D I08	Data Lines	Carries Data
DAV	Data Valid	Indicates if data lines contain stable data
NRFD	Not Ready For Data	Goes False when all devices are ready for data
NDAC	Not Data Accepted	Goes False when all devices have accepted data
ATN	Attention	Indicates if data lines carry address or data
IFC	Interface Clear	A reset signal
SRQ	Service Request	Interrupt Signal
REN	Remote Enable	Selects Front Panel Operation
EOI	End or Identify	End of transfer or polling sequence

APPENDIX F

ACRONYMS

AC	Alternating Current	BSC	Binary Synchronous Communication
ACC	Accumulator		
ACK	Acknowledge		
A/D	Analog to Digital	C	Carry
ADCCP	Advanced Data Communication Control Procedure	CAD	Computer-Aided-Design
		CAM	Contents-Addressable Memory
ALU	Arithmetic-Logic Unit	CCD	Charge-Coupled Device
ANSI	American National Standards Institute	CE	Chip Enable
		CLK	Clock
ASCII	American Standard Code for Information Interchange	CML	Current Mode Logic
		CMOS	Complementary MOS
ASR	Automatic Send and Receive	CPG	Clock Pulse Generator
		CPS	Characters Per Second
BCD	Binary-Coded-Decimal	CPU	Central Processor Unit
BCR	Byte Count Register	CR	Card Reader; Carriage Return
BPS	Bits Per Second		
BRA	Branch, go to	CRC	Cyclic Redundancy Check

450

CROM	Control-ROM	FSK	Frequency-Shift-Keying
CRT	Cathode Ray Tube		
CRTC	CRT Controller	G	(carry) Generate
CS	Chip Select	GP	General-Purpose
CTS	Clear to Send	GPIB	General-Purpose Interface
CU	Control Unit		Bus
CY	Carry		
		HDLC	High Level Data Link
D	Data		Control
D/A	Digital to Analog	HEX	Hexadecimal
DC	Direct Current	HPIB	Hewlett-Packard
DC	Don't Care		Interface Bus
DCD	Data Carrier Detect		
DIP	Dual In-Line Package	I	Interrupt/Interrupt Mask
DMA	Direct Memory Access	IC	Integrated Circuit = Chip
DMAC	DMA Controller	INT	Interrupt
DMOS	Double-Diffused MOS	I/O	Input-Output
DNC	Direct Numerical Control	IOCS	I/O Control System
DOS	Disk Operating System	IRQ	Interrupt Request
DPM	Digital Panel Meter	I^2L	Integrated Injection Logic
DTL	Diode-Transistor Logic		
DTR	Data Terminal Ready	JAN	Joint Army-Navy
D$\emptyset$-7	Data Lines $\emptyset$ Through 7	JP	Jump
E	Empty; Enable (Clock)	K	(1024) Kilo
EAROM	Electrically Alterable ROM	KSR	Keyboard-Send-Receive
EBCDIC	Extended Binary-Coded-Decimal Information Code		
ECL	Emitter Coupled Logic	LCD	Liquid-Crystal Display
EDP	Electronic Data Processing	LED	Light Emitting Diode
EFL	Emitter Follower Logic	LIFO	Last-In-First-Out
EMI	Electro Magnetic Interference	LOC	Loop On-Line Control
		LP	Line Printer
EOC	End of Conversion	LPM	Lines Per Minute
EOF	End of File	LPS	Low-Power Shottky
EOR	Exclusive OR	LRC	Longitudinal Redundancy Check
EOT	End of Text, Tape		
EPROM	Erasable PROM	LSB	Least Significant Bit
		LSI	Large Scale Integration
FAMOS	Floating-Gate Avalanche MOS	MNOS	Metal Nitride Oxide Semiconductor
FDC	Floppy-Disk Controller	MOS	Metal Oxide Semiconductor
FDM	Frequency-Division Multiplexing	MPU	Microprocessor Unit
FET	Field-Effect Transistor	MSB	Most Significant Bit
FF	Flip-Flop	MSI	Medium Scale Integration
FIFO	First-In-First-Out	MTBF	Mean Time Between Failures
FPLA	Field PLA		

MUX	Multiplexer		ROM	Read-Only Memory
			RPROM	Reprogrammable PROM
N	Negative (Sign Bit)		RPT	Repeat
NDRO	Non-Destructive Read-Out		RS	Register Select
NMOS	N-Channel MOS		RST	Restart
NVM	Non-Volatile Memory		RTC	Real-Time Clock
			RTS	Request-To-Send
			R/W	Read/Write Memory
OCR	Optical Character Reader		Rx	Receiver
OEM	Original Equipment			
	Manufacturer		SAR	Successive Approximation
OP	Operation			Register
OV	Overflow		SDLC	Synchronous Data Link
				Control
P	Parity; (carry) Propagate		SEC	Scanning Electron Micro-
PABX	Private Automatic Branch			scope
	Exchange		SEM	Standard Electronic
PBX	Private Branch Exchange			Module
PC	Printed Circuit; Program		S/H	Sample and Hold
	Counter		S/N	Signal to Noise
PCI/O	Program Controlled I/O		SOS	Silicon-On-Sapphire
PCM	Pulse Code Mod.		SR	Service Request
PFR	Power-Fail Restart		SSI	Small Scale Integration
PIC	Priority Interrupt Control		STB	Strobe
PIO	Programmable I/O Chip/		SUB	Subroutine
	Interface			
PIT	Programmable Interval-		TDM	Time-Division Multiplexing
	Timer		TDSR	Transmitter Data Service
PLA	Programmable Logic-Array			Request
PLL	Phase-Locked Loop		TSS	Time-Sharing System
PMOS	P-Channel MOS		TTL	Transistor Transistor Logic
POS	Point-of-Sale Terminal		TTY	Teletypewriter
PROM	(Field) Programmable		Tx	Transmitter
	ROM			
PSW	Program Status Word		UART	Universal Asynchronous
PTP	Paper Tape Punch			Receiver Transmitter
PTR	Paper Tape Reader		uC	Microcomputer
			uP	Microprocessor
Q	AC extension		USRT	Universal Synchronous
QPL	Qualified Products List			Receiver Transmitter
			U-V	Ultra-Violet
R	Read			
RALU	Register Arithmetic		VMOS	Vertical MOS
	Logic Unit		V_{ss}	Ground
RAM	Random-Access-Memory			
RDSR	Receiver Data Service		W	Write
	Request		WPM	Words Per Minute
RDY	Ready			
RES	Reset		X	Index
RF	Radio Frequent		XOR	Exclusive OR
RMS	Root Mean Square			
			Z	Zero Bit
			⏀	(Clock) Phase

INDEX

SYBEX BIBLIOGRAPHY

VIDEO COURSES

V1   MICROPROCESSORS (12 hours)
V3   MILITARY MICROPROCESSOR SYSTEMS (6 hours)
V5   BIT-SLICE (6 hours)
V7   MICROPROCESSOR INTERFACING TECHNIQUES (6 hours)

AUDIO COURSES

S1   INTRODUCTION TO MICROPROCESSORS (2½ hours)
S2   PROGRAMMING MICROPROCESSORS (2½ hours)
S3   DESIGNING A MICROPROCESSOR (2½ hours)
SB1   MICROPROCESSORS (12 hours)
SB2   PROGRAMMING MICROPROCESSORS (10 hours)
SB3   MILITARY MICROPROCESSOR SYSTEMS (6 hours)
SB5   BIT-SLICE (6 hours)
SB6   INDUSTRIAL MICROPROCESSOR SYSTEMS (4½ hours)
SB7   MICROPROCESSOR INTERFACING TECHNIQUES (6 hours)
SB10   INTRODUCTION TO PERSONAL COMPUTING (2½ hours)

REFERENCE TEXTS

C200   INTRODUCTION TO PERSONAL AND BUSINESS COMPUTING
C201   MICROPROCESSORS
C202   PROGRAMMING THE 6502
C207   MICROPROCESSOR INTERFACING TECHNIQUES
C280   PROGRAMMING THE Z80
D302   6502 APPLICATIONS BOOK
C281   PROGRAMMING THE Z8000
G402   6502 GAMES
IMD   INTERNATIONAL MICROPROCESSOR DICTIONARY (10 languages)
X1   MICROPROCESSOR LEXICON
Z10   MICROPROGRAMMED APL IMPLEMENTATION

SOFTWARE

6502 ASSEMBLER (Microsoft BASIC)
8080 SIMULATOR FOR KIM
8080 SIMULATOR FOR APPLE

FOR A COMPLETE CATALOGUE
OF OUR PUBLICATIONS

U.S.A.
2344 Sixth Street
Berkeley, California 94710
Tel: (415) 848-8233
Telex: 336311

EUROPE
18 rue Planchat
75020 Paris, France
Tel: (1) 3703275
Telex: 211801